Freud's Dora

# Freud's Dora

*A Biography
of Ida Bauer Adler*

MARGE THORELL

McFarland & Company, Inc., Publishers
*Jefferson, North Carolina*

**Frontispiece:** The famous sofa in Sigmund Freud's study, shown here in 20 Maresfield Gardens, the Freud Museum, Hampstead, London, where Freud fled after the Nazis invaded Vienna. The room is set up exactly as it was on Berggasse 19 in Vienna (Robert Huffstutter, Flickr).

LIBRARY OF CONGRESS CATALOGUING-IN-PUBLICATION DATA

Names: Thorell, Marge, 1940– author.
Title: Freud's Dora : a biography of Ida Bauer Adler / Marge Thorell.
Description: Jefferson, North Carolina : McFarland & Company, Inc., Publishers, 2022 | Includes bibliographical references and index.
Identifiers: LCCN 2022002709 | ISBN 9781476682792 (print) ∞
ISBN 9781476645346 (ebook)
Subjects: LCSH: Adler, Ida Bauer. | Hysteria—Patient—Austria—Biography. | Dysfunctional families. | Families—Mental health. | BISAC: PSYCHOLOGY / History
Classification: LCC RC455.4.F3 T465 2022 | DDC 616.85/240092 [B]—
dc23/eng/20220314
LC record available at https://lccn.loc.gov/2022002709

BRITISH LIBRARY CATALOGUING DATA ARE AVAILABLE

**ISBN (print) 978-1-4766-8279-2**
**ISBN (ebook) 978-1-4766-4534-6**

Front cover image: Ida Bauer, age 8 in 1890, while living at Berggasse 32 in Vienna, just up the street from Freud's apartment and consulting room (taken from Wikimedia Commons); *background* © 2022 Shutterstock

Printed in the United States of America

*McFarland & Company, Inc., Publishers*
*Box 611, Jefferson, North Carolina 28640*
*www.mcfarlandpub.com*

To my psychoanalyst,
without whom this and many other things
would not have been possible

I cannot think of any need in childhood as strong as the need for a father's protection.

—Sigmund Freud

If there is one woman who sums up for many what is both fascinating and repellent, most subtle and most bullied in Freud's relationships with women, then that woman is Dora.

—Lisa Appignanesi and John Forrester,
*Freud's Women*

# Table of Contents

*Acknowledgments*                                           ix

*Preface*                                                    1

*Introduction*                                               9

**Part I: Secrets and Lies**

  **1.** The Search for Secrets                    20

  **2.** The Secret of Freud's Women               29

  **3.** The Bauer Ménage and *Its* Secrets        36

  **4.** The Secret Life of Merano                 49

  **5.** The K's Ménage and *Their* Secrets        62

  **6.** The Nature of Secrets                     73

**Part II: Dora and Freud**

  **7.** The Teenager and the Analyst             82

  **8.** Freud's Story of the Seductions          91

  **9.** Dreams and Desires                        97

  **10.** Dreams and Hysteria                     104

  **11.** The Master                              111

**Part III: Triumph Over Freud**

  **12.** The Return                              120

  **13.** Marriage                                125

  **14.** Motherhood                              132

  **15.** The Bauer Family After Freud            137

## Table of Contents

**16.** The Politics and Power of Otto Bauer     143

**17.** World War I     147

### Part IV: The Aftermath

**18.** The New World Order     154

**19.** The Nazi Period     161

**20.** Kurt in the United States     167

**21.** Ida's Escape     172

**22.** The Aftermath     179

**23.** The Scholarship     184

*Epilogue*     190

*Chronology*     195

*Chapter Notes*     199

*Bibliography*     213

*Index*     219

# Acknowledgments

Nothing is ever done alone, at least not in my experience. For every project, whether a creative or a domestic one, there are always many people who help make things happen. In my case, I want to thank Katharina Adler, the great-granddaughter of Ida Bauer Adler, with whom I have had several email conversations and who was kind enough to provide me with some in-depth information about the story of Ida.

I am also grateful for the help I've received, over the years of working on this book, from Anne Dubuisson, who has reviewed my manuscript many times and has been most helpful in organizing my material. Also, thanks to Dannette Bock, who has proofread the manuscript, offered comments, and created the index—again, many times.

I am indebted to the Graduate Faculty of the University of Pennsylvania, Graduate School of Education, where I earned a doctoral degree and was able to create a dissertation based on psychoanalysis.

I am deeply appreciative of the work on Ida Bauer Adler (Dora) that came before me, especially Hannah S. Decker's definitive work on Freud, Dora, and 1900 Vienna. This book could not have been written without Sigmund Freud's case study *Dora: An Analysis of a Case of Hysteria*. I also was happy to find an article by Andrew W. Ellis and colleagues, who wrote about the "other couple," the Zellenkas—named Herr K. and Frau K. in Freud's case study. This article, which appeared in the *Journal of Austrian Studies* was one of the few to detail the life and exploits of the Zellenkas and their relationship with Ida Bauer's family. I am also grateful for the help and support from many people at McFarland & Company, Inc., Publishers.

## Acknowledgments

I also want to thank dear friends and family who were there for me as I was writing this book. And I could not have done this book without the help and support of my husband, Klaus. I am especially grateful for the ongoing support from Craig Lichtman.

# Preface

In September 1939, Sigmund Freud (1856–1939), the founder of psychoanalysis, having escaped the Nazis in Austria, lay dying of cancer in Hampstead, London. Up until his last moments, he saw patients, wrote, and read books. In the same year, his most famous patient, Dora, was still living in Vienna, where, as a Jewish woman, she was terrified and alone. She tried desperately to obtain a visa to travel to France to be with her beloved brother, Otto. Dora finally succeeded in traveling to France, but only after he had died. Eventually, she was reunited with her son, Kurt, in the United States. Then, she, too, died of cancer in 1945 in Manhattan—a few years after Freud.

Freud and Dora had been together a scant three months in Vienna, but she, a young girl, would be coupled for eternity to the analyst by virtue of his most celebrated case study. She was his earliest, and arguably his most famous, psychoanalytic patient—and his biggest disappointment.

Through the years, much has been written about Freud and his relationship with Dora in everything from academic journals to popular magazines. Their story has been depicted in plays and movies. Freud's behavior surrounding the case, his theories emanating from the case, the toll the case enacted on his health—all have been dissected and illuminated.

Anyone who has enrolled in a college psychology course is familiar with Freud and Dora. For many years now, the vocabulary of psychoanalysis, largely emanating from the Dora case, is part of the lexicon of the average reader, even those who are not involved in counseling, medicine, therapy, or literary criticism. Everyone, it seems, knows about transference, countertransference, hysteria,

1

Freud's home at 20 Maresfield Gardens, London NW3 5SX, in the United Kingdom was his final home and eventually of his daughter Anna Freud, a pioneering child psychoanalyst, who lived there from 1938 until 1982. The home now is the Freud Museum (Rup11, Wikimedia Commons).

displacement, penis envy, repression, and other Freudian terms. Conversely, few people are knowledgeable about the real person in Freud's well-known case study. For many, Dora remains a fictive protagonist, unknown as a person.

It is ironic that such a well-known case, one so studied, was considered by Freud an "exemplary failure."[1] And yet, despite his miscalculation, he was determined to write up the case history, initially completing a first draft in January 1901, entitling it *Traum und Hysterie* (*Dreams and Hysteria*).[2]

In the case study, which reads like a novella, Freud recounts the story of this troubled young woman, an adolescent, who was sexually assaulted by a friend of her father's. He describes Dora in great detail, creating a character that has been compared to Nabokov's Lolita. Dora, like Lolita—both children—were seduced by older men.[3]

Freud's fascinating portrayal of Dora brings to life a young girl of some complexity. He describes her physical appearance, thoughts, reactions, speech, and dreams. He also writes about how she suffered due to the entangled and highly sexualized family structure that she was forced to live in. He describes her relationship with her father and the flawed and unsatisfactory one with her mother—all this in graphic detail. Freud also recounted how Dora talked back to him, questioned his analysis, openly discussed sexual matters with him, and finally walked out on him. Freud did not seem to like her very much—suggesting that he really didn't "get" his struggling young patient. He was singularly unsympathetic toward her.

So, who was this daunting, abused, misrepresented character?

The Dora of Freud's narrative was a strong-willed seventeen-year-old who suffered with a variety of symptoms, many of which were attributed to her own nature but also were due to her entangled and enmeshed family situation. She endured loss of voice, depression, respiratory illnesses, gastric and intestinal distress, a limp, and anxiety. Certainly, the dysfunctional family structure she was forced to live in contributed to her malaise. After openly discussing her life with Freud and frequently disputing his interpretations of her ailments, she decided to abort the six-days-a-week analysis.

Freud's treatment of Dora, one of his earliest patients, was a failure, perhaps because he was singularly inept in treating her. Rarely one to admit defeat or failure, he managed to understand and even write about the mistakes he made with Dora (he never actually admitted anything to his young patient, however). He was thus able to salvage something significant from the broken interaction—his recognition of one of the more significant tenets of psychoanalysis, namely the phenomenon of transference, and ultimately countertransference.

In his defense, Freud was just starting out as a psychoanalyst and in subsequent years would have a much better understanding of women and of his own reactions to his patients, as well as to his own theories. However, as feminist scholars write today, he never really understood female psychology—and actually appeared to have had disdain for women.

Freud's analytic constructs were characterized by an unconscious redirection or misdirection of feelings from one person to another, patient to doctor—or doctor to patient, in the case of the countertransference. This significant psychic and creative discovery largely came about because of Freud's miscalculation and mishandling of his relationship with this early patient, Dora.[4]

On the subject of a therapist's knowledge of a patient, in an introduction to Freud's case history of Dora, Philip Rieff claims, "The mystery of character never submits entirely, even to the greatest masters."[5] Freud did get some things right about Dora, but he got a lot wrong, too. There was a great deal that was unknown or "mysterious" to him about Dora.

Freud does acknowledge this, admitting in the case study of Dora that he failed to understand or even discover the nature of transference until it was too late. To say the case of Dora is one of Freud's great failures is no critique of mine. Freud himself wrote, "The longer the interval of time that separates me from the end of this analysis, the more probable it seems to me that the fault in my technique lay in this omission [of his knowledge of the transference]."[6]

In her article "The Strange Case of the Freudian Case History," Anne Sealy tells us that Freud's case studies illuminate his understanding of the power of narrative and thus of human psychology. Yet his stories only provide information within the context of the case study, which is naturally influenced by the teller's point of view. This does not allow readers to see the complete, or at times most accurate, picture of the subject of the case study.[7]

Case studies, even flawed ones, have their uses of course and are effectively discussed in hospital grand rounds, a staple at university medical schools. Case studies are also used effectively within the pharmaceutical industry to discuss and illustrate the adverse events and benefits of its drugs. Much is learned of diseases and patients' responses to illness and health through case studies.[8] In the telling of these tales, while dysfunction abounds, no one, as Rieff argues, is a villain, only a victim[9]—generally of oneself.

This is surely the case with Ida Bauer, the real person behind the characterization of Dora, who was a victim of her own lack of self-awareness. And while she clearly did not understand herself, nor did Freud, today her motives are more comprehended, but only in relationship to Freud. Within analytic circles today the situation Ida found herself in would not be viewed as unique and would have been handled in an entirely different way than it was within the confines of Freud's consulting room and the medical environment of 1900s Vienna.

Ida's real-life story was only an illustrative "fragment" for Freud. And, it is true, had she not been Freud's patient, no one would have known about her or cared anything at all about her symptoms or her life. But when we understand the totality of Ida's life, we do care about her.

Today, feminist scholars have taken up the Dora case, viewing Ida as someone whose "hysteria developed as a form of protest, a silent revolt against male power," according to Toril Moi, in "Representation of Patriarchy: Sexuality and Epistemology in Freud's Dora."[10]

Reams have been written about the case and dissected by scholars, both pro and con. Some believe she was highly dysfunctional and never should have walked out on Freud. They consider that the case study of Anna O. is the much better example of a woman improving her life through analysis and shows how she survived her traumas and ended up helping to create a social environment that encouraged women.

However, although much has been written about Dora, what little we know of Ida is from Freud himself. But she does have a story to tell apart from what Freud and academic authors tell us. Her story is the tale of a Jewish Viennese woman enmeshed in a family dynamic that was not merely dysfunctional, but by today's standards would be viewed as abusive. It is also the heroic story of a woman who transcended not only her family and Freud, but the Nazis as well.

It is my intention to provide a narrative of Ida Bauer that grants her a life of her own, showing how she confronted Freud, relieved herself of her symptoms—to some degree—married, had a child, and even developed a career. Ida lived a difficult life, in a problematic world, but survived.

# Preface

In Part I, "Secrets and Lies," I illuminate not only Freud's use of secrets in psychoanalysis, but also the Bauer family secrets, of which there were many. These not-so-secret secrets created an environment for Ida that led to a number of her psychiatric ailments and symptoms. I also tell the story of others who helped traumatize Ida, such as the Zellenkas, who had their own secrets and amplified Ida's issues with their provocative and unthinking behavior toward the sensitive young girl. Additionally, I write about other women deemed hysterics by Freud, such as Anna O. And I try to shed some light on Freud's understanding of women through his relationship with his own mother. In examining the lives of other female patients of Freud, I illustrate how his adoring and unrealistic relationship with his mother—and his disdain for his father—impacted both his life and his work and clearly his relationship with Ida.

The Zellenkas, whose story is part of this one, sexually abused Ida. The husband Hans did so explicitly, and the wife Peppina engaged in a sexual liaison with Ida's father, usurping Ida's mother, and was complicit in Hans's seduction. While these sexual entanglements were being engaged in, the larger environment of Austria during both world wars and the rising tide of anti–Semitism deeply impacted not only Ida but also her family, Freud, and their world.[11]

The Bauer family was rife with illness: tuberculosis, vision problems, syphilis, gastric issues—the list of ailments various family members experienced goes on and on. Her father, her mother, her favorite aunt, and even her father's lover, Peppina, all had physical as well as psychiatric issues, which Ida apparently adopted, consciously or unconsciously.

In Part II, "Dora and Freud," Ida meets the young psychoanalyst for a second time to begin what was to be a formal analysis. Having been dragged to Freud's office by her father, the relationship between Freud and Ida was rocky from the beginning—and Ida was not afraid of Freud or unwilling to speak openly to him. While his initial knowledge about his new patient came from her father, he did question Ida about her life as she saw it. To his credit, he did not rely solely on the narrative of a family member but began the first session by asking Ida to provide him with the whole story of her life and illnesses.

Ida was fairly talkative. She spoke about her family members and particularly her beloved aunt Malvine, her father's younger sister, who had recently died. It was apparent to Freud in these first few sessions that Ida's family had provided her not only with her natural gifts—her beauty and intellectual precocity—but also with her predilection to illness. For instance, she seemed to Freud enamored of the illnesses of the women in her life: her aunt Malvine, as well as those of her mother and of her father's lover, Peppina.

From what he learned in those initial sessions with Ida, Freud believed that Ida's mother, with her devotion to cleaning and apparent lack of interest in her children, was a contributing factor to Ida's illnesses. It was Ida's interactions with both the Zellenkas, however, that caused her the most distress and exacerbated her symptoms to such an alarming degree that her father sought Freud's help for Ida, who was contemplating suicide.[12]

As Freud and Ida continued to meet, she began to speak of the seduction by Hans Zellenka, whom Freud would call Herr K. in the case history. She also spoke of her father's affair with Herr K.'s wife, Peppina (Frau K.). She expressed disgust for Hans's seduction of her and her father's affair with Hans's wife.[13] During her analysis, Ida revealed to Freud two dreams that have been made much of in psychoanalytic literature. She refused to believe Freud's interpretation of these dreams, especially the second dream, and abruptly fled therapy.[14]

In Part III, "Triumph Over Freud," I recount Ida's marriage to Ernst Adler and the arrival sixteen months later of her only child, Kurt Herbert. Ida and her husband formally left the Jewish faith as a result of the growing anti–Semitism—while remaining part of the Jewish community—after Kurt's birth and were baptized in the Protestant church. While the Bauers were never religiously Jewish, they were culturally Jewish, as was Freud. However, following the birth of their son, Ida and her husband came to understand that the situation was changing in Austria. Many Viennese Jews saw the turning of the tide. As Hannah Decker writes, "The urge to convert had strengthened at the turn of the century, as increasingly voluble anti–Semitism roused many Jews to re-consider their situation."[15]

I also tell the story here of Ida's brother and of her son, both of whom had brilliant careers, albeit with somewhat dysfunctional family lives. Her son, for instance, was married several times and was known far and wide for his fiery temperament. Ida's brother did not marry until the death of his parents, and then, although in an outwardly satisfying marriage, became involved with other women, perhaps unconsciously following the example of his father.

In Part IV, "The Aftermath," I examine the life of Ida in Nazi Austria and the repercussions for herself and her famous brother, Otto, as well as her son, a talented musician and conductor. I also describe Ida's eventual escape to the United States, via a circuitous path, and her life and death there as a refugee. Finally, I explore the interpretation of her life by feminists, Freudians, and others.

Through several years of research, including for my dissertation, and in several published articles, particularly the article I wrote about Ida's analysis with Freud,[16] I was able to develop a fuller picture of this complex woman who played such a significant role in the annals of psychiatry and psychoanalysis and, by extension, in our understanding of ourselves. For my doctoral work and while in therapy myself, I read a great deal about psychoanalysis and about Dora but knew little about Ida. This book is an attempt to learn who Ida Bauer really was—the real person behind the "Dora" of Freud's case study.

# Introduction

In 1986, the *New York Times* acknowledged that Sigmund Freud, the discoverer of psychoanalysis, was considered the greatest modern writer. By creating in the grand literary tradition, "the neurologist who sought a dynamic psychology seems today to have been a speculative moralist and a mythologizing dramatist of the inner life."[1] His case studies, for which he is justly famous, contain all the requisite elements of the novel: character, plot, setting, conflict, and sometimes resolution. These studies, now classics, exercise a certain influence on readers of them. They are unforgettable, multilayered, and multifaceted, and demand rereading to fully enjoy and understand them, just like classics of literature.

Like Flaubert's *Madame Bovary* or Tolstoy's *Anna Karenina*, Freud's works pull us into his stories of women's conflicts and struggles, as in the case histories of Anna O. and especially the young girl Dora. Although all his case studies (Rat Man, Little Hans, Wolf Man) capture our imagination, it is Dora's that stands out.

Even though his works are nonfiction, Freud, as a physician, was concerned with literary value, and also of course with the scientific. He described and came to understand the complexity of neurotic illness by analyzing his patients' obsessions, anxieties, and fantasies. He was thus able to develop his theories based on the treatment of his patients, many of whom were women. He was especially interested in hysteria—or conversion disorder as it is frequently called today—where patients who refuse to or cannot tolerate past and frequently hidden trauma convert their anguish into physical symptoms.[2] Freud and Josef Breuer (1842–1925) published a book on the subject.[3]

One of Freud's first patients, Ida Bauer (1883–1945)—named

# Introduction

Dora by Freud in his case study—was a young girl when she first met Sigmund Freud, the trained neurologist. He agreed to see Ida at her father's behest, as she had been suffering from a multiplicity of physical symptoms as early as age seven. At that time, she had a complete breakdown, which was treated by hydrotherapy and electric shock therapies. Her symptoms were brought about, it seemed on the surface, by her mother's obsessive cleanliness (which began after learning that she had contracted venereal disease from her husband). Later, when Ida was an adolescent, the family's complex sexual situation, which was compounded by another family, brought on hysteria, which manifested it itself in many symptoms.

Freud was fascinated by the results of the "talking cure" as understood in Josef Breuer's treatment of one of his patients, Anna O. Thus, Freud was excited about what he felt he was able to discover when working with one of his own patients, a girl he called Dora in his case study. On October 14, 1900, Freud wrote to colleague Wilhelm Fliess (1858–1928) about his new patient, "a girl of eighteen." (She was actually seventeen.) He told Fleiss that the case opened smoothly to his collection of picklocks.[4] As it turned out, this particular door did not open easily and was one of Freud's early analytic failures. His young patient stood up to him and abruptly left therapy before the treatment was finished. As we shall see, Breuer's patient, Anna O., did much better in her therapy with Josef Breuer and had a more productive life than Dora would come to have.

Much has been written about the relationship between Freud and his young patient, and his ensuing discoveries, but not too many know of the life of Ida Bauer. The case, as written up by Freud, is still intriguing on many fronts these many years later: the cultural context of Vienna at the time, the facets of Ida's home life, the discovery of transference—and countertransference—and eventually the gender issues that came to light in the field of literary and cultural analysis after the deaths of Ida and Freud. Even without these components, Ida Bauer is an interesting young woman in her own right.

Before elaborating on the life of Ida Bauer, it's important to understand Vienna, the Jewish situation, and the medical practice

**The Freud family, approximately 1876. Standing, left to right: Paula, Anna, Sigmund (16 at the time), Emmanuel, Rosa and Marie Freud and their cousin Simon Nathanson. Seated: Adolfine, Amalia, unknown girl, Alexander and Jacob Freud. The boy at bottom is unidentified (Wellcome Images, Wikimedia Commons).**

during the time of Freud and Ida, which I attempt to do in this work. At the turn of the century, Viennese Jews were moving out of ghettos, as they were becoming more economically successful and academically relevant. The Jewish population within the Austrian empire was in its ascendancy, rising from 6,000 in the mid-nineteenth century to nearly 150,000 in 1900.[5]

Decker writes about Vienna:

> Historical accounts of the era frequently refer to the feelings of approaching Doom that underlay the superficial air of gaiety and insouciance in fin-de-siècle Vienna. But usually these histories do not state clearly enough the extent to which pessimism about the future reflected the despair of the Jews and the liberals, as they saw the disintegration of their deeply held aspirations.[6]

# Introduction

Jews had moved into Vienna, relocating to the metropolitan area in pursuit of better living conditions, more job and professional opportunities, and less harassment, which they had experienced for centuries in their villages, large and small.

At the time, the medical profession had little understanding of the psychological impact on physical symptoms and diseases, although there were some pioneers, such as Breuer, who were looking into the issues of the mind and illness.

In working with Ida Freud's life and his treatment of his friends, his analysis, and his relationships with other women certainly impacted his interactions with his young patient. He himself had a problematic childhood, as his parents had moved from poverty to burgeoning respectability when they came to Vienna from Moravia—but not without trauma to young Freud. One might think he would have been more empathic toward his patient.

Once in Vienna, Freud's parents, while not denying their Jewish heritage, found themselves more interested in cultural and social success than in passing on their Jewish heritage. Freud grew up in a household that did not celebrate Jewish festivals, and he was not taught Hebrew. This is not to say that Freud or his parents denied their identity, but like other Jews at that time, their sense of themselves was wrapped up in their "German-ness," not necessarily their Jewish heritage or culture. This lack of a Jewish religious life would not keep Hitler's Nazis from significantly impacting the life of Sigmund Freud and his family—as well as that of the Bauer family.

The generation of Jews from which Ida's father and Freud emerged, that is to say, male Jews, tended to believe that no position in society would be denied them in political, academic, or other professional circles, even though anti–Jewish sentiment was on the rise and subtly growing in Vienna. However, being Jewish did impact Freud's choice of profession; he wanted to be a lawyer, but that was not possible, as the profession was closed to Jews. Freud felt, and rightly so, that there were more opportunities within medicine for someone like him. Because of the popularity of medicine for Jewish men, there was a call for quotas for those entering the universities, with lectures by Jewish teachers boycotted at some academic institutions and medical schools.

Thus, assimilating Jews like the Freuds and, as we shall see, the Bauers, thought that because of their academic brilliance and increasing financial assets, they could join mainstream Austrian society. This was not the case, as their lives were spent almost entirely among other Jews.

Young Ida Bauer, for example, while being educated at home, did not socialize with non–Jewish children—nor would Freud's own daughter, Anna, even though unlike Ida, Anna (thirteen years younger) attended a convent school. Neither made friends with non–Jews, so mostly the socializing of the Freud and Bauer families was within the Jewish community. Freud's practice consisted solely of Jews for quite some time, and the early psychoanalytic movement consisted almost entirely of Jewish physicians. It was not until around 1907 that there were any gentile recruits for his burgeoning therapeutic interventions.

As a result of this closed culture, it has been asserted by many that Ida's father would never have chosen anyone other than a Jewish physician for his daughter (or himself). It has been argued, too, that this social and cultural isolation set up Ida for hysteria amidst a clearly dysfunctional family background. And at that time, Vienna's society was one where even bright young women like Ida were denied any real education, so there could be hardly any outlet for her.

Thus, Ida found herself seeking psychological help, though not willingly. According to Michael Billig, Ida entered Freud's life when hers was gloomy, at the "gloomiest, most isolated point in his life."[7] Ida's family, for its part, was also experiencing dilemmas—personal, physical, and social. The Bauers came from Bohemia, where Ida's father's textile business was experiencing difficulties because of growing anti–Semitism. By moving to Vienna, the Bauers, like the Freuds, hoped to create a better life for their families and achieve professional and financial stability.

The families did not actively practice Judaism, even though the Bauers did have their son, Otto (Ida's elder brother), circumcised. You could say that both Freud and Ida were at the same place psychologically when she entered treatment with him: isolated, depressed, and hindered by the anti–Semitism of Vienna at that time.

The cast of characters who made up young Ida Bauer's life were both rich and formidable. Ida was born in Vienna on November 1, 1882. Her paternal grandparents had probably moved from Bohemia, near the Moravian border, in the late 1850s as a result of pressure following the revolution of 1848.

Ida's father, Philipp Bauer, an industrialist, was frequently ill, having contracted tuberculosis and syphilis. Her mother, Katharina (Käthe) Gerber Bauer, born in 1862 in what is now north central Czechoslovakia, had her own troubles. Some claim (as Freud did) that she was a strange woman, a pathological house cleaner, and someone her daughter disliked and did not respect. She died in 1912 of stomach cancer. Ida's father, Philipp, died shortly thereafter in 1913 from complications of tuberculosis and venereal disease.

Ida's brother and only sibling, Otto (1881–1938), would become a leader of the Austrian Socialist Party from 1918 to 1934 and was its chief Marxist theorist. In 1914 he married a divorcée with three children, and then maintained a long-term relationship with several younger mistresses, just like his father. He died prematurely of a heart ailment.

Because of Philipp's diagnosis of tuberculosis, he moved the family from Vienna to a Tyrolean resort town (today in Italy) to more easily find relief and hopefully effect a cure. It was in Merano that the family befriended another couple—the previously mentioned Herr K. and Frau K.

Ida took care of the Zellenkas' two children, along with her own sick father. At some point as he became more ill, Philipp was nursed by Peppina, and they shortly became lovers. At the same time, Peppina's husband, Hans, began his seduction of the young Ida, a girl who was continuously neurotic and neurasthenic. Following Hans's sexual advances, which no one in the family believed, or wished to believe, she developed increasingly severe symptoms of hysteria, including a cough, a limp, and loss of voice.[8]

Although she consulted Freud in 1898 at the behest of her father (who himself had seen Freud for nervous issues due to his syphilis), Ida did not go into analysis with him until the earlier part of October 1900. The case study that Freud would construct around his treatment of Ida consisted of her dreams and the foundations of her family life: the obsessive mother, the adulterous father, the mistress, and the seducer who made amorous advances toward Ida.

It is interesting to note, and very revealing about Ida's character, that a young woman of those times was willing to talk—and to argue—with Freud while undergoing treatment. She was also not afraid or embarrassed to speak of sexual topics. She was more apt to disagree with her therapist than to stay silent. This is all the more surprising as middle-class Jewish girls and women felt especially powerless in Vienna and elsewhere, since they were discriminated against both as Jews and as women. Jewish women were barred from admission to higher education and careers, for instance. This must have been particularly galling for the intelligent young woman who watched her brother, Otto, achieve educational and eventually professional success.

The progression of Ida's life was complicated by her abrupt termination of treatment with Freud after only three months of analysis. And so it was that on the last day of the year 1900, to the surprise and chagrin of Freud, she said adieu.

Ida remained somewhat symptom-free for a number of years and in 1903 married and shortly thereafter gave birth to a son. She seemingly recovered her emotional health through her own agency. Strangely, after all that had transpired between her and the Zellenkas, she maintained a relationship with Peppina, her father's mistress. They became partners as bridge masters, teaching the popular card game during the 1930s when bridge was all the rage in Vienna.

According to Sheila Kohler, who wrote a fictionalized story of Ida's life, Ida was a fierce and formidable mother who urged her gifted little boy to study music and learn foreign languages. Fearful of what was happening in Europe, she believed that his knowledge of other languages and cultures would enable him to leave Austria at the right moment.[9]

Because of her brother's Marxist affiliation, the Nazis sought Ida in the late 1930s. This was a short time after her husband's death. Fortunately, she was able to hide from the Nazis until she could secure transport to Paris, which was arranged for by her brother, who was living there, and her son, who was living in the United States. Unfortunately, before Ida could leave Vienna, she was informed that her brother had died.

Eventually, Ida did arrive in Paris, her transport arranged by friends of her late brother. She stayed there for several years. She then made her way to Casablanca, where she was taken ill. She had to delay her trip to the United States for several more months. She eventually flew to New York and then on to Chicago, where she was reunited with her son, Kurt, before she died of cancer—like her mother.

Kurt Herbert Adler, Ida's son, died in 1988. He is survived by his third wife, Nancy; two daughters, Kristin Krueger and Sabrina; and two sons, Ronald and Roman, from a previous marriage; as well as two grandchildren. Her great-granddaughter, Katharina Adler, has recently written a fictionalized life of her great-grandmother, called *Ida*.[10]

Ida's story is particularly important because she would not allow herself to be treated with disrespect by male physicians or others, even as a young woman. Her analysis, written up by Freud and published as *Dora: An Analysis of a Case of Hysteria*, portrayed her in a poor light. Years later, feminist scholarship took on Freud's inappropriate handling of Ida and the implications for Freudian analysis for women.

While feminist scholars have written about Ida, she was less a feminine role model than other Freud subjects, such as Anna O. who went on to become a famous social worker. But these writers do not delve into Ida's entire life—only the segment that reflects on Freud's use or abuse of her and other female patients. Over the years, these feminist theorists have taken up the study of Freud and Dora and have in essence created an academic cottage industry from her analysis.

Yet Ida, the real woman rather than the fictionalized Dora, led a successful life despite the trying circumstances of her family life and her own disabilities. Her family situation resulted in debilitating symptoms from which she suffered throughout her entire life. And Austrian society, led by Hitler and his condemnation and persecution of Jews, brought her to the depths of despair and poverty. Despite all this, Ida managed to create a family and a professional life. It was not until she had to leave Vienna, both because of the activities of her brother and because of the Jewish situation in Europe, that her life once again became destabilized.

Not much is known about the full life of this woman, Ida Bauer Adler, who is mostly written about simply as "Dora." Like many unsung heroes and unknown women, Ida lived a precarious life brought about by male sexual dominance, a medical profession that demeaned women, and her own mental instability due to those familial acts of abuse and ignorance. Despite all this, she managed to survive. She maintained a somewhat stable marriage and raised a brilliant son, making sure he had the skills to overcome the Nazi regime. In addition, she provided for herself after her family's money was lost following World War I. And, finally, she was able to secure a new life for herself in the United States with her son.

Ida Bauer's connection with Freud has always been the reason articles and books have been written about her. This will be the first full-scale biography of her in English and will shed light not only on her "failed" relationship with Freud and her aborted psychoanalysis, but also on her indomitable spirit. She was a remarkable girl and woman, and her story needs to be told.

# PART I

# *Secrets and Lies*

He that has eyes to see and ears to hear may convince
himself that no mortal can keep a secret. If his lips are
silent, he chatters with his fingertips; betrayal oozes out
of him at every pore.

—Sigmund Freud

# CHAPTER 1

# The Search for Secrets

Ida Bauer, Freud's Dora, was complex and confounding. She was an intelligent, troubled young woman of seventeen when she began her analysis with Freud. At the time, her family of origin and her extended family had so many problems and troubles that Ida apparently was forced to shoulder hers alone. At the time of her birth in Vienna on November 1, 1888, her family resided at Berggasse 32, just up the street from Freud's consulting room and family apartment, making her trek to see him consist of only a few steps. Freud moved there in 1891, when the building was newly constructed.

Her first visit to the esteemed Dr. Freud occurred when Ida was only fifteen years old, in the early summer of 1898—years before the start of the famous analysis. After pushing the buzzer, she and her father opened the door onto the dingy ground floor and made their way up the marble stairwell. They reached the first floor and Freud's suite of offices, entering the waiting room and then waiting for her father's psychiatrist to see her. By this time, she had been suffering for years from various symptoms and had visited many physicians, stayed at numerous spas, and had been a patient at many treatment centers. At the behest of her mother, she had tried hydrotherapy and electroshock treatments. All to no avail. Now her father wanted her to visit his physician—the up-and-coming Sigmund Freud.

But she would have none of it.

Sigmund Freud's Dora was born into a family and a culture that embraced secrets. There was a secret Austro-Hungarian plan to intervene in the Timok uprising in Serbia.[1] This had little or no impact on Ida and her family, but it is illustrative of the secrets that surrounded Austria and Germany at the time. These and the secrets Freud was studying would have far-reaching implications for Ida, too.[2] Freud himself had secret relationships that compounded and confounded his life and perhaps his patients. He also delved into the secrets of other women patients, perhaps doing a better job with these patients than he did with Ida.

As for the secrets within Ida's own family, they were legion. It was those secrets that drove Ida to Freud in the first place. Freud, a trained neurologist, was making a name for himself at that time in treating hysteria, a condition primarily seen in women. He would have far to go, however, from his initial experiments, and in his treatment of "Dora," to developing ground-breaking therapies for psychiatric illnesses using what he would eventually call psychoanalysis.

About a year before Ida's birth, Freud began experimenting with hypnosis. "During the past weeks I have thrown myself into hypnosis and have achieved all sorts of small but noteworthy successes," he wrote in a letter to his friend and colleague, Wilhelm Fliess.[3] The field of psychiatry would be changed not only hypnosis by also by using dreams, talk therapy, and the uncovering of secrets as treatment modalities.[4] But with all his burgeoning knowledge about the human mind, it would turn out that Freud did not understand his young patient's clinical situation. As Barron writes, "In the same way that he conducted a subtle search for secrets in specimen dreams, he tried to search for Dora's secrets by paying attention to seemingly insignificant details of her life. The treatment's failure led to the discovery of the deeper central secret, the transference."[5] Sadly, Ida, an ill seventeen-year-old when she started her analysis with him, only wanted peace, not psychiatric discoveries. Their coming together helped Freud understand certain concepts, but it did little for her. To understand Ida and her story, we need to begin with Freud.

Sigismund Schlomo Freud was born on May 9, 1856, in Freiberg, Moravia, in the Moravian-Silesian region of the Czech Republic. His father, Jacob Koloman Freud, was a wool and textile merchant, and his mother, Amalia, was Jacob's third wife. His father was not doing well financially at the time of Freud's birth. New regulations were being established for full freedom of trade in Austria, but especially in Vienna. Because that city's economy was growing rapidly, Freud's father thought there would be better opportunities for

Freud's birthplace, Freiberg, Austrian Empire (later Příbor, Czech Republic), was in a rented room in a locksmith's house (Jiří Jurečka, Wikimedia Commons).

himself and his family there. In 1860, they moved to the Leopoldstadt section of Vienna—the so-called Jewish ghetto—where Freud was educated, first at home with his mother and with some help from his father. Eventually, he entered a formal school and graduated summa cum laude from the Sperl Gymnasium (Leopoldstädter Kommunal-Real-und Obergymansium).[6]

Freud started classes at Vienna University in 1873 to study medicine. Although initially thinking about becoming a lawyer, he came to understand that in Vienna at that time, the wiser option would be medicine. (Jews were allowed into medical school but had difficulty entering law school.) In 1875, Freud changed his name to Sigmund, dropping Sigismund Schlomo forever. He qualified as a neurologist in 1881. From 1882 to 1883, Freud was employed at the Theodor Meynert Psychiatric Clinic in Vienna. As a practicing neurologist, Freud saw many patients while working in the lab as a cerebral researcher.[7]

Freud was interested in more than just science. Throughout his life, he reveled in Shakespeare's great tragedies, which he read in English. The works of Shakespeare, Harold Bloom informs us, cemented Freud's understanding of human nature and helped him come to an understanding of what psychology was and how it impacted people's lives.[8] This is what led to the dramatic nature of his famous case studies.

Freud's life was not all medicine and scientific theories, either. In 1882, the year of Ida's birth, he met and became engaged to Martha Bernays, the daughter of a prominent Jewish Vienna family whose ancestors included a chief rabbi of Hamburg and Heinrich Heine, the German poet, who had an international reputation and great influence in the world of literature. Martha was from an observant orthodox Jewish family, while Freud appeared to be Jewish in name only, as his family did not practice any of the Jewish rituals.

While Freud and Martha met in April 1882, they did not marry until four years later, on September 14, 1886. While they were apart during their engagement, Freud wrote close to nine hundred letters to his beloved. The engagement was tumultuous, but the marriage of fifty-three years would be harmonious, according to many biographers of Freud—but perhaps not as successful as one would imagine.[9]

As their engagement was a long one (Freud would have little money for marrying for some time), he was able to work on his ideas and projects. Freud's inquiring mind was always researching and experimenting—sometimes with disastrous results, as in his skirmish with cocaine.

In 1884, thinking cocaine could be a miracle therapy, he began to study the physical and psychological effects of the drug; however, he misunderstood its addictive properties. Shortly after experimenting on himself with it, he left Vienna somewhat in disgrace for his attempts to use cocaine therapeutically.

On a scholarship, Freud was able to travel to Paris to work with famous neurologist Jean-Martin Charcot from October 1885 to February 1886. This travelling scholarship enabled him to study the effects of nervous diseases under Charcot at the Salpêtrière Hospital in Paris. Freud was fascinated by Charcot's work on traumatic hysteria and took from it the notion that one of the principal forms of neurosis came about when a traumatic experience led to a process of unconscious symptom formation.[10]

Charcot was using hypnosis to work with patients diagnosed with hysteria, a term used for many different ailments, such as depression, epilepsy, and multiple sclerosis.[11] At the time Freud was learning about hysteria, it was understood that the condition mostly affected women. It was

Jean-Martin Charcot, who is considered the father of French neurology and one of the world's pioneer neurologists (National Library of Medicine, Wikimedia Commons).

through this work with Charcot that Freud came to understand how powerful the role words play in the treatment of mental illness as well as physical ailments.[12]

However, even before Freud's departure in 1885 for Paris and his work with Charcot, Freud had begun what would be an auspicious relationship with Josef Breuer, a physician working in neurophysiology. It was Breuer who sowed the seeds of hypnosis and the so-called talking cure in working with patients diagnosed with hysteria. Breuer had briefly discussed with Freud his work with some of his patients, especially with Bertha Pappenheim, whom Breuer treated from 1880 to 1882.[13] We will learn more about Bertha and other women that Freud treated as a way of understanding what may have gone wrong with Freud's treatment of Ida.

Following his return from Paris in 1886, the same year he married Martha, Freud opened a private practice specializing in nervous disorders. By this time, he was convinced that hypnosis, and what he was hearing of the talking cure used by Breuer in his treatment of Pappenheim, could be a useful therapeutic tool. He was just waiting for the opportunity to use it on one of his patients. Freud was convinced that this could be used with patients suffering from the many symptoms brought on by hysteria. The therapy involved treating mental disorders by delving into a person's unconscious thoughts and motivations. He was "profoundly impressed" with what he learned from Breuer and was determined to try it himself.[14]

In early 1886, Freud had an opportunity to employ Breuer's therapy with Mathilde Schleicher, a twenty-seven-year-old musician and the daughter of the Viennese painter Cölestin Schleicher, one of Freud's earlier patients.

**Bertha Pappenheim (Josef Breuer's Anna O.) in 1882, when Bertha was twenty-two years old (archive of Sanatorium Bellevue, Kreuzlingen, Germany; Wikimedia Commons).**

She had become seriously ill after abandonment by her fiancé, developing what was described as a nervous illness. She had been recommended to Freud by Breuer because of her migraines and nervous disposition. Freud had only recently, in April 1886, set up in private practice as a doctor treating nervous disorders, a so-called "nerve doctor." Freud saw Mathilde for three years using talk therapy and hypnosis, after which both she and Freud thought she was cured.[15]

In gratitude, she gave him a history book: *Germania: Two Millennia of German Life*, by Mikkel Borch-Jacobsen, author of many works on the history and philosophy of psychiatry, psychoanalysis, and hypnosis. She had inscribed it, "To the excellent Dr. Freud, with my affectionate memory. As a token of the deepest gratitude and the deepest respect. Mathilde Schleicher, June 1889."[16]

Unfortunately, Mathilde's story did not end there. Shortly after treatment with Freud, she developed mania and again became agitated, sleepless, and grandiose. She was ultimately committed by Freud on October 29, 1889, to the private clinic of Dr. Wilhelm Svetlin, where she was given, among other drugs, sulfonal, a pharmaceutical that neither Svetlin nor Freud understood well.

Unfortunately, Mathilde Schleicher died on September 24, 1890, an ugly death, with her urine filled with blood, indicating liver damage. She was buried two days later in the Jewish section of Vienna's Central Cemetery. Freud was puzzled by her death, which came about because of a too-high dose of sulfonal over a long period of time, which caused the liver damage.[17]

During the treatment of Mathilde, and undeterred following the disaster of her death, Freud continued discussing his cases with Breuer and how talk therapy might be a viable treatment strategy. In 1888, they decided to document a case Breuer worked on and discussed intensely with Freud—the Anna O. case study. They described in their book the cathartic talk therapy that had been employed by Breuer with Bertha Pappenheim, the patient of the case study.

While Freud was becoming established as a neurologist, but publishing little, Bertha had been explaining to Breuer her symptoms: paralysis of the limbs, disturbances of vision and speech, and an inability to drink water. These had begun following the nursing of her dying father, whose illness began in mid–1880. Her father died on April 5, 1881, after which Bertha's symptoms became so much worse that she was admitted—against her will—to a sanatorium. Her treatments over the years with Breuer resulted in some periods of stability, but relapses caused her to return to a sanatorium several times.[18]

During Breuer's treatment of her, he noticed that Bertha's symptoms either reduced or disappeared as she spoke about them. As Bertha told more stories, Breuer was able to gain insight into her state of mind. He concluded that the traumatic experiences from her past brought on her symptoms, which contributed to his diagnosis of hysteria. On October 29, 1882, her condition improved enough for her to be released from treatment, although she continued to suffer for years, saved perhaps by her own indomitable spirit.[19] As the years went on, it was instructive to see how well she survived following her treatment and how much she accomplished as a professional woman, despite having symptoms until she died. Her recovery was unlike Ida's in her treatment with Freud.

While conversing with Breuer and studying his methods, Freud was himself developing a mixed reputation for his theories. He started publishing his few pieces of writing and was working with patients where the emphasis of his treatments was on the sexual. Even though the works Freud published were frequently ignored or maligned, he still managed to connect with a coterie of like-minded physicians who thought his revolutionary ideas had merit, such as Wilhelm Fliess, the Berlin physician with whom he would eventually have lengthy discussions about Ida.[20]

By 1891, having married and established both a practice and a framework for his theories, Freud moved into his new building on Berggasse 19, near the Bauers. He was treating patients using hypnosis and the talking cure. He had several patients, including Anna von Lieben (called Cäcilie M. in his writings about her) and Elisabeth von R. It was not until this time that he was able to write up the Anna O. case study, which he and Breuer published in *Studies in Hysteria* in 1893.[21]

In 1900, Freud wrote what would later become known as his

groundbreaking work, *The Interpretation of Dreams* (*Die Traumdeutung*), where the term *psychoanalysis* was first used.[22] Following this, Freud began analysis on himself, believing that dreams shed light on feelings and hidden desires. He followed up self-analysis by treating his family and friends, and found that their repressed wishes could be analyzed in terms of their symbolism.[23] He would use his understanding of dreams in his analysis of Ida and in the published case study where he wrote about two dreams that she described to him in the three months they spent together.

And what of Ida during these years that were so complicated and challenging for Freud?

While Freud was struggling to make a name for himself, his most famous patient was also struggling with issues that would remain intermittently with her for the rest of her life. Ida Bauer, the Dora of Freud's most famous case study, was more than a character in a short story, as she is sometimes viewed by those reading the study. In fact, she was a troubled young woman who found that Freud could not help her, so she had to help herself.

But before we look intimately at Ida's life and come to some understanding of her relationship with Freud, we need to understand his relationship with women—particularly with his mother.

## CHAPTER 2

# The Secret
# of Freud's Women

As with many men, perhaps all men, the quality of their relationships with parents impacts their other relationships, depending on what those parental relationships were like. Boys learn about relationships with other women from their mothers, especially in seeing how their parents interact with each other, while they learn to live in the world from their fathers—at least that's how it was in Victorian times.[1] Ida, too, learned relationships from watching her parents, and the family dynamic within the Bauer household proved traumatic, and perhaps complicated her eventual relationship with Freud.

It would be impossible to discover anything about Freud and his relationship with Ida without first examining Freud's relationship with the other women in his life—especially his mother and eventually his wife, sister-in-law, and daughter. How well mothers and fathers cared for each other impacts children's lives, as a loving couple imparts a certain sensibility to children that carries through to friends and partners.[2]

While I might argue that Freud's lifelong connection with his mother impacted his interaction with female patients, his father also contributed to Freud's personality and psychoanalytic theories, but in a negative way. And because Freud had somewhat complicated relationships with both his parents, all of that played out in his life, his work, and with his analytic patients.

The tension within Freud was apparently because he harbored a lifelong disappointment with one parent and adored the other, although neither assessment of Freud's was totally based on reality. However, the parental conflicts and unresolved issues Freud experienced affected all his connections, both professional and personal.

On the surface, Freud seemed to enjoy male companionship and entered into a number of fruitful and meaningful relationships with many of his professional male colleagues—for a time. He would begin these relationships, mostly professional but which turned personal, with deep conversations and intimacy, but sooner or later, Freud, always competitive, would have a falling out, and he would reject his friend forever, as he did with Wilhelm Fliess and Carl Jung, to name just two of the people he loved and then pushed away.[3]

It seems that his relationships with men were more fraught than those with women. Because of the feeling that his father let him down and did not provide the emotional support and the modeling that he needed, Freud always wanted to be the most successful and knowledgeable partner in any relationship with men. Freud's relationship with his father was more complicated than with his mother, which was less nuanced. He judged his father harshly, by all accounts, because of his father's financial ineptitude, among other real or perceived failings.[4]

Jakob, Freud's father, entered bankruptcy and was forced to move his family first to Leipzig in 1859 and then to Vienna in 1860, pulling his son away from Freiburg, where he had family and friends. Jakob had hopes of making a better living and providing a happier life for his family because of this move. Freud was about four years of age at the time and later wrote that he felt lost and alone, losing everything of importance to him at this very young and impressionable age. This would also be true for Ida, who at the age of six left a stable home life because of her father's illness and moved away from Vienna.

For most of his life, Freud feared poverty, which he believed was due to his father's lack of financial success. "All his life, Freud masked his disappointment in his father, even from himself," Ernest Jones tells us.[5] Freud eventually became wealthy, while Ida started out rich but saw the family fortune obliterated following first one war then another.

Once in Vienna, Freud's family apparently lived somewhat

harmoniously in Leopoldstadt. A second child was born, then others. Freud felt jealous of the new arrivals, and his feelings of competition for his mother's love also stayed with him all his life. Jakob and Amalia retained their Orthodox Jewish roots in Vienna but did not foist their religious beliefs on their children. Freud would end up distancing himself from the religious side of Judaism but would remain Jewish culturally, also like the Bauer family.

Freud's mother, Amalia Malka Nathansohn, was born on August 18, 1835. She grew up in Odessa—the home of her mother—and was the third wife of Jakob Freud, who was forty at the time Sigismund, as he was originally called, was born. (Ida's mother would also be the child of her father's third marriage.) Freud was his mother's first-born and came on the scene when Amalia was twenty years old. At the time, Amalia and Jakob were living in Freiberg in Moravia, where Jakob was engaged in the textile business.[6]

Freud's birth was special. He was born with a caul, literally a "helmeted head," which is a piece of membrane that covers a newborn's head and face. It is a rare phenomenon, harmless, and some said it signified that the child would be special. Birth with a caul is rare, occurring in fewer than 1 in 80,000 births. (David Copperfield, one of Freud's favorite characters, was also born with a caul.)[7]

Amalia would go on to produce seven other children (one died in infancy), but seemingly, Sigmund was always her favorite. She also tried to be a mother to some degree to the two sons from Jakob's first wife—Emmanuel and Philip. (Jakob's second wife had not produced any offspring.) Jakob's two sons were adults when Amalia and Jakob married, and when "Sigi," as he was called, was born, one brother already had a son of his own. This boy, who was born a few years before Freud, became one of Sigi's favorite playmates. It was this nephew, John, whom Freud believed influenced all his subsequent relationships with other men, which, while being friendly, were also confrontational, loving, and hateful. The two vied for leadership throughout their relationship, with neither one ending up being the leader.

Freud was educated by his mother during his early years. His mother was the major force in the family. Amalia, a strong-willed

woman, was said to be intelligent, quick-tempered, and egotis-
tical but also lively and humorous. According to Ernest Jones, she
called her eldest son *"mein goldener Sigi."*[8] If Amalia thought the
world of her Sigi, he thought the world of her, and her domineering hold over him would last a lifetime and was never fully analyzed
by him, according to many. He eventually came to believe that the
mother-son relationship was nearly perfect, the most ideal of all
human relationships.[9]

It has been argued that Freud turned his unsolved and suppressed negative feelings for his mother onto other relationships,
specifically his fiancée and later wife, and his professional colleagues. He ultimately had an intensely close relationship with his
sister-in-law, as well as with his daughter, Anna, who followed in
his professional footsteps, becoming a pioneering child psychiatrist.

While he was never able to fully maintain adult male relationships, his female relationships seemed to be less complicated on the
surface. Yet even his relationship with his wife, arguably his most
important connection, seemed distant (perhaps partly due to his
close association with Minna, the sister of his wife). Perhaps because
of his adoring yet unrealistic relationship with his mother, he frequently engaged in close and intimate relationships with women—
except for Ida. From the case study he wrote, it seems as if he never
really felt an affinity for this troubled young woman.

Freud's understanding or misunderstanding of women can in
some ways be illustrated by his famous question, "What do women
want?" Freud also seemed to believe that women were inferior to
men, which aligned with the prevailing opinion in Europe at the
time, so this was not something exclusive to Freud.[10]

It is little wonder, then, that he had such difficulties with the
high-spirited and neurotic Ida Bauer, who had tried to educate herself and who lived with feelings of inferiority caused in part by her
adoring yet envious relationship with her brilliant brother, Otto.
Ida's feelings of inferiority were reinforced by Austria's—and the
rest of Europe's—sense of women's place in the world. We also must
remember that Ida was one of Freud's first female patients, and he

experimented on her with the new techniques that he had been learning about and thinking about with Breuer and Charcot.

Before he even opened his own practice, or first saw Ida, Freud had some sense of a woman's emotional and psychological life because of Bertha Pappenheim and her relationship with Josef Breuer. As Freud spent time with Breuer discussing Bertha, they ultimately wrote up her case study, calling her Anna O. From that case study and other works, feminist scholars have said that Bertha should be noted as the better feminist psychiatric heroine and role model—rather than Ida—because her recovery from her hysteria was much more successful than Ida's. Bertha's life was more profound and meaningful than Ida's, as Bertha accomplished much. Was Breuer a better analyst than Freud? Or was Bertha a more resilient woman than Ida could ever hope to be?

Born in 1859, Bertha was the third daughter in a traditional Jewish family, with a merchant father and an heiress mother. As just "another Jewish daughter," Bertha was conscious of the fact that her parents would have preferred a son; one did arrive a few years later.

Her life, within an apparently loving family, had its own traumas: her elder sister died of consumption when Bertha was eight years old. Her younger brother, born a few years after Bertha, was the son everyone had always wanted, as was Ida's elder brother Otto. He attended school to prepare for a distinguished professional life, as did Ida's brother. Bertha, relegated to household and cooking duties with her mother, was jealous of her brother although she loved and admired him, similar to how Ida felt about Otto. (Bertha had been forced to leave school at sixteen years of age, while Ida never even went to school.)[11]

As has been mentioned, Bertha became ill upon the illness and death of her father, and between 1880 and 1882 was in treatment with Breuer. Eventually, after many hospitalizations and setbacks, and her long-term treatment with Breuer, Bertha began to think about writing, ultimately publishing in 1888 under a pseudonym. Her work and her writing were both political and social. She worked in a soup kitchen and in an orphanage for Jewish girls, which she would later oversee. She established educational activities for the girls in her care because she wanted to help young girls see that there were other avenues for them besides marriage. Bertha remained for the rest of her life a champion of women's rights, even translating Mary Wollstonecraft's *A Vindication of the Rights of Woman* from English into German. She worked tirelessly for women's causes until she died in 1936.[12]

Freud, of course, did not treat Anna O., but he did write about her case in detail with Josef Breuer, so he had to have some appreciation for her greatness. Surprisingly, he did not seem to bring that appreciation of women's potential into his treatment of Ida.

After his publication of the therapy of the two women, Bertha Pappenheim (Anna O.) and Ida Bauer (Dora), Freud would work with other female patients: the poet HD (Hilda Doolittle), Maria Bonaparte, and others, as well as analyzing his own daughter. Anna Freud, Freud's sixth and youngest child, would be considered the founder of child psychology and was perhaps the closest to Freud of all his children.[13]

Like Ida Bauer, Freud's daughter, Anna, never had a close relationship with her mother. She was nurtured instead by her nurse. She never got along well with her siblings, either. Anna had a history of illnesses like Ida's, such as those of a psychosomatic nature, and she was made to rest at home and was sent to spas—again like Ida. She may also have suffered from depression, which caused eating disorders. Born in 1895, some thirteen years after Ida, Anna was only five years of age when Freud was seeing Ida. At sixteen, then, when Anna might have been going through her difficult times, and thus might have had some empathy for Ida, Freud was no longer treating Ida.

To be fair, Freud would learn a great deal in the years following his involvement with Ida, not only from his theoretical work and analysis of numerous patients, but also from his relationship with his daughter, who continued to experience health issues. She began her professional life as a teacher but resigned from her post in 1920 because of multiple episodes of illness. Had Freud been working with Ida in 1920, he might have had a better understanding of her based solely on his reflection of his own daughter's illnesses. Of course, as is well known, Anna, like Pappenheim, went on to have a brilliant career, becoming an outstanding child psychiatrist and analyst, an exceptional woman in her own right, and a person whose lifelong partner was another woman.[14]

In Freud's analysis of Ida, he determined that she had suppressed lesbian tendencies and desires. In the case study where he discusses this potential side of Ida, he does not seem condemnatory. Did he know, perhaps intuitively, that his beloved daughter and mentee would eventually engage in a lesbian relationship, one that would last until the end of her days? Unfortunately for Anna, he was not so merciful toward his own daughter regarding her potential homosexuality as it seemed he was with Ida. Freud wrote a paper about his daughter and her sexuality and read it to a group where Anna was in the audience.

Anna later sat in the audience as her father read that paper to the public. Though he did not share her name with the audience, he did make it clear that he thought it unlikely that her case would end well, and it was unlikely she would ever be able to reach "sexual normalcy"—meaning, of course, that a lesbian relationship could not provide women the sexual intimacy and satisfaction that they desired.

This experience of Freud presenting a paper covertly about her, in front of her, was what finally ended Anna's analytic sessions with her father. Hurt and betrayed, she focused even more on her own work.[15] Nonetheless, regardless of Freud's clinical assessment, Anna and her partner Dorothy Burlingham forged a meaningful life partnership, by all accounts.

And what of Ida during those years when she was reaching adulthood, as Freud was raising a family and accomplishing much in his professional life? Ida was growing up in a family that would determine the course of her life. That family consisted of an adulterous father, a punitive and withdrawn mother, a brilliant brother, and several women (including her mother) who had compromising psychiatric conditions. Ida would not only measure herself against these women but mimic them.

It is with this history of Freud's relationships with women, both before his interactions with her and after, that we finally come to Ida's story.

## CHAPTER 3

# The Bauer Ménage
# and *Its* Secrets

Ida Bauer was the product of two parents who never seemed to be completely satisfied with each other. The many complications that each brought to the marriage caused Ida difficulties for most of her life.

Ida Bauer's parents came from the same area of central Europe, and both families were involved in the textile business, so they might have been compatible due to their shared heritage. However, that was not to be the case. Her parents were dysfunctional almost from the beginning of their marriage, if not their courtship. And from an early age, Ida and older brother Otto were aware of the disharmony within their parents' marriage.

Ida's father, Philipp Bauer, was born on August 14, 1853, in the small market town of Pollerskirchen in the eastern part of Bohemia, a woody, verdant area. Interestingly, he lived only 120 miles from the small town where Freud was born. Bohemia, located in the westernmost and largest historical region of what is today the Czech Republic, has a rich history.[1]

Philipp Bauer's family had been established for generations in Bohemia and was involved in the manufacturing of wool. He was the son of Jacob Bauer and Babette Mauthner,[2] his father's second wife. Philipp had two brothers, Karl and Ludwig, and a younger sister, Malvine. His sister was born in 1856 when Philipp was three. Malvine would come to be influential in the life of Ida, Philipp's only daughter.[3]

When Philipp was still only a toddler, possibly around 1855 or 1856, his father, like Freud's father, made the fateful decision to move the family to Vienna from the countryside, following in the steps of

Bohemian Jews who sought greater freedom and acceptance in the Austrian capital.[4]

There were periods throughout Bohemia's history when Jews were persecuted, murdered, expelled from the area, or forced to resettle elsewhere. At the same time, however, some Jews in some locales were tolerated, which caused conflicting ideas about their place in Bohemia and society. Because of this, Bohemian Jews felt separate from the rest of the population.[5]

Most Jewish families at the time did not completely identify with being Jewish. Although the Bauers spoke Czech, as well as the prevailing German language of the area, they did not use Yiddish, if they knew it at all, as the use of both Yiddish and Hebrew were eliminated in business records. According to the *Yivo Encyclopedia of Jews in Eastern Europe*:

> By the close of the 1860s, the Jews of Bohemia and Moravia had already experienced one modernization: a restructuring of religious practices, political identification, and economic profile that had been set in motion by the reforms of the 1780s. Though still predominantly rural, Jewish society had abandoned most of its premodern forms. The community had no juridical autonomy; traditional Jewish education had fallen into disuse, as had the Yiddish language; and Bohemian and Moravian Jews no longer suffered from residential, demographic, or occupational restrictions.[6]

Because of these and other cultural tensions, the Bauers, like many soon-to-be-prosperous Jews, depended on the good will of their community. They continually feared the political swings and turmoil at the national level, and there had been many changes to the status of Jews over the years, mostly not in their favor. It was not until the ascension of Emperor Joseph II, king of Hungary, Croatia, and Bohemia, that things changed for Bohemian Jews, especially in Vienna.[7]

Emperor Joseph had enlightened ideas about Jews and wanted them to be more useful for the state. On February 13, 1782, in the Edict of Tolerance (*Toleranzpatent*), he decreed new laws that would help the Jewish population while also helping him. Although these laws and edicts were not specifically designed for the improvement of the status of Jews and did not offer them any special advantages, they allowed Jews to be treated like other citizens under most laws.

37

Joseph opened all forms of trade and commerce to Jewish participation, encouraged Jews to establish factories, and urged them to
engage more fully in the artisan crafts and agriculture. Yet Jews were
still not allowed to own rural property or attain the rank of master or
citizen in the crafts.[8]

All these political and administrative improvements would
come to benefit the Bauer family. And while there were still restrictions—for instance, the requirement to have a German elementary
education to obtain a marriage license or permission from authorities to build a synagogue—individual Jews were slowly allowed to
be encircled in the general culture. The result was that Jews felt as
if they were earnestly invited to become citizens in many parts of
Austria.[9]

However, it was the development of modern machinery in the
textile mills in the mid–1860s that ushered in the burgeoning Bohemian textile industry, resulting in increased wealth for some, like
Philipp Bauer and his family (and as we shall see, his wife's family).
While Jews now had the opportunity to be more agrarian under the
new edicts, they had little experience with farming or agriculture. As
they had been peddlers for centuries, a move toward textiles, such
as linen, wool, and cotton manufacturing, seemed to make the most
sense.[10]

The move to Vienna by Philipp's parents, from a country to
an urban environment, might have caused stress to the family
and to the toddler. According to Decker, although Philipp was "a
pleasant-looking child, he was, however, slightly handicapped from
birth by vision in only one eye."[11] A move from familiar and calmer
surroundings to the frantic life of the city could have been frightening, especially given that Vienna at the time was political and sometimes difficult for the Jewish families who arrived continuously in
search of housing and job opportunities.

At this time, in approximately 1855, a few years following the
Revolution of 1848, many Jewish intellectuals welcomed the opportunity to agitate for the emancipation of their community. For the
first time in their history, Jews would be accorded the unrestricted
right to reside in and practice their religion throughout Austria via

the constitution. Consequently, the Jewish community in Vienna grew rapidly: in 1860, the Jewish community numbered 6,200; by 1870, that number had already risen to 40,200; and by the turn of the century, to 147,000. Jewish families understood that on the surface Vienna supported Jews, with Leopoldstadt being the center of Vienna and Judaism. Those arriving in the capital congregated there, in areas that would today be considered ghettos or slums.[12]

Vienna's Second District, Leopoldstadt, developed into the center of Jewish life at this time.[13] While somewhat of a hectic, crime-ridden, and dirty area (*Judenstadt*, or Jewish ghetto), this section of Vienna, virtually an island in the heart of the city, provided arriving Jews with everything they needed: housing, taverns, shops, and employment opportunities. Furthermore, Leopoldstadt was the terminus for the Northern Railway, which meant cheap transportation from Bohemia and Moravia to Vienna. By 1860, when Philipp Bauer's father moved his family there, Leopoldstadt already had a strong Jewish sensibility, with not only essentials for living, but also established synagogues. Almost every arriving Jewish family had relatives in Leopoldstadt with whom they could stay upon arrival—as Freud and his family did.[14]

Families like the Bauers and the Freuds would eventually have a great impact on Vienna society as they became more economically successful and academically influential. The large number of Jewish inhabitants, mostly in the Leopoldstadt section of Vienna where the Bauers settled, led to the area being called *Die Mazzesinsel* (Island of Matzo), referring to the unleavened bread eaten during Passover. There were several important synagogues there, as well as schools, yeshivas, Orthodox Jewish educational establishments, and stores.[15]

Leopoldstadt, in the heart of Vienna, was initially home to fabric and tailor's shops. It is the site of the *Wiener Prater*, a large public park, and the home of Vienna's *Riesenrad*, a giant wheel, which was constructed in 1897. At the time that the Bauer family lived there, it was a robust area that maintained, among other things, numerous beer gardens, one of which was where the original Czech Budweiser draught beer was sold. The park was always filled with emigrating Jews straining to become middle and upper class, which was possible

In the Prater, Vienna, Austria,—the largest park in Europe.
Copyright 1896 by Underwood & Underwood.

**This postcard shows the *Wiener Prater*, Vienna, Austria, with the famous *Riesenrad*, the giant Ferris wheel, in the background. As noted on the card, at the time, the Prater was the largest park in Europe (Library of Congress).**

in Vienna at the time. It was the main source of entertainment for these somewhat impoverished Jewish families.[16]

As the Bauers and other families moved into Vienna society, they had the opportunity to practice Judaism, but only in a limited way. However, because they thought of themselves as progressives and as Germans, rather than primarily as Jews, they abandoned many religious and cultural traditions and practices, even though they were more likely to be allowed to engage in these activities in Vienna than they were in the Austrian and Czech countryside.

Philipp Bauer and Sigmund Freud's generation of Jews hoped that nothing would be denied them in political, academic, or other professional circles, even though anti–Jewish sentiment was on the rise and growing, albeit subtly.

Unlike Freud, Philipp, fortunately, did not have aspirations that were denied to him (that we know of); yet, not all of Austrian and Viennese society was open to him. For instance, he was easily able to enter his chosen profession of textile manufacturing because of his family's established factories, and he was by all accounts resourceful, forceful, ambitious, and enterprising. (He would have been a "captain of industry" if he were living in the United States.) Yet, he still lived among his own Jewish community—not within the wider Viennese society.[17]

Such was the environment in which Philipp Bauer grew up in Vienna. Little is known more specifically about his childhood, other than he was surrounded by extended family who had also moved to Vienna. Hard-working and energetic, young Philipp was by all accounts happy, as his family was socially and financially on the upswing.

As he came to adulthood, Philipp worked in his father's textile factories and enjoyed the social life of Vienna. Because men in Philipp Bauer's time did not marry until they were in their late twenties or thirties when they were more financially settled, they often chose to have sex with prostitutes or women from poor families, as it was generally frowned upon to engage sexually with women from their own station in life; that is, marriageable women. Consequently, like other young men, Philipp contracted syphilis at an early age. Some twenty percent of all young men in Vienna were so afflicted at the time.[18]

There was no cure for venereal diseases during Philip's time, but, according to Decker, there was no shortage of medical practitioners offering various ineffectual treatments: "Walking through doctors' neighborhoods one could read on every sixth or seventh door: 'Specialist for Skin and Venereal Disease.'"[19]

Syphilis has three distinct stages. In stage one, the infected patient has very few symptoms: no pain, and only a sore around the mouth or genitals that can last two to six weeks before disappearing. In the second stage, the patient experiences a rash and sore throat, which also tend to disappear after a few weeks, with the infection going into a latent or hidden phase. This stage could last for years. The third stage is when considerable damage occurs to the eyes, brain, and entire body.[20]

Philipp was probably in the second, asymptomatic, stage when he met and married his wife and conceived children. In about the tenth year of his marriage, he would enter the third stage and experience blindness and paralysis, which would catapult his marriage into a state that would have disastrous effects on his daughter Ida, if not his entire family.

At age twenty-six, Philipp met, courted, and became engaged

to the nine-years-younger Katherina Gerber, or Käthe as she was called.[21] Born in 1861 in Koniginhof, a mountainous village in Bohemia, Käthe, Jewish like her husband, had also come to Vienna with her family as a young child. Käthe's mother, Jeanette Gerber Pick (called Joanna), was the third wife of Bernhard Gerber, a cotton manufacturer. Käthe was the youngest of Bernhard's six children but the eldest of her parents' marriage.[22]

According to some reports, Käthe had a strange disposition, a myth perhaps perpetrated by Freud's assessment of her in the case study of her daughter. And while there is little written about her, one can perhaps assume that, as the youngest offspring of older parents, she might have been quiet and lonely and used to working within the home to help her aging parents. There is some indication that she was considered disagreeable and, as her marriage progressed—in problematic directions—she chose to overlook what was happening to her daughter and to her marriage right in front of her.[23]

What little we know about Käthe comes more from Freud than anyone else. In his writings, Freud is disparaging, describing her as a woman with "housewife psychosis."[24] Although he never met Käthe, he wrote that she was largely confined to the household and was obsessed with order and cleanliness. Strangely, he seemed to have a limited understanding of a woman's role in upper-middle-class family life and took a demeaning tone regarding Ida's mother, who did perform on the surface as most upwardly mobile housewives did, maintaining the household and not necessarily being active outside the home. Freud describes her as somewhat pathological, and some of the descriptions of her behavior toward her children do bear this out. But all this was to come later.

What we know about Käthe's childhood is that she seemed to have a desire to pass unnoticed, and once she married Philipp and became a mother, she stayed within the confines of her perfectly ordered house. As a Jewish girl, and later woman, perhaps she thought it best not to call attention to herself. And as the youngest child of a large family and the daughter of her father's third wife, Käthe may not have had the easiest life. Her mother was thirty-seven years old at the time of Käthe's birth, and while not old by today's standards, then it was considered the beginning of old age and a loss of vitality. And the move from Koniginhof to Vienna sometime in the late 1860s might have been unsettling for not only Käthe, but for her mother as well. Little is documented about Käthe's early years, so one can only speculate.

Käthe's father, a cotton manufacturer, was also engaged in wool processing and no doubt known to the Bauer family. The early 1860s witnessed a growing increase in Jewish investment and industrial ventures in textiles, with Jews leading in technological innovations and business organization methods. In Bohemia, Jewish participation in the textile industry reached its peak, with approximately fifty percent of all textile factories being owned by Jews.[25]

Because of early Jewish peddlers who bought and sold rags, becoming leaders in the textile industry was not so much of a leap. At the end of the nineteenth century, Jewish peddlers bought up raw materials in villages and supplied them to Jewish traders, who then sold fabrics and clothes in the villages.[26]

On the surface, textile manufacturing in Bohemia seemed ideally suited for people like Käthe's father and the Bauers. By 1867, Jews were allowed unrestricted rights to reside and practice their religion throughout Austria, especially in Vienna, where Jewish communities were growing rapidly. At different times, both the Bauer and Gerber families emigrated from Bohemia to that section of Vienna. It seemed that keeping textile and cotton mills in Bohemia, while living in the more cosmopolitan Vienna, gave Jews the best of both worlds.[27]

The Bauers and the Gerbers were part of a rapidly burgeoning Jewish middle class. On the surface, Vienna was liberal, secular, and metropolitan. Jews could develop a cultural identity, which has been seen as the most fascinating phenomenon in Jewish history. Erika Weinzierl, who died in 2014, was the second director of the Department of Contemporary History and a professor of history at the University of Vienna. She writes that as Jewish merchants, physicians, accountants, and bankers began moving up both socially and economically, they moved to the Ninth District, known as Alsergrund, forsaking the so-called Jewish ghetto. The Alsergrund area ranked third in number of Jewish inhabitants. It consisted mainly of doctors who settled in the vicinity of the General Hospital, where the Bauers and the Freuds eventually resided, around the area of Berggasse.[28]

Because both Philipp and Käthe's families resided in the very congenial if crowded Leopoldstadt, and both fathers were engaged in cotton, textile, and lumber manufacturing, it is not surprising that Philipp would become engaged to Käthe. Was it an arranged marriage? It is hard to say, as there is little known about what kind of courtship they had. We do know from historical narratives of Bohemian marriage patterns that they preferred to marry partners from the same area, as did Galicians and others from around Austria. And couples seemed to have little choice in who they married.[29]

According to one historian, "the majority of Viennese-born men refused partnerships with women born somewhere else; they preferred to marry Viennese-born women. Because many 'Western' Jews looked down on the *Ostjuden* (eastern Jews), why would they marry one of them?" And of those Viennese-born women, they seemingly had to come from the men's home districts.[30]

It is possible that the engagement of seventeen-year-old Käthe to Philipp was arranged and the two-year courtship uneventful. It also appears that Käthe had no knowledge of her husband's venereal disease when they married. Ultimately, in marriage, Philipp and Käthe were seemingly joined together by illness and dysfunction. For her part, Käthe suffered from gynecologic disorders and gastric and bowel distress. Still, she was able to get pregnant despite her illnesses and Philipp's venereal disease.

The Bauers' first child, a son, Otto, was born on September 5, 1881, at Leopoldsgasse 6–8, while the family lived in the Leopoldstadt area.[31] And while not actively practicing Judaism, they did have their son circumcised a week after his birth. Little is known about Otto's early life, although he would become a famous figure in Austrian politics.

According to Decker, five months after the birth of Otto, Käthe was again pregnant. She gave birth to Ida on November 1, 1882. At that time, the family had moved from Leopoldstadt to an apartment at Berggasse 32 (doors away from where Freud's apartment and consulting rooms would be housed about nine years later). This move was a signal to the tiny world of Jewish Viennese society that the Bauers had arrived, as the Berggasse area was deemed special and affluent.[32]

For Ida's birth, her mother was assisted by a midwife, Anna Eichenthal, which was customary at the time. Due to the prosperity of the textile mills owned by Philipp and his family, the move to the more affluent Alsergrund section of Vienna was a testament to the family's increased wealth and status. It also meant that the Bauers were now considered a respectable middle-class Jewish family.[33]

Little is known of the early years of the Bauers' marriage or of their life together. Freud would write later about Ida's father, however, as a shining object and seemed to think that Philipp was an exemplary figure. He treated him accordingly in his case study, while other writers saw Philipp differently. Patrick Mahony, for example, describes him here:

> A wealthy textile manufacturer, he could impress with his shrewdness and perspicacity. But he appeared crippled in both body and mind—and reportedly was impotent. Sickly in youth, Philip [*sic*] underwent a series of serious maladies in middle age. He was also given to hypocrisy and self-serving secrecy; he preferred "deviousness and a roundabout way." Philip's premarital syphilis in every way affected relations with his wife, and he transmitted it to her as part of an unexpected dowry.[34]

In 1890, Ida Bauer, age 8, with her beloved brother Otto (age 9), while living at Berggasse 32 in Vienna, just up the street from the Freuds's apartment and consulting room (**Wikimedia Commons**).

Because of Ida's family drama—a mother who was primarily focused on herself and housework and a duplicitous father who was mainly concerned with his image and his business—both Otto and Ida had problems in their youth. Otto was considered by Mahony as somewhat humorless with effeminate gestures and unkempt dress, although otherwise agreeable and quite bright. He was adored by both parents.[35]

Ida and Otto, only fourteen months apart in age, were very close and continued that intimacy for most of their lives. And they shared some unfortunate symptoms, too: they both wet the bed, which continued long after the age when children were in school, and both were frequently ill. One might assume that the bedwetting particularly inflamed their meticulous mother, who would have had to continuously change the children's bedding and garments.[36]

As the family drama unfolded, Ida tended to side with her father and Otto would take his mother's side if he had to; however, he frequently refused to get involved at all. Mahony tells the story of how Otto, studying in his room in winter, had to wear an overcoat, hat, and gloves because his mother felt that keeping the windows open, even in the dead of winter, was a healthy thing to do. As he told one of his visiting cousins, he did not necessarily think this strange.[37]

The two siblings studied together and were considered precocious—both bright and engaging, one active, the other more inward-focused. Otto was studious while Ida was a tomboy and rambunctious until she was about six. Ida adored her brother: she followed him around and perhaps even thought of herself as a boy. In her early years, she exhibited what in those days would be considered boyish ways, running, jumping, roughhousing, and was not the least bit modest or shy. Then an unexplained climbing accident changed her behavior. This event came at a time when her father, whom she worshipped, was away on a trip. Freud recounts this event, while describing Ida's first bout of chronic dyspnea.

> The first onset occurred after a short expedition in the mountains and was accordingly put down to over-exertion. In the course of six months, during which she was made to rest and was carefully looked after, this condition gradually passed off. The family doctor seems to have had not a moment's hesitation in diagnosing the disorder as purely nervous and in excluding any organic cause for the dyspnea; but he evidently considered this diagnosis compatible with the aetiology of over-exertion.[38]

## Chapter 3. *The Bauer Ménage and Its Secrets*

The family was still living in Vienna at the time, but their difficulties were increasing, both emotional and physical. While Philipp's business continued to be financially stable, he began having significant health issues. At the same time, Ida's mother was becoming more and more obsessed with housework, almost to the point of neglecting her children to keep the home pristine. The children, however, were surrounded by Philipp's family, and Ida was particularly close to her father's younger sister, Malvine. Some of the dysfunction of their own nuclear family was mitigated by the closeness and affection from their extended family, particularly from the Bauer relatives.

According to Decker, the Bauer family lived an unpretentious but affluent life in Vienna in a four-story dwelling, with Philipp exuding "the air of a solid citizen. He exemplified the liberal values of Vienna at that time, belonged to the Freemasons, and involved in charitable activities." He has been described as someone who did not "appear Jewish" and was charming, friendly, and intellectually alive.[39]

But all of this changed when at the age of thirty-five Philipp discovered that, in addition to his syphilis and his ongoing vision problems, which he had had since childhood, he had contracted tuberculosis. Because of his increasingly poor health, Philipp made the decision to move his family to Merano, the Tyrolean resort and spa town. This meant that Ida would have to leave the support of her beloved family—grandparents, uncles, cousins, and especially her aunt Malvine—at a time when Ida was having her own health problems, which appeared to be of a nervous nature.

In 1888, when Ida was six years old and her brother had just turned seven, the family made the move to Merano, a town more salubrious for Philipp's debilitating tuberculosis as well as his other conditions, but not so healthy for the rest of the family. Once established in Merano, Käthe was not able to visit her friends and family in Bohemia so easily because of the demands of her ailing husband and her dissatisfied family. By all accounts, Ida's mother ultimately became even more reclusive, escaping family outings and involving herself less in Philipp's care. It was here in Merano that she appeared to devote her entire life not only to housekeeping but also to her own illnesses, which were becoming more debilitating for her.[40]

As if Ida Bauer did not have enough trouble in her life, including poor health, mental instability, parental discord, an autocratic and demanding father, and a somewhat distant mother, the move to the small insular spa town was problematic. Merano was in many ways a strange place for children, with secrets of its own.

## CHAPTER 4

# The Secret Life of Merano

Due to the health issues of Ida's father, the family's relocation from Vienna to Merano was unsettling. They had to leave their comfortable home on Berggasse and access not only to their extended family but also to the cultural activities of Vienna. There, Otto and Ida were happy. However, Philipp had a huge business empire to deal with, with factories in both Náchod and Warnsdorf, which necessitated his getting well in order to take care of his business. He felt that if his health allowed, he could care for them in Merano.[1]

His life and that of his family were different in Merano. And although it was not better for the family as a whole, the more healthful way of life was helpful for Philipp. In his thirties at the time and feeling that he should think of his two young children, who were closely involved with their extended family, he thought that maybe he should turn the business over to the management of his brother, Karl, especially as he found that his own health continued to deteriorate even after the move to Merano.[2]

Merano, a mountain-encircled spa town, is both tranquil and enchanting and has a rich history. Located within a basin, it is protected from cold, wind, and rain in what is today South Tyrol in northern Italy. An ancient settlement, its history started in 15 BC according to some histories, and in more modern times was once the capitol of the County of Tyrol, until Duke Friedrich VI of Austria moved the Tyrolean court out of Innsbruck in 1420. According to the official homepage of Merano,

> The blooming markets of Meran lost their importance and the whole city gradually turned into an anonymous "cow-town," whose inhabitants were mainly craftspeople or peasants. The situation started to change first in 1809, with the struggle led by Andreas Hofer to free the Burggrafenamt

**The Tappeiner Promenade (*Tappeinerweg*) is situated in the middle of the city and was built for Empress Elizabeth. This health trail is still popular today (JFKCom, Wikimedia Commons).**

district. The host from the Passer valley and the chanters and travelling merchants who went all around Europe were the first sort of advertisers of Meran as a touristic destination. Soon famous scientists and doctors started to study the mild climate of the city recommending a stay in Meran to recover from various diseases. The dawn of a new era for tourism in Meran is to be considered the year 1836, when the countess Mathilde von Schwarzenberg, warned by Johann Huber, her personal physician, came from Vienna to receive treatment in the city of the river Passer. Back in Vienna, Huber published a writing recommending the climate of Meran, therefore producing—so to say—the first advertising leaflet about the Kurstadt. Shortly after and also thanks to the enthusiasm and the vision of some shrewd town leaders, Meran turned into an international high class health resort.[3]

When the Bauers came to Merano, Austria, in 1888, it was widely renowned for its tuberculosis cures. Its residents consisted of many international Jewish patients, who flocked there.[4] Strangely, despite this large influx of Jews, there was not a synagogue in Merano until 1901, when the first was inaugurated.[5] Providing physical rather than spiritual comfort was apparently the first goal of the Merano community. According to the *Judische Gemeinde Meran* (Jewish Community of Merano), hotels and sanatoriums were constructed to cover the needs of the poor and ailing Jewish community, complete with walking paths and promenades for relaxation and distraction. The first of these sanatoriums was built around 1893 at the villa Steiner.[6]

It took only a few years for Merano to become internationally renowned and frequented for its thermal health treatments. Many famous and important personalities spent their vacations in Merano to undergo the various treatments offered. For instance, Freud, his wife, and his sister-in-law came to the spa town several times, as did Franz Kafka in 1924, who suffered from lung disease.[7]

With torrents of people pouring into Merano, there was a demand for hotels, villas, restaurants, shops, and entertainment. The need for these establishments was exacerbated by visits from the popular Empress Elizabeth of Austria, called Sissi, who paid visits to the town between 1870 and 1897 "seeking rest and recuperation

**Franzensbad Spa in Czecho-Slovakia: the interior of the Francis Spring, where people stand to drink water drawn from the central circular point by female attendants in white uniforms and caps (Wellcome Images, Wikimedia Commons).**

This statue of Empress Elizabeth of Austria sits in a public park in the town of Merano. The park was created in 1860 and named in honor of the empress, who was also queen of Hungary. She was assassinated by an anarchist in Geneva on September 10, 1898 (Gryffindor, Wikimedia Commons).

for herself and her daughter, Princess Valeria." With Sissi's implicit endorsement, Merano became one of the Austro-Hungarian Empire's most prestigious health resorts.[8]

Merano, as lovely as it was, had its secrets. As the city became more affluent, the Jews established themselves as a secret power in the town. Eventually, as things worsened due to anti–Jewish feeling, they were considered responsible for everything negative. Although their wealth insulated them to some degree, enabling them to live peacefully, they knew they had to be careful. After the First World War, a secret treaty (the Treaty of London) between Italy and the Allies would give south Tyrol to Italy. Merano, which had rich Jewish traditions, would be compromised because of the Nazis. According to the Jewish Virtual Library:

# Chapter 4. The Secret Life of Merano

Between 1933 and 1939, hundreds of Jews escaped Nazi persecution and found shelter in Merano, and Jewish schools were established for them. When the fascist regime adopted the Anti-Semitic laws of the Nazis, and the Germans moved into South Tyrol, foreign Jews were expelled.

The first deportation of Jews from Merano occurred immediately after Italy's surrender. The Nazis subsequently occupied the country and ruled this region as a part of Great Germany (September 1943). Meanwhile, more than 80 Jews perished in the Nazi extermination camps, mainly Auschwitz, in the concentration camp Reichenau near Innsbruck, or in the concentration camp established in 1944 by the Nazis in Bolzano.

Merano was in these years, also a main transit point for Odessa, the secret Nazi organization helping war criminals and political leaders to escape. Adolf Eichmann and Joseph Mengele were among those who passed through Merano.[9]

And during those years (1945 to 1947), more than fifteen thousand Jewish survivors of the Shoah found a temporary haven in Merano and the sanatorium, then being run by the American Joint Distribution Committee. Many of these Jews immigrated secretly to Palestine with the help of the citizens of Merano. In 1947, three thousand Jews crossed—by night and on foot—the ten-thousand-foot-high Alps near Bruneck, coming from Austria. Today, the Jewish community of Merano is one of the smallest in Italy, and the synagogue of Merano is the only one still in use in the entire region.[10]

However poorly they were treated later, in the first half of the nineteenth century, early Jewish families of Merano made a name for the town and contributed significantly to its fame and wealth. One such family, which had an impact on the Bauers, was the Biedermann family, who opened a bank and a money exchange office. Daniel, Jakob, and Moritz Biedermann, who came from Hohenems and settled in Merano in the 1840s, were related to Peppina Zellenka (Heumann), who would become the infamous Frau K. in the case study of Dora. As we shall see in later chapters, Peppina and her husband, Hans, would have a deleterious effect on Ida's health and would maintain a long-term relationship with her father.

In addition to the Biedermann clan, the Bermann and Schwarz families also helped to develop South Tyrol and Merano. Not only did these families contribute to the health, tourism, and commerce of the town, which was at one time a small provincial enclave, but the Schwarz family also established a railway connection throughout the area. They also built a funicular railway that opened in 1907 and was Europe's steepest. So, the Jewish community when Ida and her family arrived there were the prime movers of the development and cultural richness of the town.[11]

Although Merano had a tumultuous and rich past, it would have a shameful future, and the Bauers' stay there would in some ways become problematic. However, at the time of their arrival, Merano was a lovely, thriving spa town. Nonetheless, it was not a place the Bauer children wanted to live. At their young ages, Ida and her brother were forced to give up their enriching life in Vienna for a life of no friends and a sick father. Ida especially felt the loss of her father's family. Leaving Vienna had come at a time when both Ida and her aunt were having health problems, and for both, their illnesses appeared to be of a nervous nature.

Ida was much too young to be so unsettled, and so was her brother, Otto. And Käthe, their mother, was not happy with this move either—she had no desire or inclination to nurse her sick husband, or, it would seem, even notice that her daughter was not doing well. As she could not travel, she was relegated to keeping her house as clean as she possibly could, no matter how disruptive it was for her children. This move clearly did not improve her disposition.

Merano was a wine-growing area, and the waters there were thought to have curative powers. There was a lovely promenade in town, the *Wassermauer*. The fairs, market days, and religious holidays provided pleasant diversions. The hotels were opulent, and families could play croquet, listen to concerts, and go for enchanting walks.[12]

Philipp, meanwhile, appeared to be regaining his health and thrived in Merano for a brief period of time. His health improved enough that he could travel to his factories when he felt up to it. Still, he experienced one setback after another, as he had several medical conditions and experienced many symptoms. His eye problems returned, necessitating that he stay in a darkened room. This was four years after the family had moved to Merano. And then, turning the family's world completely upside down, Philipp's "syphilis entered the tertiary stage, and he suffered a meningeal inflammation that caused some paralysis and mental disturbances."[13]

Otto found it all to be trying for the family and, as an adult, wrote that it was "the evil time out of my childhood."[14] Ida experienced that time as unsettling, too, especially as it was hard for her to see her beloved father so ill. She adored her father and, at this time, she was the primary nurse for him, which was no doubt unhealthy for an impressionable six-, seven-, and eight-year-old child, especially as her own nervous illnesses returned during this period.

Eventually, the family made their peace with living in Merano; Ida and Otto continued their close connection with each other, perhaps even more so since they had only each other now. They played together and slept in the same bedroom, enjoying each other's company until they were in their teens. The love between brother and sister would endure for as long as they lived, with only a few periods of emotional separation. "Dora remembered catching from Otto all his infectious childhood illnesses."[15] This seemed to please her—that she would be following in Otto's footsteps.

The two siblings experienced many parallels in their childhood years: they received formal instruction together, being schooled at home with governesses; they each wet the bed; and they struggled together to understand the family illnesses and their parents' relationship, which was becoming more and more strained with each passing year—especially having tried to navigate a life together in Merano, a new environment for all of them.

In Merano, Ida became less playful than she was previously. She began wetting the bed again, after having stopped for a while. Otto had only stopped this habit at the age of ten. Ida's bed-wetting lessened around her eighth year, but then she began having migraines. She also had shortness of breath. These conditions seemed to have no physical cause, and no medical treatments appeared to help.[16]

One thing that was not a problem in Merano at the time was

being Jewish. Interestingly, because of increased religious tolerance and accessibility, spa towns like Merano allowed Jewish patients to thrive. According to Zadoff,

> Even for a Jewish community the atmosphere was unique. People from diverse Jewish backgrounds and practices joined together in these towns to take the cure as well as to socialize. Synagogues were built in these towns during the 1870s and 1880s as the Jewish populations during peak spa season from May through September grew. As time went on, Jewish businesses emerged, such as hotels and restaurants. With the rise in anti–Semitism elsewhere in Europe, the policy regarding religious tolerance that various spa towns like Bad Reichenhall as well as Carlsbad, Marienbad, and Franzensbad were known for, led Jewish communities to view these locations as safe havens where they could intermingle with fellow Jews from all over the world.[17]

While living in Merano had its downside, it did afford Ida the opportunity to become closer to her father, whom she adored. As his own illness progressed, and he was confined to the home, Ida spent as much time with him as she could. For several years, she continued to be her ailing father's main nurse. She spent hours with Philipp, and they developed a close relationship. As Philipp could not work and had trouble reading because of his chronic eye problems, Ida was not only his companion and nurse, but his entertainment as well, telling him stories, reading to him from the daily papers, and staying with him constantly—in the absence of his wife. According to Katharina Adler, Ida's great-granddaughter, Käthe believed that nursing her husband was a job even the servants didn't want, so she would not care for her husband, leaving that chore to her daughter.[18]

As nurse to her father, Ida spent most of her time bringing Philipp food and drink, changing his linens and bedclothes, and keeping his room dark and quiet due to the detached retina, which had been diagnosed during one of his worse sieges of illness. No doubt she also brought gossip and spring flowers to keep him from getting depressed about his conditions.[19]

Philipp was very proud of Ida because, despite her ailments, she was an intelligent young girl, as well as a loving companion to him who received little in the way of affection from his wife. Ida read early as a young child and discussed with her brother his

The Franzensbad Spa, which was frequented by Ida Bauer and her mother, is in the former Czechoslovakia. These two paths lead to the inner part of a c-shaped building which houses the Natalie Spring (photograph by Zuber, Photo-Atelier; Wellcome Images, Wikimedia Commons).

studies and classroom activities and homework, as Otto had begun to attend school in Merano. As they were very close, Otto shared many things with his sister, including, as best he could, his intellectual development.

While Ida loved being with her father, she had enough understanding of the family dynamic to recognize that their closeness put a strain on the already-problematic marriage of her parents. Käthe became jealous of the attention Philipp paid to their daughter, yet doing nothing to change that dynamic.

Although happy to be with her father exclusively, Ida continued to have the symptoms that she would experience for most of her life: loss of voice, insomnia, various fears, and depression, symptoms from which her father was also suffering.[20] Father and daughter developed a special affinity during Philipp's illness since Ida's mother did not take on those responsibilities of nurse and refused to be a companion to her husband. By this time, Otto was immersed in his studies and schoolwork and refused to get into any discussion about the troubled family's interactions. Once Philipp's conditions became more debilitating, his work was nonexistent, as he was too ill to travel or take care of the family business—so it was just Philipp and Ida.

About this time, Freud would relate in the case study of Dora,

> During the girl's earlier years her only brother (her elder brother by a year and a half) had been the model which her ambitions had striven to follow. But in the last few years the relations between the brother and the sister had grown more distant. The young man used to try so far as he could to keep out of the family disputes; but when he was obliged to take sides he would support his mother. So that the usual sexual attraction had drawn together the father and daughter on the one side and the mother and son on the other.[21]

At as early as the age of eight, Ida developed additional neurotic symptoms in Merano, which coincided with her mother's illnesses. She suffered the usual childhood complaints but as she entered her adolescence, she began to suffer from hemicranial headaches "in the nature of migraine, and from attacks of nervous coughing." These symptoms were always together initially, but as she got older, the migraines lessened and the cough, or *tussis nervo*, as Freud called it, continued for years.[22]

As she entered her teens, Ida continued to exhibit other worrisome symptoms such as sleeplessness, anxiety, and sinus and digestive issues (her mother suffered from gastric and digestive issues as well). Even before this, the family had begun to feel the repercussions of their increasingly dysfunctional lifestyle. Ida's father had always been somewhat unhealthy due to his vision problems, tuberculosis, and then with syphilis, as well as other issues, but his health was now becoming progressively worse. And as her mother's phobic housecleaning took on epic proportions, she became stranger and more reclusive.[23]

Ida's mother has been described, even by Ida's great-granddaughter, Katharina Adler, as overstretched and cold toward her daughter. She was living with the fact that her husband had already been infected with syphilis before their wedding, and she herself also had many ailments for which she spent much time at the spas in Merano and the surrounding area. According to Adler, she was also good at maintaining facades.[24] Perhaps Ida's mother's frantic and somewhat psychotic housecleaning was due to her desire to keep up the image of a perfect family. One can only suppose.

Käthe's cleaning phobia grew worse in Merano. This was probably because it was there that she first found out that her husband had a venereal disease and, worse, that he had infected her with it. In addition, she had no real sense of her children's interests or who their playmates were as she basically did nothing but clean and clean again—even household items that had no need of cleaning.[25]

In his case study of Dora, Freud described Ida's mother, whom he never met, as being

> an uncultivated woman and above all as a foolish one, who had concentrated all her interests upon domestic affairs, especially since her husband's illness and the estrangement to which it led. She presented the picture, in fact, of what might be called the "housewife's psychosis." ... This condition, traces of which are to be found often enough in normal housewives, inevitably reminds one of forms of obsessional washing and other kinds of obsessional cleaning. But such women (and this applied to the patient's mother) are entirely without insight into the illness.[26]

The seemingly abnormal need to clean of Ida's mother led to estrangement not only from her husband but also from Ida. The mother and daughter's only connection seemed to be through their various illnesses. One of Käthe's preferred destinations for both herself and Ida was the town of Franzensbad, which was noted for its cures for women's disorders and nervous conditions. It was also popular among middle-class Jewish women at that time.[27]

Franzensbad, a bathing spot in Bohemia and a spa town, dates back to 1707 when it was first used for bathing. With approximately twenty-four mineral springs of saline, alkaline, and ferruginous waters—the oldest spa being the Franzensquelle—healing various diseases and conditions was its aim. The waters, whose temperature was between fifty and fifty-four degrees centigrade, were reputedly good for healing cases of anemia, nervous disorders, sexual disease (especially for women), and heart conditions. Another health attraction there was the mud bath that was prepared using the peat of the Franzensbad marsh, rich in mineral substances such as sulfates of iron, soda, potash, and other organic compounds. Franzensbad was also home to several parks and a hospital for poor patients.[28]

## Part I. Secrets and Lies

As mother and daughter tried to cure their ills and find some common ground, Philipp slowly improved. It was still an anxiety-ridden time for his family, as everyone was concerned about both his future health and the well-being of the rest of the family. The children worried about where and how they would go to school, and in Ida's case, if she would even attend school. Käthe wanted to return to Vienna, where she felt more stable being surrounded by relatives. Also, there were few children for Ida and Otto to play with in Merano. Otto seemed to accept the situation in which he found himself: the lack of playmates, the dissention between his parents, and the chronic familial health problems, possibly because he had academic outlets, as he was going to school, while Ida became more symptomatic.

Even with the reconciliation she experienced with her mother during their spa trips and the return of her father's health, Ida was not happy. Ida and her mother continued to feel secluded and unsettled in Merano, leading a life far different from the one they had had in the capital. Contributing to Ida's feelings of isolation was Otto's attending school in Merano. This left Ida alone at home with only her father as a companion.

Otto was by now considered a boy genius. As Decker writes:

> Just ten, he [Otto] wrote a five-act play, *Napoleon's End*, as a Christmas present for his parents. Among other themes, the drama dealt with the plight of a daughter caught between her husband's and father's rivalry and with the emotions arising from the triangle of a husband, his former wife, and his present wife. The capriciousness of fate also occupied Otto. The play revealed a profound absorption in history and literature for one so young.[29]

In 1892 at age eleven, Otto entered the Gymnasium in Merano, which was open only to boys from age ten to eighteen. It was the first time the two emotionally attached siblings were separated.[30] While Otto attended an academically challenging school, studying Latin, Greek, German language, literature, history, geography, mathematics, and physics, Ida was probably educated at home by a governess, who would later play a role in Freud's case study.[31]

Without Otto, it is unlikely Ida had any friends, as it was not possible for a Jewish girl to socialize with non–Jewish children—even in

60

Merano. The contrast between Otto's education and Ida's "had academic, social, and psychological significance."[32]

This was not only unjust but also difficult for Ida, as she was a very bright young girl and would have benefited greatly from an education such as the one allowed to her brother. She was very inquisitive and had a pronounced sense of curiosity. She read a great deal and was happy to spend time with older people whose conversations were advanced for a young girl. Unlike Otto's future, Ida felt that hers would not be very substantial. Those graduating from the Gymnasium became members of an elite group where entry into Austrian's hierarchical society was assured. Upon graduation, Otto spoke four languages, and he would decide to dedicate his life to socialist causes and public service. By contrast, Ida was dominated by her illnesses and was beginning to despair of life.[33]

And if all this was not enough—basically losing her brother and not being allowed to study in the same way Otto could—her family started a relationship with the Zellenka family, which would exacerbate Ida's already shaky mental state and upend the family's already questionable stability.

## CHAPTER 5

# The K's Ménage and *Their* Secrets

While in Merano, the Bauers had become increasingly and intimately involved with Peppina and Hans Zellenka, who would be called "the Ks" in Freud's eventual case study of Dora. The subtle but ever-present anti–Jewish sentiment on the rise in Bohemia caused Hans and Philipp to bond together, as they were both business professionals with connections, whose various enterprises could be jeopardized by anti–Jewish feeling.

And while there were many Jewish families in Merano with whom the Bauers could have associated, their social life was limited due to Philipp's health issues. At the same time that the Bauer and Zellenka families were becoming closer, the Bauers' loveless marriage was virtually in tatters, with both partners hobbled by their significant medical disorders and with totally different viewpoints on life and raising children. Philipp was interested in his children's lives, while Käthe seemed indifferent to them and their progression through life.

The Zellenkas' marriage was also somewhat dysfunctional, and at some point they would not even be living together. Their relationship mirrored that of Philipp and Käthe's in the coldness between the partners with limited sexual activity and intimacy. What is known about Peppina is that she was considered beautiful and possibly had a millinery business.[1] Hans, a prepossessing man, made his living as a commercial agent and traveled frequently as a result. He initially went to Merano for employment. Peppina had been living there since she was six years old. They met and subsequently married in 1889. Although the Zellenkas gained fame—or infamy, depending on your point of view—due to the Dora case study as the Ks, little was known about them until recently.[2]

Of the two Zellenkas, Bella Peppina Heumann, known as Peppina, had the strongest ties to Merano, moving there when she was six years old. She was born on March 24, 1870, in the coastal town of Ancona on Italy's Adriatic Sea. Her parents had previously left their strong Jewish community in Hohenems, Austria, which was established in the early seventeenth century and was near the border of Switzerland.

Hohenems's strong Jewish ties began early: A charter of protection, created in 1617, established the legal basis for the settlement of Jewish families and the construction of institutions within a Jewish community. Soon a synagogue would be built, along with a *mikvah* (a ritual bath), a school, a poor house, and a cemetery. Jewish businesses followed, consisting of a coffee house, bank, and insurance company. The year of 1862 was considered the golden era, when the town had nearly 600 Jewish citizens—12 percent of the population.[3]

On the surface, life appeared to be good for Jews. It was during this time that Peppina's parents met and married even though Jews were segregated to the *Judengasse*—two streets in Hohenems. Because the constitution of Hohenems allowed Jews to settle freely all over Austria, many left, going not only to cities in Austria but also to Switzerland, Italy, Germany, and America. This meant that there would ultimately be limited work for those left behind.[4] Thus, the move to Ancona, which Peppina's father thought would provide a better and more prosperous life.[5]

Peppina's father, Isidor Heumann, born in 1826, married his own niece, Jeanette Biedermann, in Hohenems in 1868, at the age of forty-two. His bride's father, Moritz, was the master baker in Hohenems; her mother, the daughter of Isidor's sister Julia. At the time of their marriage, there was very little work in the town of Hohenems, so Isidor and Jeanette decided to travel to the port of Ancona on Italy's Adriatic coast. Bella Peppina, as she was called as a child, was born there, as was a son, Marco. Another son was thought to have been born there, also, but died in infancy.[6]

Even though Peppina's parents had intended to stay in Ancona, this was not to be, as they were still looking for financial security, which they did not achieve there. When Peppina was about six, her family moved to Merano, where Jeanette's family, the Biedermanns (mentioned previously because of their development of Merano) were making a name for themselves—namely, the brothers Jakob, Daniel, and Moritz, the aforementioned baker of Hohenems, and Peppina's maternal grandfather. All three brothers had recently settled in Merano, where they opened first a small shop in a hotel selling jewelry and leather goods and then, as a side enterprise, exchanged money for foreign visitors. This eventually led to the creation of the Biedermann Bank, which shortly became quite a prosperous enterprise.[7]

According to Andrew Ellis:

> It was Jakob and Daniel's good fortune that in 1837, Johann Nepomuk Huber, doctor and resident of Meran, published a pamphlet in Vienna extolling the benefits of Meran's moderate climate and cool, dry air for tuberculosis sufferers, of which there were a great many at that time. Huber's pamphlet increased the number of people wanting to visit Meran and hence the demand for hotels, villas, restaurants, shops, and so forth. That demand was further boosted when the hugely popular Empress Elizabeth of Austria, known as "Sissi," paid four visits to the town between 1870 and 1897, seeking rest and recuperation for herself and her daughter, Princess Valeria. With Sissi's implicit endorsement, Meran became one of the Austro-Hungarian Empire s most prestigious health resorts, with the Biedermann Bank at the heart of its development.[8]

Because Jakob and Daniel never married, they worried that there would be no one to take over the management of their businesses when they were too old to continue working or when they died. It was because of this that Peppina's father, Isidor, husband of the brothers' niece, was asked to come to Merano to become a director of the bank. And so, because of this great opportunity, Peppina's family left their coastal Italian home for Merano.

At the time, Peppina's mother was twenty-eight years old and Peppina and Marco were six and four years of age, respectively. The Heumanns would add several more children once they became settled in Merano—Moritz and the twins, Julian and Rosa—all three of whom would die at relatively young ages.[9]

As a side note, it is interesting that Peppina, who would come to have a huge effect on Ida, also had experienced numerous neurotic symptoms in childhood—symptoms which were similar to Malvine Bauer's symptoms. This loss of proximity to her aunt was perhaps one reason why Ida did so poorly in Merano and gravitated toward Peppina, as it seemed that she was looking for a maternal figure, given that she had little respect or fondness for her own mother.

A word about Malvine: At the age of twenty-three, she married Edward Friedmann, a twenty-six-year-old goldsmith born in Hungary. As Ida had spent a great deal of time with her aunt as a child, while the Bauers were living in Vienna she was almost like a member of their family. Malvine had two daughters around Ida's age, and the marriage was an unhappy one, similar to the marriage of Ida's mother. Malvine was also frequently ill. While never having Malvine as a patient, Freud, who knew the family in Vienna, diagnosed Malvine as having a severe form of psychoneurosis "without any characteristically hysterical symptoms."[10]

It appears that Malvine found respite from her sadness and ill health in her relationship with her niece, as Ida was bright and fun-loving and no doubt lavished love on Malvine and her two girls. Ida loved being a part of Malvine's family and played with her cousins frequently when she lived in Vienna. They were so intimate that Malvine openly discussed her marriage and ill health with her young niece, when Ida was still barely a teenager, making Ida feel special and loved. (Peppina would repeat this pattern, too, of inappropriate conversations with her young friend.) Ida's original role model for female behavior, her mother, was replicated by both her aunt and her father's lover.[11]

The attachment Ida and Malvine shared was a peculiarly emotional one. Ida experienced great sadness when they moved away from Malvine, and would subsequently recapture that female intimacy with Peppina. Freud would record in the Dora case study that she took on the symptoms of her aunt, as well as that of her mother and Peppina. Ida seemed to develop a strong connection with ill women.[12]

Freud seemed to think that Ida mimicked the illnesses of these women because of her devotion to them. But her symptoms were also brought on by stress and lack of openness about her family situation. Everything would come to a head for Ida, however, when Hans and Peppina, each in their own way, brought Ida to a place so dreadful that she eventually contemplated suicide.

Peppina—like these other women in Ida's life to whom she was closely aligned—suffered the same type of nervous disorders. Ellis writes:

> The future Frau K grew up from the age of six as part of a small but influential Jewish community in a fashionable health resort with a father who was a director of the increasingly prosperous Biedermann Bank, a younger mother, two brothers, and a selection of aunts, uncles, and cousins. Freud says that at some stage Peppina had "been an invalid and had even been obliged to spend several months in a sanatorium for nervous disorders because she had been unable to walk." Freud does not provide any further information about the nature of Peppina's illness, but he does note that she made a good recovery and matured into a "young and beautiful woman" who was "healthy and lively."[13]

As Peppina got older and entered womanhood, she apparently left her disabilities behind her. And as a beautiful woman from an increasingly wealthy and important Merano family, there was a question of whom she would marry. Unfortunately, at the time, there were but a few healthy Jewish men residing in Merano whom the family would consider appropriate for Peppina. It was at this time that Hans Zellenka entered the picture.

Johan Zellenka, or Hans (or Hanns) as he was called, was born in Vienna on December 22, 1860. Like the Bauers, his father, Ignatz, had moved from a small town in Bohemia to Vienna, where they, too, settled on Leopoldstrasse with other emigrating Jews. It was here that he met and married Hans's mother, Charlotte (Lotte). She had previously been married to a merchant "called Wilhelm Beer" with whom she had two children, Leopold and Regina. Wilhelm Beer died in 1857, leaving Charlotte in her late twenties with two young children. Three years later, she married Ignatz Zellenka in the Leopoldstadter Tempel.[14]

Hans's father was a dealer in medicinal leeches (his wedding recorded him as a "*Blutegelhändler*").[15] Because he was both ill and financially unsuccessful, Hans's mother was forced to open a little shop selling women's underwear. Hans's early life was not easy due in part to his father's ill health, poor business skills, and frequent moving within Vienna, leaving Hans and his mother with limited financial or emotional support. Eventually Hans's father disappeared, leaving his mother to support herself and her children. To make ends meet and to find some stability, they moved many times, ending up in working-class Ottakring, a town in the Sixteenth District, some distance away from Leopoldstadt. His older stepbrother eventually found a job in a bank to help the family out. Hans's life was in stark contrast to that of his future wife, who lived in Merano in the lap of luxury.[16]

Where Peppina was beautiful, Hans was unattractive; where she came from a wealthy and loving family, he came from a poor and dysfunctional one. It was only due to his mother's example of providing for her family that Hans and his half-brother, Leopold, were prepared for the world of work. And it was in Merano that he found work that would lead him to his future bride.

In Merano, Hans took several jobs before managing to impress one Philipp Haas, the owner of a progressive company with "a well-developed social conscience."[17] It was in the circle of Daniel Biedermann, Isidor Heumann, and Friedrich Stransky, the leaders of the Haas Company, that Hans began his career working for this prestigious company, where he was seen as an ambitious young man with potential, not as just a shopkeeper as he would be portrayed by Freud in the Dora case study. As Ellis writes, "He was clearly considered a suitable match for Peppina Heumann."[18]

Hans and Peppina married in Merano on Sunday, September 22, 1889, at the Merano synagogue, about a year after the Bauers had moved to Merano. Interestingly, the wedding was attended by the Bauer family, including Ida and Otto. As they had been invited to the wedding, they may have become friendly before the Zellenkas were even married. But as the Jewish community in Merano was small, perhaps all the influential Jewish families of Merano were invited to the celebration.

At the time of the wedding, Hans was twenty-eight years old and Peppina only nineteen; Ida was seven. Fifteen months after the wedding, on January 5, 1891, Peppina gave birth to a son, Otto, and then eleven months later to a girl, Klara, who was ill from birth with a congenital heart condition. The couple continued to reside in Merano at Pfarrplatz 8, "adjacent to the cathedral and close to Peppina's parents' home on Postgasse, as well as to invited to Hans's office and the Biedermann Bank on Habsburgerstrasse."[19]

It seems clear that the Zellenkas, had they not befriended the Bauers, would not even be a footnote to history. According to Ellis, "The Zellenkas would be long forgotten were it not for the fact that they became involved in Meran with Dora and her family."[20] As the families became closely entwined, Ida was a frequent visitor at the Zellenka home, taking care of Hans and Klara, the Zellenka children. Peppina often spent time in a sanatorium. Ida would note that Peppina's illnesses appeared to ebb and flow. Ida was quick to also note that Peppina would be well when Hans was away—which was often, as he traveled for his job—and ill when he returned. Ida was an observant child to have noticed this change in Peppina's health based on the travels of her husband.[21]

As for the Bauers, while living in Merano and when feeling reasonably well, Philipp became involved in the active and wealthy Jewish community by joining the board of trustees of the Königswarter Foundation. The family would spend eight or nine months "staying in hotels or rented villas"[22] and found this organization, the Königswarter Foundation, to be the very center of Jewish life.

The foundation was started in 1872 by Baron Isaak and Lisette Königswarter to honor their son, Emil, who had died suddenly and unexpectedly. They capitalized on the foundation's money and influence, which helped them purchase property, including a plot of land that served as the Jewish cemetery. The Königswarter money was also used to construct a sanatorium to treat impoverished Jews.[23]

Following his marriage to Peppina, Hans became regional agent for possibly the most important retailer of quality textiles in the Austro-Hungarian Empire. And because of Philipp's involvement in the resident Jewish community, he had frequent contact with Isidor Heumann and Friedrich Stransky, co-directors of the Biedermann

**Merano, view toward the northwest, with Zielspitze (center) and Tschigat (right) in the background (Noclador, Wikimedia Commons).**

Bank, and thus with Hans, as well as with the family of the lovely and charming Peppina.

Through their bank, Peppina's family also was involved in improving the quality of the life and health of the many international Jewish people, patients who at the time were flocking to Merano. The Jewish people who eventually settled in Merano, began to change its society for the better. The creation of spas, hotels, boardwalks, parks, and coffeehouses brought guests, both ill and well, to stay in Merano for months at a time, traveling from one spa to another, just as Ida and her mother did.

While Merano was thriving, conversely, things were getting worse again for Philipp Bauer, who in 1892 suddenly lost vision in his good eye. Ellis writes, "His other eye had never functioned well, so Philipp faced the prospect of being almost blind. The oculist who treated Philipp was overheard discussing with him the possibility that his eye condition might be linked to a long-standing syphilis infection."[24]

Up until this time, Philipp's wife had no idea that her husband had contracted a venereal disease in his premarital days. She was not only shocked by his condition, but also found out that he had infected her, which led to further estrangement between the couple that was never resolved. It was at this time that Peppina stepped into the breach.

> The recommended treatment for Philipp's condition was prolonged rest in a darkened room. Käthe declined to nurse her husband, who turned instead to Peppina Zellenka, now twenty-two years old with two small children. Philipp's eyesight improved considerably, while a mutual attraction between Philipp and Peppina flourished in the darkened room. The affair that ensued was conducted with little attempt at concealment: Dora told Freud that her father would visit Peppina "every day at definite hours, while her husband was at business," adding that "everybody had talked about it." ... Dora also admitted to Freud that she had been complicit in the affair, helping to look after Peppina's children while Peppina and her father were together.[25]

Eventually, Philipp became so unwell as to necessitate a return to Vienna to visit a physician—none other than Sigmund Freud, who was becoming famous for his effective treatment of patients with psychosomatic conditions. Freud had also made a study of syphilis and its effect on the nervous system. After only one visit, Freud diagnosed Philipp's many symptoms as the result of chronic tertiary neurosyphilis and set about combating the symptoms with an "energetic" course of treatment that would have involved the administration of mercury salts in the form of pills, ointments, or injections. Philipp made a good recovery. Freud believed that the success of this treatment was the reason Philipp brought his daughter to him for treatment six years later.[26]

Philipp had been accompanied to Freud's consulting office by Hans Zellenka, of all people. Later, when Freud began his treatment of Ida, he had an insider's understanding of the familial situation, having met the major players (with the exception of Ida's mother). At the same time that Philipp and Käthe were no longer enjoying conjugal activities, neither were Hans and Peppina. As Ida noted, Peppina was often too ill to be with Hans when he returned from his business travels—but not too ill to interact with Philipp, sexually and otherwise.

By the time Ida was thirteen years old, she was quite attractive. Perhaps as a way of getting back at Philipp—and Peppina—because of their affair, which was conducted fairly openly, Hans began the seduction of Ida. The first time was when he lured her, under false pretenses, into his place of business on Habsburgerstrasse in Merano and kissed her on the lips. Ida was disgusted; she tore herself free from the man and hurried past him.[27]

As for Ida's parents, they thought Hans's attention to their daughter was simply avuncular interest in an intelligent and interesting young girl. Decker writes that Ida herself had ambivalent feelings about her relationship with Hans Zellenka. "It certainly was pleasant—considering the deficiencies of Meran for a young, intelligent girl, as well as the handicaps her fluctuating health imposed on her activities—to have a dependable and attentive walking companion and to receive regular letters and gifts from a man highly regarded by her father."[28] These thoughts occurred to Ida before the encounter in Hans's office. Once that happened, Ida became somewhat fearful of Hans.

Ida did sense, or perhaps even knew, that the relationship with Herr K., as Freud would call him, was inappropriate. After other encounters that left her somewhat unsettled, she determined not to be alone with him, and she again developed phobic symptoms. Unfortunately, this was not something she felt she could discuss with her parents; consequently, she never mentioned the encounter until she met with Freud in the fall of 1900—and she continued to accept frequent gifts and letters from Hans.[29]

This was a time in which Ida was very lonely. Otto was busy with schoolwork, her mother was ill, and her father was either away on business or ill himself. Ida, although wary of Hans, began to feel connected to Peppina. With Peppina she developed a strong and intimate relationship in which they discussed sex, emotions, jewelry, clothing, and even children, as Ida took care of the Zellenka's two small children, similar to how Peppina was taking care of Philipp. It was Ida's task to mind the Zellenka children while Peppina was with Ida's father, who had begun taking over the nursing duties from Ida.

The Bauers continued their relationship with the Zellenkas, which, when looked at from the perspective of an outsider, was quite bizarre and complicated: Ida's mother kept her distance from Philipp; Philipp was sexually involved with Peppina; Hans continued his sexual pursuit of Ida, the daughter of his wife's lover; and Ida was looking after Peppina and Hans's children.[30]

Ida continued to be very careful around Hans—never allowing herself to be alone with him—as her phobic reactions were exacerbated by her encounters with Hans. As Decker explains, "From then on she would not walk near a man and a woman who seemed attracted to each other."[31]

# CHAPTER 6

# The Nature of Secrets

By crashing into each other's lives, the Bauers and the Zellenkas created a world that exacerbated many of Ida's symptoms, most of which would be with her for the rest of her life—and had been with her since she was about six years old. Ida's persistent distress was complicated by secrets, those held close to the hearts of Ida's father, her mother, Hans, Peppina, and even those of her own. Adding to all those secrets, Sigmund Freud had his own secrets, which would not only complicate his eventual analysis of Ida, but would contribute to his own failure as therapist in his analysis of his young patient.

It appears that there was little or no apparent concern from the adults about the gross and abominable secret perpetrated against the pubescent Ida—seemingly agreed upon by both her father and her father's friend, Hans, with tacit understanding from her mother and Peppina. Ida therefore had no recourse but to acquiesce to Hans's importuning. Ida hid the facts of Hans's gross advances until she could no longer keep it to herself and divulged to her mother what was happening with Hans.

One of the more distressing events happened when Ida was fifteen years old, in the summer of 1898. The amorous encounter took place against the backdrop of the not-so-clandestine relationship between Hans's wife and Ida's father.[1]

Philipp and Ida were visiting the vacation home of the Zellenkas in the Austrian Alps. The plan was that Philipp would return alone to Merano and Ida would be left with the Zellenkas to care for their two children—odd, since a young German governess was also in residence there. The governess was hired to provide lessons for Otto and Klara. We shall come to see how this added to the sexual drama at the Zellenka home.

## Part I. Secrets and Lies

Hans, up to his old tricks, had successfully seduced—and made declarations of affection toward—the governess, who had given in to his passionate inclinations and believed that there was a future for her with Hans. It is hard to believe that she would think that Hans would leave his wife and two children for a governess, but that apparently was her fantasy.

Immediately having made the conquest of the young woman, Hans dropped her—possibly because Ida was on her way to the Zellenka summer villa or perhaps just because he felt he was finished with her. Hans was not a particularly nice person, even as the young German woman was foolish. When asked to leave the villa, the governess refused. Even though she claimed to hate Hans, she was hopeful that he would return to her. She eventually saw that he had discarded her, and she did leave the villa, but not before she told Ida about her own encounters with Hans.[2] It was in this atmosphere that Ida once again experienced a seduction by Hans.

Ida had been apprehensive about her visit to the Zellenkas because of the situation with Hans—both the earlier seductions and her ambivalence about being alone with him—and because her coughing spells, headaches, and aphonia[3] had not abated since they had come to Merano. Also, hearing the sordid tale from the governess and how he used the same words with her as he had with Ida, "I get nothing from my wife," was disheartening.[4]

It was on one of the little boat trips on and around the lake that Ida and Hans took shortly after she and her father arrived at the Alpine villa that things fell apart for Ida. Hans, true to form, made an advance and used the same line he used with the governess—that he got nothing from his wife. Ida was irate and slapped him in the face and walked off. While she wanted to return to the villa on her own, she realized it was a two-and-a-half-hour jaunt, and so she returned to the boat and Hans, who begged forgiveness and asked her not to tell anyone. He wanted it to be their secret, I suppose.

That, of course, was not the end of it. Upon returning to the villa, Ida took a nap. "She lay down in the bedroom and fell asleep but suddenly awoke to find Herr K. standing beside her. She asked him 'sharply' what he was doing there."[5] As she would later tell Freud,

## Chapter 6. The Nature of Secrets

Hans arrogantly and unrepentantly told her he would not be prevented from coming into his own bedroom. The next night Ida asked for a key to the room, but soon she found the key gone and assumed that Hans had taken it so he could continue to enter her room at will.[6]

Ida surely must have felt totally unprotected and uncared for by the adults in her world: her parents and the family for whom she was babysitter and quasi-governess. For while she was being sexually harassed by Hans—afraid to get dressed or undressed for fear he would enter her bedroom—her father and Peppina were having their own amorous adventures. Philipp had decided for his own reasons not to stay at the villa but was residing at a nearby hotel, which allowed Peppina to join him for early morning walks and day-long excursions. When it came time for her father to leave, Ida determined that she would return with him, despite the plan that she would stay with the Zellenkas.[7]

Once home, Ida waited a few weeks before telling her mother of Hans's sexual advances. Her mother then told Ida's father, who spoke with his older brother, Karl. It was because of the pressure from his wife that Philipp first wrote to Hans demanding an explanation. Two of Philipp's brothers confronted Hans, who denied ever having an encounter with Ida. Hans went so far as to speculate about Ida's mental state, claiming that Peppina had told him that Ida was obsessed with sex. He said that Ida had aroused and over-excited herself by reading sexually oriented books—textbooks, as it turned out—and that she imagined the whole scene with Hans.[8]

Ida continued to be unnerved by her experience with Hans and realized that she was being used as a pawn: if her father could have Peppina, then Hans could have her. Ida's symptoms returned in full force, and she continued to see physicians who prescribed hydrotherapy and electrotherapy. At the time, both these therapies were common practice, especially in places like the spa town Merano.

As early as age twelve, Ida's physician had recommended that she undergo intensive sessions of electrotherapy. Under examination, her larynx was normal, but her adductor muscles were partially paralyzed, even though when she coughed the adductors were able to come together. As Gilman writes:

This would have been seen through the use of the laryngoscope. To treat her the physicians would have applied current directly to the larynx, but—as was clear when Freud examined her—without any long-term success. Electrotherapy simply did not work, as it should have done. Dora's physicians were expecting a lesion; Freud came to understand the psychogenetic nature of her illness. ... Freud saw in this case of failed electrotherapy a return to early childhood patterns, not a lesion of the nervous system. "Many of my women patients who suffer from disturbances of eating, globus hystericus, constriction of the throat and vomiting, have indulged energetically in sucking during their childhood" (SE, 7: 182). This was his new reading of the loss of voice, a core symptom in the case of Dora. Freud's complicated account of this case stressed the sexual fantasy that lies at its core. But his treatment was the talking cure. Electrotherapy was never considered.[9]

The electroshock treatments had taken place in Vienna. While the family was living in Merano, Ida also tried hydrotherapy, probably at a spa in Franzensbad, the Bohemian spa visited by both Ida and her mother in 1890.[10] But with limited success.

Experts recommended above all the general douche—a jet of water to the body; the force of the water was considered as efficacious as its temperature. Brief bursts of water at forty-five degrees Fahrenheit were given for fifteen seconds, or bursts of water at fifty degrees for twenty to thirty seconds. If the patient could not tolerate the cold water or its pressure, then the "Scotch" douche was tried. Warm water (100 degrees Fahrenheit) was sprinkled on the patient for as little as one-half minute to as long as three minutes. Then, when the patient was felt to be ready, the cold-water jet was introduced.[11]

Other hydrotherapy treatments existed: transition douche; wrapping patients in cold, wet sheets; hot sheets. It is unclear which if any of these treatments Ida received; we only know that none of them worked and both types—hydrotherapy and electrotherapy—helped to alienate Ida from the medical profession.[12] By the time she was fifteen years old, these treatments had resulted in her hating medical treatments and those who performed them. It was at this time that she apparently saw Freud for the first time at his office up the street from her own home on Berggasse 19.

She was in the midst of one of her coughing attacks, and at that time saw Freud, probably because her father thought highly of his doctor and pushed her at least to meet the man and talk to him—what could she lose? So it was that Dora [Ida] met Freud who summed up her history as "merely a case of 'petite hystérie.'" Freud proposed psychological treatment; Dora said she

**Home of Sigmund Freud at Berggasse 19, Vienna, Austria, now the Freud Museum, where Ida Bauer met with Freud six times a week (Gryffindor, Wikimedia Commons).**

would think it over, and then when the episode passed, she declined on the grounds that she was better.[13]

By now, Ida was exhausted by her disabilities and by the chronic secrets and seductions within her own family enclave. Ida had been seeing physicians since she was six years old and, once in Merano, went for treatments to the spas and health resorts with her mother. She was sick of seeing physicians and found that they did not help her. "Although Freud proposed treating her with entirely novel methods, she was adamant that she would not begin yet another round of fruitless appointments and refused any treatment," according to Decker.[14]

This was a time in Vienna, and indeed in Europe, when women were not necessarily treated fairly by physicians. In many ways, Ida was right in refusing treatment when she was first brought to see the Vienna physician. Ida had a great love for her father, but she had distrust and disdain for men in general and for doctors in particular. At that time, most physicians were men and non–Jewish. Jewish female physicians, who might have had empathy for Ida, made up only one fifth of the female physicians in Central Europe.[15]

Because of Freud's emerging interest in psychoanalysis, a science of the mind, he was a fairly good choice of physician for Ida. Vienna in 1900 was the greatest medical center in Europe—and psychiatry was being vigorously aligned with neuroanatomy, which many doctors thought was the source of Ida's condition. Psychotherapy was first introduced in Vienna by Richard von Krafft-Ebing in 1889 at around the same time as Freud was becoming increasingly interested in the science of the mind. Freud's approach to treating patients was moving toward psychoanalysis and away from neurology, his area of expertise and education. At the time he first saw Ida and her father, Freud was aligning his ideas not just to the work of Jean-Martin Charcot and Pierre Marie Félix Janet but also to others in the Vienna medical circle. Both of these French theorists practiced at the Pitié-Salpêtrière Hospital in Paris, where Freud went to study as a newly minted neurologist.[16]

The Salpêtrière was originally a gunpowder factory, but at the time that Freud worked there, it was one of France and Europe's most esteemed institutions, as it is today. Many studied and worked there over the centuries, such as Charles Darwin and Georges Gilles de la Tourette, and many especially came to work with Charcot to witness his clinical demonstrations. Freud was 29 years old when, while on scholarship, he worked in Charcot's labs. It was Freud who translated Charcot's lectures into German and whose interpretation of Charcot's lectures on hysteria formed the foundations of Freud's own understanding of how the mind works.

This may have been the perfect time for Ida to visit Freud and work with him to undertake analysis that could help her with her symptoms, which many physicians besides Freud saw as psychosomatic. As Philip Rieff writes, she was the daughter of a sick father, who had a sick mistress, who had a sick husband, who proposed himself to the sick daughter as his lover.[17]

The first time she saw Freud, Ida wanted none of what Freud had

**This photograph shows the Mazarin entrance to the Pitié-Salpêtrière Hospital, Paris, a teaching hospital in the 13 arrondissement, where Freud worked with Jean-Martin Charcot (Vaughan at English Wikipedia).**

to offer. Still, she did not know how to deal on her own with the consequences of the many familial, as well as societal, secrets swirling about her. Freud would eventually conclude that she simply refused to give up those secrets. He felt that if she would do so, she would be happier and more functional.

While Ida was hiding her secrets, Freud was hiding his as well. He was discovering the secrets of dreams and had begun to analyze his own dreams. Although dedicated to unearthing the secrets of both nature and of the people he saw in consultation, he was "ambivalent about revealing secrets about his private life."[18] That being said, Freud's pivotal consideration in psychoanalysis was that secrets must be expressed, no matter how excruciating they might be, for him or for his patients.

Nonetheless, Ida held firm in her distrust. She would divulge two critical dreams to Freud in her short and aborted analysis, but she refused to agree with Freud as to the implications of those dreams.

# PART II

# *Dora and Freud*

A child in its greed for love does not enjoy having to share the affection of its parents with its brothers and sisters; and it notices that the whole of their affection is lavished upon it once more whenever it arouses their anxiety by falling ill. It has now discovered a means of enticing out its parents' love and will make use of that means as soon as it has the necessary psychical material at its disposal for producing an illness.

—Sigmund Freud

CHAPTER 7

# The Teenager
# and the Analyst

Since girls were not admitted to the Gymnasium, or even to the *Realschulen*, which was "the more recently established and slightly less prestigious secondary school,"[1] Ida was in all probability being further educated at home by a governess, while her brother, Otto, was attending school. Some authors have argued that Ida went to the convent school in Merano, but her great-granddaughter, Katharina Adler, disputes this. In an email, she wrote,

> I know of no records showing that Ida actually attended the convent school in Merano although I am aware this convent school has been mentioned in a couple of publications without mentioning any sources. More likely Ida did not go to school at all. Instead she was educated at home by a governess who also plays a role in Freud's text.[2]

Whether in school or at home, Ida was lonely. As a Jewish girl, she would not have made friends with the non–Jewish young women in Merano, and in any event, the spa town did not have an overabundance of young people inhabiting it. Since she had lived in Vienna and Merano in Jewish enclaves, it would have been at school where she would have been exposed to anti–Semitism. In Austria, teachers, students, texts, and curricula degraded and vilified Jews. According to Harold Blum, Jews were seen at the convents and other places as being "Christ killers."[3] Perhaps it was good that she did not go to school.

Bright as Ida was, she was no doubt envious of Otto who, by attending school and studying exciting subjects, was able to intermingle with people who would become important to him later in life. With her many interests, Ida was both worldly and intelligent, but

82

she was "locked in a repressed society with limited opportunities for Jewish people in general and for Jewish women in particular."[4]

You could say that Ida did not have viable female role models, since women in nineteenth-century Vienna and elsewhere had restricted access to education and employment. There were few professional women or female university students until the end of the nineteenth century.[5] Ida entered young womanhood with ineffective female role models: Peppina Zellenka, her aunt Malvine, her mother, and her final governess, who was infatuated with her father. All either betrayed her or modeled illness and mental instability—and Ida appeared to be easily influenced.

As a result, instead of experiencing enriching activities that school might have provided for her or having the example of achieving women, she continued to jump from one ailment to another. Her most serious illnesses began around the age of twelve, when she suffered from migraines, loss of voice, and a chronic cough. In between bouts of illness and seeing one doctor after another, Ida was educated by governesses.

Ida initially liked one governess who was with Ida until she reached the age of seventeen, the last one to be employed by the Bauers. The governess has been described as an older and well-read woman, perhaps thirty or forty years of age. She held liberal views and discussed sexual subjects with Ida and suggested that Ida read books with mature content. The governess, whose name has not been identified, appeared to know about Philipp and Peppina's affair and urged Ida—and her mother—to put a stop to it. She told Käthe that it was incompatible with her (the governess's) dignity to tolerate such intimacy between her charge's father and his lover.[6]

The governess and Ida engaged in subversion; the governess shared her very mature reading views with Ida but "cautioned against letting her parents find out."[7] Although Ida's parents recognized after some years that the governess was educating Ida somewhat beyond her years, they did not stop it. The governess seemed to have a sense of the family dynamic: keep everything secret.[8]

Peppina was a second governess for Ida and, as Decker explains, "filled the 'no questions asked' role." While Peppina was viewed as a family friend, she, too, was providing Ida with materials that her parents and perhaps Viennese society would not have approved of. She shared Mantegazza sex manuals and other books with explicit sexual content with her young friend. All of this was also kept secret (until Hans, in an effort to defend himself against the seduction charge, told her family about Ida's reading habits).[9]

Apparently, Ida still had mixed feelings about the women in her life. Despite the fact that Ida was still fond of Peppina, she was ambivalent about whether or not to break off relations because of the situation with Hans. Ida also believed that the governess was more interested in Philipp—perhaps even as a lover—than in her.[10] Thus, it was the governess's indifference to Ida that caused Ida to turn her against her. Ida believed that the governess pretended to like her but was actually enamored of her father, because her voice and conduct would change around Philipp.

The affair between Philipp and Peppina obviously impacted both families and anyone associated with the family. Once, while the Bauers and Zellenkas were vacationing together and taking a suite of common rooms in a hotel, Philipp and Peppina both complained about their rooms; Peppina, because she was sharing her room with her children. Philipp soon gave up his room and they both managed to occupy rooms at the end of a long corridor in order to keep their amorous goings-on private from their respective families. As Freud pointed out in the case study, "They had both moved into new rooms—the end rooms, which were only separated by the passage, while the rooms they had given up had not offered any such security against interruption."[11] Once back in Merano, the couple became open about their relationship. Ellis tells us that the "affair was conducted with little attempt at concealment," with Philipp visiting Peppina every afternoon in Merano. Ida would later admit that everyone talked about the two lovers, and she felt complicit in the affair since she was helping to look after Peppina's children while the two were together.[12] Nonetheless, Ida enjoyed looking after the Zellenka children: Otto was a bright young boy about eight years younger than Ida, and Klara was eleven months younger than him. Although Klara was often ill because of her cardiac issues, Ida spent enjoyable times with both children, functioning as a quasi-governess for them as well as playmate.[13]

While Philipp and Peppina conducted their affair openly,[14] Peppina avoided conjugal duties with her husband, using the excuse of her alleged illnesses.[15] The two families continued in this way for some time, with Philipp's wife ignoring the situation and Peppina's husband attempting a sexual relationship with Ida.

The affair between Ida's father and Peppina went on for many years while both families were living in Merano (and even later in Vienna). Philipp often showered Peppina with money and gifts, and because of such obvious largess, he felt the need to spend an equal amount on his wife and daughter to make his gifts to his mistress less conspicuous. Consequently, Peppina, who "had been obliged to spend months in a sanatorium for nervous disorders because she had been unable to walk, had now become a healthy and lively woman."[16]

Ida continued to have a great deal to contend with: her illnesses, her father's illnesses, the strain of her parents' relationship, her father's ongoing relationship with his mistress, the aftereffects of Hans's sexual advances, and her feelings of betrayal by her adored father. To make matters even worse for Ida, her aunt Malvine, her favorite role model, was ailing. Now, after years of being ill, she took a turn for the worse.

Sometime around February or March of 1899, Ida traveled on her own to Vienna to visit her aunt when she was dying. Psychosomatically, Ida developed a high fever and abdominal pains, which were misdiagnosed as appendicitis. Freud would later tell Ida that her attack was a fantasied childbirth since it occurred nine months after Hans's sexual advances. It could also be that she was turning grief into symptoms, for she knew that her beloved aunt was dying. And indeed, it was following these symptoms that Malvine died on April 7; "Dora stayed on for a while with her uncle and the two Friedmann girls who were close to her in age."[17]

Sometime in the same year, the Bauers briefly moved to Reichenberg, the site of one of Philipp's mills. The town had a twisted history where Jews were concerned. Before 1860, while they were permitted

The town of Liberec, August 2009, called Reichenberg in the 1890s. Philipp Bauer had several textile mills in the surrounding area, and the family stayed there during part of 1899 (Daniel Baránek, Wikimedia Commons).

to trade there, they were not allowed to live there. Yet it was the Jewish fabric distributers and factory workers who developed the city's textile industry. By the time the Bauers moved there from Merano, Jews were more or less tolerated, the Jewish population being 3.5 percent of the city. In addition to business concerns, Philipp also wanted his son, Otto, to "attend the local textile technical college there and then 'join the family firm.'"[18]

The Bauer family stayed only a short while in Reichenberg. Otto had decided not to enter the family business, demanding to attend university in Vienna. Also, and perhaps given the family history, even more reason to move back to the capital, Peppina had decided to leave Merano and move to Vienna. Thus, in 1900, the Bauers permanently returned to Vienna. Ida had wondered about the abrupt return to Vienna, but she knew the reason when she found out that the Zellenkas had also returned to Vienna. Hans had taken a new

Reichenberg i. B.
Bismarckplatz.

**A postcard of the town of Reichenberg, Bismarck Plaza, 1900. The Bauer family stayed here for a bit following their stay in Merano, as Philipp Bauer had textile plants in the area (Zeno.org, Wikimedia Commons).**

"position with the flagship store of Philipp Haas and Sons in central Vienna that was similar to his role in Meran (regional agent) but on a much larger scale."[19]

The Bauers' return to Vienna could have been an interesting and exciting time for Ida, as women were now being admitted to university and were also afforded other opportunities. According to Decker, Ida "was both stimulated and discouraged," but all of this while experiencing frequent illnesses and depression. It was difficult for her to take advantage of these new freedoms that could have been invigorating and engaging for the bright and curious young woman. She was also unhappy because she saw what kind of life her brother was making for himself at university. Nonetheless, she began to travel a bit and tried to engage in the cultural activities and progressive climate that was emerging in Vienna.[20]

Ida persevered in trying to educate herself. She attended art exhibitions. She traveled to Dresden and went to the Zwinger, the famous art museum. She also seemed to seek out controversial exhibitions, such as the Gustav Klimt exhibit during the summer of 1900. As Decker explains:

> Klimt, formerly an Establishment artist but now a leader of the Secessionists, had been commissioned by the Ministry to Culture and Education in 1894 to design three ceiling paintings for the University of Vienna. ...Klimt had radically altered his style, one new feature of which was the sensual portrayal of women with seductively long hair. ...Eighty-seven faculty members signed a petition ... [Ida's] interest [was] piqued by the scandal.[21]

With this cultural and artistic progression in Vienna, Ida should have been happily pursuing an intellectual life. But there was strife and conflict in Austria. In a town close to Philipp's former village of Pollerskirchen, there were attacks by the military because of violence sparked by labor troubles in factories and mills. This exacerbated Ida's already despairing nature, feeling that she had very little control over her personal life, as some of the agitation in and around the family's village was due to anti–Semitism.[22]

It wasn't long, however, before Ida began to give in to her fears (Vienna was ruled by an anti–Semitic mayor) and began to isolate. Further, she started to consciously dislike her father after years of having affection and great love for him. Her continuously poor relationship with her mother worsened and she experienced depression, irritability, tiredness, and a loss of appetite. She "even lost her fondness for jewelry and stopped wearing any." It was during this period that she began actively to think about killing herself and went so far as to write a suicide note that she made sure both parents would find. She did not actually attempt suicide, but a day later became very ill: she lost consciousness, became delirious, and had convulsions—then remembered nothing of the incident.[23] It was time, her father told her, that she must see Freud.

In late October of 1900, Ida, also concerned about herself, finally agreed to be analyzed by Freud. Upon meeting Ida for the second time, he wrote in his famous case study that she was "by that time in the first bloom of youth—a girl of intelligent and engaging looks. But she was a source of heavy trials for her parents."[24]

Some authors have written that Freud failed to appreciate how young Ida was, evident in both his manner and his interpretation of her.[25] Freud himself wrote that she was eighteen years old, but she was seventeen and should have been treated as an older adolescent or a young girl—not as a woman. It can be argued, and many have, that Freud was prone to male prejudice and lacked empathy for women, which is evidence of his limitations as an analyst.

Freud learned from Ida that she was dissatisfied with both herself and her family. She had become disenchanted with her beloved father and continued to feel disdain for her mother. Before Ida even had a chance to talk about herself to Freud, her father had given Freud a sense of things. He mentioned to Freud that Ida had discussed with her mother the two incidents of attempted seduction by Hans Zellenka. Freud wrote that Philipp went on:

> She keeps pressing me to break off relations with Herr K. and more particularly with Frau K., whom she used positively to worship formerly. But that I cannot do. For, to begin with, I myself believe that Dora's tale of the man's immoral suggestions is a phantasy that has forced its way into her mind; and besides, I am bound to Frau K. by ties of honourable friendship and I do not wish to cause her pain. The poor woman is most unhappy with her husband, of whom, by the way, I have no very high opinion. She herself has suffered a great deal with her nerves, and I am her only support. With my state of health I need scarcely assure you that there is nothing wrong in our relations. We are just two poor wretches who give one another what comfort we can by an exchange of friendly sympathy. You know already that I get nothing out of my own wife. But Dora, who inherits my obstinacy, cannot be moved from her hatred of the K.'s. She had her last attack after a conversation in which she had again pressed me to break with them. Please try and bring her to reason.[26]

By now, the Bauers were living on Berggasse in Vienna's Ninth District, just up the street from Freud's apartment at Number 19, where he kept his office on the first floor of his family's apartment. At the time that Freud began analyzing Ida in earnest, he was perhaps in his unhappiest, least successful period: he was struggling in gaining professional approval and had significant financial difficulties. According to Billig, this was when Freud was at the most isolated point in his life, "when he was experiencing a bitter sense of rejection from mainstream, or Christian, Austrian society."[27] Ida, of course, was also having issues: she was living in a society that disparaged Jews and she had a father who did not believe her when she told of Hans's seduction of her—not to mention having the myriad physical ailments previously mentioned.

And so it was that the two came together at a time that was not ideal for either: a teenage girl who had frustrations about being a woman who was compromised by lies and deceit and a frustrated physician who could not achieve the recognition he so dearly sought.

## CHAPTER 8

# Freud's Story
# of the Seductions

It seems appalling that a grown man with two young children of his own and a wife—be she adulterous or not—would attempt the seduction of a close friend's young daughter, a teenager who was the babysitter of his children. But that's just what Hans Zellenka did, according to Ida. Perhaps he felt entitled due the seduction of his own wife by his close friend, Philipp, but that seems like a specious argument, and I am sure it did not comfort poor Ida at all.

While Ida's father was engaging in a sexual liaison with Peppina, a woman described by many as young and beautiful, he foisted her husband, Hans, on his own daughter. From the time Ida was thirteen, Hans had made sexual overtures. It was following an especially repugnant sexual encounter with Hans—and her father's subtle insistence that she continue the relationship with him—that she developed severe symptoms and considered suicide, as detailed previously.

During this time, Ida was practically acting as a mother figure to the two Zellenka children.[1] While Peppina had been tending to Ida's father, Ida cared especially for Klara, as she suffered from a debilitating illness and needed a great deal of care, which her mother left to the young Ida. This job of babysitter also more or less entailed keeping the children away from the lovers, Peppina and Philipp, which is why Ida came to detest her father. Even though Ida knew of her father's adultery with Peppina, she herself continued to be "intimate friends with Peppina, to the point where, on the joint summer holidays the families would take, Ida shared a bed with her, while Herr Zellenka was evicted from the marital chamber."[2]

## Part II. Dora and Freud

No wonder she attempted suicide, even if it was purely a call for help, not really a wish to die. Clearly, she needed help, which is why her father sought out Freud—again.

It was in 1896 that Sigmund Freud first used the term *psychoanalysis* (*"psychoanalyse"*) in a French journal. The article, "L'hérédité et l'étiologie des névroses," referred to a new idea in clinical psychology.[3] The beginning of his theory of the mind resulted in Freud's coming to understand how psychoanalysis could work, which he did by embarking upon self-analysis. This theory of his emanated from the work that both he and Breuer had developed from their joint studies involving early trauma in their patients.

Then in 1899, a year before he began analyzing Ida, Freud published what would be one of his most important and long-lasting works, *The Interpretation of Dreams*. Here, he described what he called dream work, where what happens at night in sleep was seen by Freud as a type of "wish-fulfillment." Freud considered dreams the royal road to self-knowledge. He believed that the dreamer would ultimately be able to access an unconscious part of themselves, thereby having the ability to resolve conflicts. Freud believed that many desires were unacceptable to the conscious mind and were thus disavowed. Within the dream world, Freud would argue, the mind's act of censorship would weaken, allowing forbidden desires to become visible and thus capable of being understood through symbols and metaphors. It was in *The Interpretation of Dreams* that Freud's most significant contributions to psychology emerged: the Oedipus complex and the elaboration of his model of human psychology, for instance.[4] It was into this scholarly world that Ida entered when she was more or less forced to visit Freud following her significant thoughts of suicide.

In accepting Ida as a patient, Freud saw a way to illuminate his new theories and experiment with them. His ultimate analysis elucidated "aspects of the cultural matrix that informed Freud's theory building," according to Adele Tutter. She argues that Freud used not only the data from the case history itself but also an in-depth examination of literary fiction. One such novel, *Madame Bovary*, Flaubert's masterpiece, dissects an unhappy sex life coupled with a desire for romance by a fantasy-driven young woman. Freud, who only wrote one case study of a woman, turned to fiction about women:

> It is posited that the suggestive text in *Dora* acts both as a literal agent of dangerous suggestion, and as a figurative symbol of the occult literary influence that intrudes upon the text, impacting Freud's formulation of his subject; his documentation of her case; and his ensuing conceptualization of the transference. The author [Tutter] ventures that literary fiction and other cultural products function as important objects, shaping our fantasy life, object representations, and transferences.[5]

Ultimately, Freud would fictionalize Ida—giving her the pseudonym of Dora for good reason. He did not do well with his young patient. When she departed from analysis before it was formally terminated, Freud was distressed and distraught. Philipp, who had been treated by Freud earlier, had hoped that Freud would be able to help his daughter. When he initially broached the subject of treating Ida, Philipp suggested that the "supposed" seduction by the lake, which Ida attributed to Hans Zellenka, never took place.

Much of the Dora case study was fictionalized—contributions from which came from Philipp Bauer, Hans Zellenka, Peppina Zellenka, and Freud himself. And so, much of Ida's life was fictive because of the interpretations of her father especially and also of Hans Zellenka. One wonders where her mother was in all of this. Other than telling her husband about the "seduction" as reported to her by her daughter, there is very little about her response regarding her daughter's situation and her health.

Of course, by now we know that Ida's father was indeed having a sexual relationship with Peppina and that Hans had been propositioning Ida for a number of years—while her parents and the Zellenkas pretended that the seduction was "all in her head."[6] That is to say, again, a "fiction."

It should be noted that Freud was just beginning to think about psychoanalysis and how he could work with patients using this new technique. "Freud enthusiastically greeted Ida as a patient who would provide him with a suitable test of his theories of hysteria, his techniques of analysis and of the interpretation of dreams."[7] It would appear, too, given he was a prolific writer, that he knew immediately that he was going to write up the case of "Dora."

## Part II. Dora and Freud

In the treatment sessions, Freud pushed Ida to discuss the sexual aspects of her relationship with Hans Zellenka. Given that the scene at the lake was explicitly sexual, Freud (and Breuer) believed that such an unambiguously sexual scene could be a traumatic event that pushed Ida further into hysteria mirroring Hans's pushing his erect penis against her body.[8]

Years later, other writers "protest at Freud demanding of Ida" that she address and respond to the erect penis of Hans. Ida was disgusted and expressed her disgust, but Freud insisted that she was repressing her real feelings, which might have had the response of a grown woman—in other words, that she would have been titillated by this event.[9] Freud consistently refused to acknowledge that Ida was a young girl, not a woman.

There was also much triangulation in the treatment of Ida. Freud knew the major players in her life, some of whom he met socially, but others, like her father and Hans, he met in the consulting room. He listened to an account by Ida's father prior to his analysis of her, recalling that Hans was told by his wife that Ida was only interested in sexual matters. In discussing this with Ida's father, Hans apparently made reference to Ida's reading of sexual manuals, which were very popular in Vienna at the time (such as Mantegazza's *Physiology of Love*).[10]

By this time in his career, Freud had a sense of the personality dynamics of those who came to him for treatment. To his credit, while he listened and internalized the information received from others, he assumed that most of what Philipp was telling him was not true. He noted, too, later in the case study, that Philipp tried to put the blame for Ida's distress on her mother, whose peculiarities made the "'house unbearable' for everyone."[11]

And so it was that Philipp, in some desperation, marched his daughter from their apartment to Freud's apartment and consulting room at Berggasse 19. The family worried about Ida's suicidal desires. Freud began to listen to his patient, to the "other side"—Ida's side—rather than relying upon what Philipp told him about his daughter. "Her father's words did not always quite tally" with what Freud knew to be true and with what Ida herself told him.[12]

## Chapter 8. Freud's Story of the Seductions

Over the years, other authors have weighed in on Freud's handling of his young patient. M. Guy Thompson, for example, argues that Freud used Ida as an experiment. Unfortunately, if true, it was one that did not produce the results that he wanted: "What he got instead was a lesson in how unpredictable an analysis can be!"[13] While Freud was apprehensive about accepting Ida as a patient, he thought he understood enough about dreams, hysteria, secrets, and desires to be able to help her. "But how many patients would enter in to analytic treatment in the first place if they understood from the beginning that its success depended on revealing their best-kept secrets to a person they didn't even know?"[14]

So it was that Ida entered Freud's consulting room, a young woman "in the first bloom of youth—a girl of intelligent and engaging looks."[15] What Freud learned was that she was on bad terms with her mother, she had withdrawn from social activities, and she was quite unhappy; she had shifted her attitude from loving her father to being on unfriendly terms with him.

The analysis began with Ida's telling about her earliest interactions with Hans. She spoke to Freud of her disgust at the situation that Hans put her in over the course of several years. She somatized her feelings. She had kept most of these encounters secret until she relayed them to Freud, although she did mention the situation by the lake to her mother. "She declared that she could still feel upon the upper part of her body the pressure of Herr K.'s embrace." Freud explains:

> I believe that during the man's passionate embrace she felt not merely his kiss upon her lips but also the pressure of his erect member against her body. This perception was revolting to her; it was dismissed from her memory, repressed, and replaced by the innocent sensation of pressure upon her thorax, which in turn derived an excessive intensity from its repressed source. Once more, therefore, we find a displacement from the lower part of the body to the upper.[16]

This situation with Hans brought on strange behaviors in Ida: she did not like walking past any man whom she thought was in a state of sexual arousal. She constantly lived with disgust, the sensation of feeling pressure on the upper part of her body, and she avoided any men who seemed to be engaged in affectionate conversation. From reading the case study, it seems that Freud and Ida initially had good communication. She was always frank and prompt in her answers and discussions about the sexual details of her symptoms.[17]

Ida was open to discussing her symptoms, her fear and disgust, and her understanding of sexuality, if not her own sexuality. She told Freud that although she had knowledge of the sex act, she didn't quite understand it. Freud thought this was important, as he saw sexual issues and the repression of sexual issues as central to his understanding of the symptoms of hysteria. But much of what would later fall apart between them was due to the lack of understanding of the transference. As Lakoff and Coyne write, Freud did not understand until later that Ida "had fallen in love with him as representative of her father ... and Herr K., whom—according to Freud—she had desired and wished to marry, himself a stand-in for her father."[18]

One could say that the therapy of thirteen weeks limped along in the beginning: Freud was engaged in discovery without much interpretation; at least, this was what Ida thought. He did have thoughts about what was going on with her, though. He felt that Ida's understanding of her father's relationship with Peppina was for the purpose of suppressing Ida's own love for Hans, which had once been conscious. It also served to conceal her love for Peppina, which was, in an even deeper sense, unconscious. Freud theorized that "these masculine or, more properly speaking, *gynaecophilic* currents of feeling are to be regarded as typical of the unconscious erotic life of hysterical girls."[19]

Even though Freud was not convinced that seeing Ida would be revelatory for his theories and hypotheses, as he considered her case one of *petite hystérie*, he did think that an analysis of Ida's dreams would help resolve some of her symptoms, if not her conflicts, which were unknown to her.[20]

# CHAPTER 9

# Dreams and Desires

On some level, Ida and Freud were in similar situations when they met; they both had their dreams and their desires—she for health and normalcy, perhaps; he for respectability and acceptance. You could say they were paired for their seductions, too. While Ida was trying to deal with and keep secret the unwelcome attention she was receiving from Hans Zellenka, it has been alleged that Freud was secretly seducing his sister-in-law, Minna Bernays.

The irony of their combined situation is that in the summer before Freud's second and final treatment period with Ida, he "had just spent five glorious days with Minna" at Lake Garda, the site of Hans's second seduction of Ida, which had sent Ida into a tailspin—and onto Freud's couch.

In the foreword to Romano's *Freud and the Dora Case*, Rudnytsky writes, "This circumstance must have decisively impacted Freud's treatment of Dora."[1] The meaning of this, of course, was that Freud himself was allegedly involved in an extramarital affair with an unmarried woman. It isn't only Romano and Rudnytsky who have suggested that Freud was involved with his sister-in-law at the time of treating Ida. Other scholars and authors have also suspected that something was going on between the two.

Minna had been nursemaid and governess to Freud's six children since 1896, which was when she moved in with Freud and his wife, Martha, at Berggasse 19. If indeed it is true about his affair with his sister-in-law, perhaps Freud felt some guilt about treating Ida, who was in an analogous relationship.[2]

Minna, four years younger than her sister, Martha, was the youngest in the family, born on June 18, 1865, in Hamburg. Minna was four years old when the family moved from Hamburg to Vienna, following her father's four-year jail sentence for bankruptcy fraud. Little is known about her childhood.[3]

We do know that when her father died in 1869, she was taken care of by her mother and, strangely enough, Sigmund Pappenheim, the father of Bertha Pappenheim—better known as Anna O. (Pappenheim was legal guardian to all the Bernays children, given that the two families had been close for years.)[4]

Minna suffered from tuberculosis, never married, and worked briefly as a tutor and companion. She had been engaged to Ignaz Schonberg, a scholarly friend of Freud's, until he died of tuberculosis in 1886, after which Minna resigned herself to her single state. She took care of

The Bernays sisters: On the left, Martha (holding hat on her lap). The two sisters, with Martha seated and Minna standing. The photograph was created on January 1, 1882 (Library of Congress).

her mother in Hamburg and worked as a lady's companion until, in the mid–1890s, she moved in with the Freuds at Berggasse 19, a welcome permanent guest. She was "Aunt Minna," who lived through her nephews and nieces, taking them to spas, and suffering (she once told Freud) from "obligatory migraines."[5]

It was after many attempts at finding a place for herself in the world that she moved in permanently with the Freuds. She remained there for the rest of her life, taking care of the household and the children, especially given that Freud's wife was often absent from the home.[6]

## Chapter 9. Dreams and Desires

While it is known that Freud and his sister-in-law traveled for an extended time without Martha, it still appears to be speculation as to whether they had a love affair. It does seem that they were close. And there is evidence that they signed into a hotel as "*Dr. Sigm. Freud u Frau*," registered to room 11, on Saturday, August 13, 1898. While suspicious, this on its own does not necessarily indicate that they were lovers. To be fair, others dispute this, claiming that letters between the two "do show a relationship of mental and personal intimacy, as between siblings, but they do not in any way hint at a love affair."[7]

Whether or not they had a sexual relationship, they did have an intimate one, living in the same household (and Freud implored her to move in with them) and corresponding sometimes secretly for years. Peter Gay writes:

> The two were close enough, indeed, to exchange letters in secret, keeping Minna Bernays' mother from reading them. "Dear Minning," Freud wrote on April 28, 1887, "my effort to appear as an affectionate son-in-law, in addition to my lack of time, has led to the cessation of our private correspondence...." He wanted to resume it, especially since he sensed that she was in a bad mood "...for which I do not want to be even partly responsible." Again he canvassed the possibility of her visit, which both Freuds so cordially desired. In fact, he told her in confidence, they wanted more: "We firmly intend to keep you with us until you establish your own household or after you, following our previous discussions, begin university studies at thirty." He pleaded: "Dear child, don't be grumpy. Come to us and let us consider together how we can move Mama here." These were not matters the two could discuss openly, since Frau Bernays, exacting and pious, would feel uncomfortable in the Freud household.[8]

If Freud had a close relationship with his sister-in-law, he always had an interesting one with his wife. Much more has been written about the connection between Freud and his wife. Their letters show a couple devoted to each other who worked in a united way: she raised the six children and ran the household (with a great deal of help—much of which came from Minna), and he established himself as a professional physician, scholar, and author. It should be noted that following the birth of the last child, the couple resigned themselves to practicing abstinence as a means of contraception. "Martha was clearly a strong, capable woman who had to stretch her affections across the Bernays ménage, a narcissistic husband, and six children." By all accounts she did that exceedingly well, with or without sex with Sigmund.[9]

Decker makes an interesting point about Freud's relationship with his wife and his description of Ida's mother. Like Philipp, she writes, Freud acceded to the rule of his wife within the household:

> Furthermore, in light of Freud's personal experiences with his wife, one can see why he was not sympathetic to Käthe Bauer's predicament and lacked insight into the dynamics of the Bauer family's pathological constellation. Martha Freud, too, seems to have been a compulsive cleaner. If not so drastic a one as Käthe, she nonetheless resembled her in having "unremitting" call to domestic duty. Freud took note of Martha's ways immediately following their honeymoon and wrote to his new sister-in-law, Minna Bernays, after four months of marriage: "My wife scolds only when I spill something or leave something lying about in disorder, or when I lead her across a filthy spot on the street. It is generally said that I am henpecked. What should one do against that?" The words might have been Philipp Bauer's as a newlywed.[10]

**Sigmund and Martha, in June 1885 (Library of Congress).**

All of this about Minna and Martha and Freud should be taken with a grain of salt, but you could say, given the possibility of an affair between Freud and Minna, that the lives of both Freud and Ida appeared to be involved in sexual activity and seduction around Lake Garda. Because of this, perhaps unconsciously, Freud began asking Ida about dreams that had something to do with the lake visit with Hans. The first dream they discussed had to do with that holiday. This was a recurring dream of Ida's, but until she recounted it to Freud, she had not recollected that it was indeed recurring. Here is the dream:

> A house was on fire. My father was standing beside my bed and woke me up. I dressed myself quickly. Mother wanted to stop and save her jewel-case; but Father said: "I refuse to let myself and my two children be burnt for the sake of your jewel-case." We hurried downstairs, and as soon as I was outside I woke up.[11]

Freud explained to Ida that she should take the dream apart, bit by bit. As she had already had some training in dream analysis, Ida knew that this way of looking at her dream might elicit new material. From the case study:

> "Something occurs to me," she said, "but it cannot belong to the dream, for it is quite recent, whereas I have certainly had the dream before."
> "That makes no difference," I replied. "Start away! It will simply turn out to be the most recent thing that fits in with the dream."
> "Very well, then. Father has been having a dispute with Mother in the last few days, because she locks the dining-room door at night. My brother's room, you see, has no separate entrance, but can only be reached through the dining-room. Father does not want my brother to be locked in like that at night. He says it will not do: something might happen in the night so that it might be necessary to leave the room."[12]

After suggesting to Ida that she "pay close attention to the exact words you used. You may have to make use of them," he asked her about the risk of fire. She then remembered about that trip to the lake and how there was no lightning conductor on the house that the Zellenkas were staying in. This caused her father some distress, she recalled. They continued analyzing the dream and the issue of fire, and how her father was openly afraid of fire and concerned when he saw the Zellenkas' wooden home without that "lightning-conductor," or lightning rod, as we know it today. She further allowed that she had this dream several times while she was with the Zellenkas at the lake. After discussing the dream with Freud, she also remembered that while they were at the lake and following the seduction at the lake, she had returned to the cottage and taken a short nap.

IDA: I suddenly awoke and saw Herr K. standing beside me....

FREUD: In fact, just as you saw your father standing beside your bed in the dream?

IDA: Yes. I asked him sharply what it was he wanted there. By way of reply he said he was not going to be prevented from coming into his own bedroom when he wanted; besides, there was something he wanted to fetch. This episode put me on my guard, and I asked Frau K. whether there was not a key to the bedroom door. The next morning (on the second day) I locked myself in while I was dressing. In the afternoon, when I wanted to lock myself in so as to lie down again on the sofa, the key was gone. I am convinced that Herr K. had removed it.[13]

In Romano's chapter "The Dream of the Burning House," his explication of the Dora case and the first dream is that the dream "had been instigated by the episode on the lake with Herr K., while on the second occasion, it occurred when the patient was clarifying 'an obscure point of her childhood' with her analyst."[14] He goes on to suggest that while the dream replicates Ida's experience on the lake with Hans, it also has a connection with "what is happening in the analysis"—and also what happened during Ida's childhood, which Freud decides he "will not satisfy the reader's curiosity on this point, as he does not reveal what he knew or had deduced about the nature of this obscure childhood episode."[15]

Freud's analysis of the dream continues with his interpretation of Ida's father standing over her bed not as a protector but as a voyeur, while it is Hans who in reality stood at her bed as a voyeur. Freud also understands the issue of the father's etiology in hysteria and the link between Hans and Dora's father of standing over her bed in the dream.[16]

According to Freud, the participants in Ida's dream, the father and the would-be lover, signified an unconscious desire on Ida's part to engage in a sexual act. Freud believed that Ida was in love with Hans, despite her protestations, and he used the "jewel-case" of the dream to illustrate that. In fact, Decker explains, "One of the presents K. had given Dora was an expensive jewel case, which was also a slang expression for a woman's genitals." There was to be an exchange—his gift for her vagina. Freud used this dream and the many interpretations he made to argue that Ida was preoccupied with sex, either through intercourse or masturbation.[17]

During one of their sessions, Ida came in with a purse hanging from her waist. Ida kept opening and closing the purse and playing with it. Freud concurred that her actions mimicked what she wanted to do with her own genitals—to masturbate.[18]

Freud spoke openly about sexual issues with Ida, and he informed her that he had trained himself to detect all kinds of symbolism. He said, "Before him, 'no mortal [could] keep a secret. If [the patient's] lips are silent, he chatters with his finger-tips; betrayal oozes out of him at every pore.'"[19]

Unfortunately, from the beginning of her analysis with Freud, Ida conflated her father and Hans, both of whom she believed used her in a sexual way. While Freud was not sexual with Ida, he certainly had no hesitation in speaking of sexual matters to the young woman. According to Decker:

> Freud intensified Dora's identification of himself with the other two older men, and, indeed, heightened her fears of adult sexual involvement, by his insistence on discussing sexual matters with her very early in the psychoanalysis. It was never clear to Dora what Freud's motives were for seeing her and what was the basis for his inquiries about her sexual knowledge and thoughts.[20]

It seems that Freud had some sense that Ida was wary of his sexual discussions, but he never really came to understand her uneasiness about these talks, especially those brought on by his analysis of the first dream, which was detailed in the case study. As the dream was interpreted, Ida felt threatened by the thought of Hans standing at her bed (instead of her father, as in the dream), but also of Freud himself. It was this unease, Freud would tell her later, that led to her ultimately deciding to leave analysis. Decker suggests, "It was not until Dora left Freud and he was writing up the case did it occur to him that he had overlooked the feelings Dora had transferred from Hans onto him."[21]

However, before Ida left her analysis with Freud, there was a second dream to analyze.

# CHAPTER 10

# Dreams and Hysteria

It was several weeks later that the second dream occurred, which Freud used in the Dora case study. It was the analysis of this dream that would terminate the relationship between Freud and Ida. This second dream was more extensive and complex than the first dream. Here it is in its entirety, as presented in the case study.

> I was walking about in a town which I did not know. I saw streets and squares which were strange to me. Then I came into a house where I lived, went to my room, and found a letter from Mother lying there. She wrote saying that as I had left home without my parents' knowledge she had wished to write to me to say that Father was ill. "Now he is dead and if you like you can come." I then went to the station [Bahnhof] and asked about a hundred times: "Where is the station?" I always got the answer: "Five minutes." I then saw a thick wood before me which I went into, and there I asked a man whom I met. He said to me: "Two and a half hours more." He offered to accompany me. But I refused and went alone. I saw the station in front of me and could not reach it. At the same time I had the usual feeling of anxiety that one has in dreams when one cannot move forward. Then I was at home. I must have been travelling in the meantime, but I know nothing about that. I walked into the porter's lodge, and inquired for our flat. The maidservant opened the door to me and replied that "Mother and the others were already at the cemetery [Friedhof]."
>
> To this she subsequently made an important addendum: "I saw a monument in one of the squares."
>
> To this came the addendum: "There was a question-mark after this word, thus: 'like'?"
>
> In repeating the dream she said: "Two hours."
>
> In the next sitting Dora brought me two addenda to this: "I saw myself particularly distinctly going up the stairs," and "After she had answered I went to my room, but not the least sadly, and reading a big book that lay on my writingtable."[1]

This dream is clearly more involved than the first, and, as Freud recounts, there was some difficulty with the interpretation. This was partly due to the fact that Ida had been asking Freud about the "con-nection between some of her actions and the motives which presum-ably underlay them." She wanted to know why she waited so long to tell anyone about the scene by the lake, and why she even bothered to tell her parents.[2]

Freud's answer to this was to wonder aloud why she would ask such questions, suggesting that a "normal girl" would deal with this situation by herself. But Ida was only seventeen years old—a mis-understanding that Freud consistently called out in the case study, assuming that Ida was a woman, not a girl.[3]

In Freud's assessment of the dream, he began by trying to iden-tify the town she was in, which turned out to be not Merano but a town that Ida had seen in photographs in a book sent to her by a friend. The young man who sent her the book was a quasi-suitor, someone who probably was more interested in Ida than she was in him.[4] Walking around in the strange town was in some way related to her first visit to Dresden, when she wandered the city on her own, specifically to visit the *Sistine Madonna*. Her cousin had wanted to show her around, but Ida wanted to be alone. She remained for two hours in front of the *Sistine Madonna*, according to Freud, "rapt in silent admiration."[5]

In the dream, Ida asked "about a hundred times" where the "sta-tion" was, which Freud interpreted as looking for the jewel case, i.e., the genitals. Ida related to Freud that on the evening before the dream, the Bauers had company. Her father asked her to fetch him a brandy, so Ida asked her mother where the key to the side-board was. When her mother, deep in conversation, did not answer, Ida exclaimed impatiently, "'I've asked you a hundred times already where the key is.'" Since this replicated her query about where the station was in the dream, Freud came to the interpretation that the station equaled the jewel box, which equaled genitals.[6]

Freud then went on to discuss the letter in the dream indicat-ing that Ida's father was ill, and the discovery that he had died. Freud associated this with the letter that Ida herself had written to her parents about wanting to kill herself, which gave her parents such a fright that her father took her to see Freud as soon as he could.

According to Freud, Ida's intent in writing that letter was to shock her father into giving up Peppina—or to take revenge on him for his association with her, who, strangely enough, Ida still cared about. (Freud took Ida's father "craving the brandy" to imply that it replicated Ida's craving for revenge.)[7]

Freud went further into the dream, suggesting that the question mark after the word "like" ("Now he is dead and if you like you can come"), which Ida added in the addendum, signified her recollection of a letter received from Frau K. inviting Ida to the lake for a visit, saying, "If you would like to come." Freud then writes, "Here we were back again at the scene by the lake and at the problems connected with it." He then asked Ida to describe the scene at the lake in detail.[8]

Ida again described in detail the scene at the lake where Hans had inappropriately attempted to seduce her, forcing himself on her. She recalled that she tried to leave him but found that walking back to the villa from where they were would take two-and-a-half hours, so she went back to Hans, who begged her not to tell anyone. Freud pulled out the significant words: *bahnhof* (train station), *friedhof* (cemetery or peace-court), and *vorhof* (vestibulum; literally, forecourt; an anatomical term for a particular region of the female genitals).[9]

"This might have been no more than a misleading joke. But now, with the addition of the 'nymphs' visible in the background of a 'thick wood,' no further doubts could be entertained. Hers was a symbolic geography of sex!"[10] Anyone, Freud claimed, who used these terms and those above as Ida did must have taken them from an encyclopedia—"the common refuge of youth when it is devoured by sexual curiosity." Thus, Freud concluded that this must be the fantasy of defloration, of a man seeking to force an entrance into the female genitals.[11]

Freud added one more point about the dream which had somehow been forgotten; it had to do with a piece of the dream where she said, "She went calmly to her room, and began reading a big book that lay on her writing-table." Ida further explained to Freud that her dream determined that the book was an encyclopedia (which he put in a footnote in his case study). Believing this to be true and adding to the mix that children didn't tend to read forbidden subjects such as she might have found in the encyclopedia, Freud and others believed that since her father was indeed dead—in the dream—she could read whatever she wanted to read: "She could read or love as she pleased."[12]

These meetings between Ida and Freud where her dreams were analyzed, including the second dream, took place between October 14 and late December 1900. In his interpretations, Freud took many liberties with what he believed was Ida's unconscious. He was sure that Ida was in love with Hans and that her protestations were merely her resistance in acknowledging that. Following these revelations and interpretations that Freud found or thought he found, especially in the second dream, which he tied to her hysteria—or as I might argue, her so-called hysteria—things went from bad to worse for Freud and his patient.

Freud believed the two sexual attacks perpetrated by Hans Zellenka were "the traumatic roots of her hysterical symptoms," according to Sharon Heller. Freud reasoned that Ida thought that Hans was attractive and alluring; thus, the first kiss, which she said disgusted her, only hid her sexual interest, which Freud further argued was the root of Ida's "hysterical" reaction.[13]

Freud claimed that this disgust is not uncommon—albeit neurotic—given that the male sexual organ reminds some women of urination. Ida's long-standing chronic and nervous cough displaced the positive sensation of arousal from genitals to mouth. Hans Zellenka would likely have had an erection when he assaulted Ida. She told Freud that she hallucinated that she experienced Hans's embrace on her upper body but felt it in her lower body.[14]

Freud's leap from mouth to genitals fit with his newly developing libido theory in which the mouth was the first erogenous zone. A thumb sucker for many years, Ida had a memory of sitting contentedly on the floor as a child, sucking her thumb as she tugged at her brother's ear. Freud theorized that Ida continued to derive sensual pleasure from sucking through her middle childhood years and speculated that she unconsciously fantasized oral sex between her father and Frau K. Apparently, Ida believed that her father was frequently impotent and that Frau K. used oral stimulation to satisfy him sexually. These sexual fantasies produced an oral symptom of hysteria: her persistent cough. After Dora "tacitly accepted" Freud's interpretation, the cough disappeared.[15]

Just as Freud was getting to the point of analyzing Ida's hysteria in depth, she decided to leave treatment. He asked her when it was that she first began to think about leaving, to which she replied that it was two weeks prior—this on the day she left him. Freud interpreted this to mean that she was giving a two-week notice, like what the governess for Hans Zellenka's children had given—after Hans had rejected her sexually and otherwise. This is the same young woman who fell in love with Hans Zellenka, then felt betrayed by him since he did not divorce Peppina and stay with her as she had hoped. Freud believed this was not only the governess's wish, but Ida's as well— that Hans, her nemesis, would leave Peppina and marry her. Freud felt this was a replaying of the oedipal conflict: Ida loved her father and was jealous of her mother, which in many ways is a universal feeling in early childhood—one which Ida had discussed.[16]

Ida refused to believe Freud's theory. Interestingly, particularly for a young woman of those times, Ida was willing to talk about the most personal of subjects in her life—and to argue with her therapist about his theories, at least as Freud interpreted her discourse. She was generally more apt to verbally disagree with Freud than to stay silent, and she was not afraid or embarrassed to speak about sexual topics. This is all the more surprising as middle-class Jewish girls and women felt especially powerless, being discriminated against as Jews—and as women.

It is entirely possible that Freud's theory was a misrepresentation of his young patient. According to Katharina Adler, Ida's great-granddaughter, "This is the way Freud presented it in his case study. However, there are strong indications that this might have been spurious. Freud may have misrepresented some details here in order to protect himself."[17]

At the Library of Congress, there is an interview with Ida's cousin, Elsa Foges, who claims that Ida told her during the time of her analysis that it was Freud who informed her how babies were made. This disavows Freud's claim that Ida had good sense of sexual activities prior to entering treatment.[18]

Freud's analysis of Ida was thwarted by her abrupt termination of treatment nearly three months after it began. In many ways, Freud's inability at the time to understand the transference—where Ida looked upon both Freud and Hans Zellenka as her father—was what drove her from analysis at a time when she very much needed the guidance and interpretation of the transference. Freud, too, would have benefited from having a better understanding of his own countertransference, which he did not completely understand until sometime after the analysis ended.

Freud had tried to communicate to Ida the configuration of the people in her life, but he was woefully unable to do this adequately. Freud's assessment was that Ida could be helped by admitting to her sexual desires—that she was leading on Hans and that she did in fact want to have sex with him. He expressed that she could freely submit herself to the acknowledgment of this situation without any guilty feelings. Ida disbelieved Freud's assessment, as she was consciously repulsed by Hans Zellenka. Years later, many would argue that Freud had set up a situation of mastery and submission—and Ida would have none of it. As Niall Boyce wrote in the *Lancet*:

> Freud's way of seeing things was understandably unpalatable to Dora, who walked out, and it is to his credit that he was not afraid to discuss his defeat, and to reconsider what it meant for his practice—in this case, in terms of the phenomenon of transference. Perhaps this frankness, persistence, and ability to cope with setbacks by learning from failure is one of the reasons psychoanalysis is still going strong, albeit at some remove from mainstream psychiatric practice, of which it is frequently critical. Are those who continue to use it historical re-enactors, the mental health equivalent of the Sealed Knot society? I don't think so: whatever one's view on the clinical effectiveness and publicly funded provision of psychoanalytic services, Freud's work is still relevant for modern mental health. That does not mean that *Dora* should be taken as an instruction manual.... I would say that Dora remains shocking, infuriating, enthralling, and inspiring. It is an indispensable text for anyone wanting to get to grips with psychiatry.[19]

Since Ida did not believe Freud's interpretation of her or her dreams, she was done with Freud. Her last visit with him was on December 31, 1900, following his interpretation of the second dream. This conversation with Freud about the dream had upset Ida. Her abandonment of him and the analysis came as a complete shock to Freud. He began writing his case study of her almost immediately and apparently finished early in 1901, calling it "Dreams and Hysteria." He then sent it off to the *Journal of Psychologie und Neurologie*.[20]

# CHAPTER 11

# The Master

Freud's narrative of his treatment of Ida, his longest case study, combines his recitations of her life with his interpretations of her life and the events it comprised. Because she was happy with neither his perceptions of her nor his way of interacting with her, she left him after seeing him six days a week for about three months.

Freud was upset that she left, and there is some suggestion that he was angry with her. It may even be said that he was not emotionally centered enough to engage adequately in an analysis with his young patient. As noted earlier, Freud diagnosed Ida as being hysterical; he looked at her physical symptoms as a path to her psychological difficulties. Prior to seeing Freud, Ida had been diagnosed by two physicians as having appendicitis when she presented with symptoms of cramps and stomach pain. Freud, however, disagreed and speculated that she had a case of hysterical pregnancy—given that she had those encounters with Hans Zellenka around the time of the so-called appendicitis attacks. Many have written that Freud bullied his young patient, demanding that she admit her sexual attraction for Zellenka. He also told her that she suppressed her sexuality, given that she masturbated. And most damning of all perhaps was when he told her that he knew all her secrets. As one author put it, "all her dirty secrets."[1]

But what about *his* secrets? Freud was forty-four years old, three years younger than Ida's father, at the time he began his analysis of Ida. As noted earlier, there have been more than several suggestions that Freud was having an affair with his sister-in-law, Minna Bernays. And while he may not have had intercourse with her, he was involved with her emotionally. Minna was his confidante, and it seems that he turned more to her than to his wife. If this wasn't enough "baggage" to bring into the consulting room, he was also experiencing bouts of depression and anxiety. Shortly before Freud began treating Ida, his father, Jacob Freud, had died in October 1896 at the age of eighty-one, following an illness that began in June. Freud would call the death of a father—his father—the most significant event of a man's life. He wrote to his friend, Wilhelm Fliess, "I do not begrudge him the well-deserved rest that he himself desires. He was

Sigmund Freud at the age of eight with his father Jakob (Wikimedia Commons).

an interesting human being, very happy with himself, he is suffering very little now, and is fading with decency and dignity." He also told Fliess that the death of his father affected him deeply. Yet, while he could extoll the virtues of his father upon his passing, Freud had not had such sanguine feelings for his father during his lifetime.[2]

Shortly thereafter, Freud began the practice of analyzing his own dreams, slips of the tongue, lapses of memory, and everyday occurrences, which helped him with his continuous experimentation with theories, eliminating ones that did not seem to work, like his seduction theory of neurosis. According to Peter D. Kramer, "By the late 1890s, an analysis of his own mental functioning had become Freud's central project."[3]

One thing that Freud did believe in was a child's desire for "an exclusive relationship with the parent of the opposite sex and jealousy—even hatred—of the parent of the same sex, which perhaps he came to from this examination of his own life and his relationship with his parents. He thought the child's feelings were complicated by simultaneous love and animosity toward both parents. This understanding was a new idea that would come to be known as the theory of instinctual infantile sexuality."[4]

In dealing with his patients' "demons," Freud had to look into his own. And if his multiple symptoms are any indication, then his demons were manifold. He was a man of deep fears, especially of dying, and had unresolved issues regarding his parents. He continued to be deviled by phobias that remained with him for most of his life, like his fear of travel. He had migraines. He fainted. He examined his earliest dreams and memories, many of which were both exciting and dangerous, but became "grist for the psychoanalytic mill. His pinnacle discoveries reveal both the man and the origin of key ideas."[5]

With regard to

Freud apparently idealized his mother, who bore eight children, but considered her son Sigmund *"mein goldener Sigi."* Freud was sixteen years old when this picture was taken (Wikimedia Commons).

his residual feelings toward his father, or lack thereof, Freud analyzed them exhaustively. According to Freud, his father was weak and ineffective and, indeed, had lost a great deal of money over the years, which threw the family into poverty. Because of his father's disposition, Freud's mother, Amalia, became the head of the family. Freud also believed that his father did not appreciate him, his own son, and this belief dominated Freud for most of his life.[6]

As Freud's self-analysis progressed, darker and more sinister depths of his unconscious spilled out beyond hostile feelings for his father. Freud discovered a sexual interest in his mother, jealousy of an older brother as his rival, and a wish for the death of a younger sibling—in short, the makings of Freud's own oedipal stirrings and the fodder for his quickly evolving ideas of the then-preposterous notion of childhood sexuality.[7]

Despite struggling with all his fears and anxieties, just before working with Ida, Freud was extremely creative, writing and publishing works that are still relevant and important today. Yet even with this success, he continued to feel discouraged and deprived. During the period before Philipp Bauer brought Ida to be analyzed, Freud suffered one of his most hurtful and recurring professional defeats, which contributed to his feelings of worthlessness.

In September 1900, he was once again passed over by the Ministry of Education for promotion from lecturer to associate professor. This promotion was important for a physician and conferred great status as well as the ability to earn much higher fees. Freud believed that he was denied tenure because of being Jewish. These societal concerns about anti–Semitism in Vienna, as well as his personal concerns, worried Freud. He feared for his children's future in a society that abused and debased Jews. If this were not enough, he was despondent about the poor reception of his epic work, *The Interpretation of Dreams*. This tome, recognized by many as the definitive work on dreams, was virtually ignored for years.[8]

Freud believed that the path to understanding oneself was to analyze one's dreams, which he continuously did. In *The Interpretation of Dreams*, he presented himself as the detective, a Sherlock

Holmes, "detecting the obscure in the seemingly obvious and the obvious in the obscure."[9]

As to Freud's discoveries about himself, at the turn of the century, he found that he was extremely unhappy about being "middle aged." According to Decker, nothing made him happy—not his famous cigars, sexual intercourse, or his contact with people. In May, on his forty-fourth birthday, he told himself that he was "an old somewhat shabby Israelite."[10] Apparently, he could not analyze himself into feeling better about the aging process.

A word about the cigars: Freud was "fatally addicted to his cigars, smoking twenty a day for years."[11] Beginning when he was about twenty-four, like his father before him, he became a heavy smoker, and continued until he was eighty-one. He had many symptoms caused by the cigar smoking: nasal catarrh and breathlessness, to name but two. There has been speculation as to why Freud continued to smoke when he knew it could eventually cause him to develop cancer. Wilhelm Reich speculated that Freud's denial was a result of his unhappy sex life with his wife, Martha. Freud considered that smoking was a substitute for the so-called primal addiction, masturbation, although he has also famously said, "Sometimes a cigar is just a cigar."[12]

When Freud began analyzing Ida, he brought into the consulting room all his anxieties, fears, phobias, disrupted relationships, and hostilities. With his own mental and emotional issues, was it any surprise that Ida would quit therapy? She no doubt had entered a therapeutic relationship with him in the beginning, not only with hopes to resolve some of her symptoms, but also in the "hope of a sympathetic ear to her position as a pawn in an adult chess game of sexual trade-offs." Instead, she was told that she unconsciously wanted to bed the scoundrel who had taken advantage of her innocence and who repelled her, and that the person she really wished to have sex with and marry was her father.[13]

Freud was domineering and unsympathetic toward Ida—surprising, given that some of his issues were similar to her issues, such as that she wanted to marry her father and he wanted to marry his mother, and she was symptomatic because of unexpressed thoughts and he was symptomatic because of repressed thoughts.

## Part II. Dora and Freud

While Freud did think Ida was an engaging young woman (perhaps because she was the daughter of a wealthy and successful manufacturer), he certainly did not seem to care for her. He was also careless about details concerning her life, writing that she was older than she was. She was, after all, only thirteen years of age when Zellenka first attempted to seduce her. Freud did not really account for how young she was and thought that she should have acknowledged that when Zellenka's penis pressed against her thirteen-year-old body, she might actually have felt desire, rather than displacement—with a sensation upward, reversing excitation into disgust.[14]

As mentioned, Ida did not like his interpretations, and this annoyed Freud. As Kramer writes:

> So annoyed was Freud that when his young patient approached him sixteen months later over a facial neuralgia, he refused to tend to her. In the interim, Bauer had made progress on her own, by confronting the Zellenkas. She got the husband to admit to having propositioned her, while the wife tacitly acknowledged the affair with Bauer's father. Freud wrote that though he would not treat Bauer further, he "promised to forgive her for having deprived me [him] of the satisfaction of affording her a far more radical cure for her troubles."[15]

So much for Freud's technique and empathy. However, the failure of Freud's analysis of her allowed him to develop his theories of transference and countertransference, so the three months he spent with Ida were not wasted—at least not from his perspective. It was some time after she abruptly left therapy with him that Freud came to an understanding of what had happened. Even though he was furious at her when she left, believing that she was taking the revenge on him that she wanted to take on her father and Hans Zellenka, he was able to create a historic case study that is still examined and reflected upon today.[16]

In the postscript to the case study, Freud explains that he called the study a "fragment," and goes on to explain that "the reader will have discovered that it is incomplete to a far greater degree than its title might have led him to expect." Freud remarks that much was omitted because the "work was broken off."[17]

While Freud takes great pains to explain the analysis and the aftermath in his case study, much is left out—Freud's thoughts about

**116**

Ida, for one thing. And it was Freud's contention that patients like Ida needed to use words, not body language, with Ida being a master at body talk versus word talk. However, it could be that if Ida talked with her body, it might have been because no one listened to her words. In fact, according to Kuriloff, "If Dora speaks with her body because she feels unheard in any other way, Freud's imposing meanings on her behavior perpetuated this familiar, unfortunate sense of herself with others."[18]

Freud himself was not too willing to engage with Ida. Kuriloff goes on to explain:

> Freud was ambivalent regarding therapeutic embroilment. With Dora, he recognized that the thorny path of transference was a resistance. Later, in 1912, he knew that it was the road to cure, providing the assurance that, rather than burn the neurosis "in absentia or effigie"—or interpret the embodied fantasy and attendant fears with words alone—transference ensured the reliving of the patient's desire and conflict in the moment. The inference here is that transference's immediacy, akin to that of pointed bodily sensation, provides something more than words—that psychoanalysis is an acute unfolding between two people. In this way, Freud was really the first interpersonal psychoanalyst.[19]

While Freud knew that Ida's leaving analysis did not allow her to complete the journey of finishing her treatment with him, he knew only too well that his own errors had caused her to abandon him, and now it might be too late to help her.

# Triumph Over Freud

The great question that has never been answered, and which I have not yet been able to answer, despite my thirty years of research into the feminine soul, is "What does a woman want?"

—Sigmund Freud

## CHAPTER 12

# The Return

Even as Ida left Freud's couch at the end of 1900, offering a warm good-bye to her doctor, she was ever the gracious Viennese young woman. With a "Happy New Year," she sailed out of his office, down the steps, and out to the street, knowing she would not be returning to him in the New Year. Despite urgings from her father to continue with Freud—six days a week of treatment—Ida demurred. She sensed that her father only wanted her to continue analysis so he could continue unimpeded in his amorous relationship with Peppina. (Philipp had hoped that Freud would convince Ida that the relationship with Peppina was a positive thing for all concerned.)[1]

Treatment with Freud did not remove the obstacles of dysfunction and loss from Ida's life. Her parents, while somewhat concerned about her health, were more interested in fulfilling their own impulses and fantasies—her father with his mistress and her mother with her fanatical housecleaning. About a year before Ida began analysis with Freud, she had lost her aunt Malvine, whom Freud would describe in the case study as a woman who "gave clear evidence of a severe form of psychoneurosis without any characteristically hysterical symptoms."[2] Ida had loved and emulated Malvine.

Freud would continue to write in his "fragments" that Ida's sympathies had always been with her father's family. He suggested also that Malvine's symptoms were incorporated into Ida's psyche—that she had been a role model of dysfunction for her young niece.[3] Given that Malvine and Ida were close, and that when Ida was in Vienna she spent a great deal of her time with her aunt and her two cousins, it would make sense that the impressionable girl would adopt the characteristics of the woman she admired. Sadly, in April of the year before Ida began analysis with Freud, Malvine died. Ida had returned to Vienna from Reichenberg, where her family had moved after leaving Merano, to be with her ailing aunt. Following her death, Ida stayed in Vienna for several weeks to be with her two cousins.[4]

Prior to her analysis and during it, Ida was also missing her brother, Otto. The two siblings had been so close that their bedwetting occurred in tandem, as did the development of other childhood illnesses and symptoms. As Otto entered adolescence, he removed himself somewhat from the family dynamic, and from his sister, to concentrate on schoolwork and studies. Otto was ambitious and was not going to let his family's significant issues get in the way of his professional advancement.[5]

Ida brought all these losses into her analysis with Freud, but once Ida abruptly terminated the analysis, the same grief and issues remained: family promiscuity, ill health, loss of intimacy, inability to flourish, and repression of women in Viennese society. Despite all this, Ida did begin to thrive within the first few months of her departure from Freud's couch. "Her attacks of aphonia and coughing became less frequent and her depression lifted."[6]

Then, a tragic event occurred, one that led Ida to getting the affirmation she desired. On May 17, 1901, Klara, the ill daughter of Peppina and Hans, died from congenital heart disease. Ida decided to make a call of condolence to the Zellenkas and was greeted by the two as if nothing had happened between her and Hans or between the two families. It was her decision, however, not only to pay her respects to the family but also to demand answers and accountability from the grieving parents.[7]

Ida got what she came for. Peppina acknowledged that she and Philipp had, and continued to have, a love affair, and, more surprising, Hans confessed that he had made an overture of a sexual nature to Ida when she was younger. As Decker writes, "She then returned home and gave this news to her father. Unfortunately, we do not know his reaction."[8]

This "confession" by the two Zellenkas must have eased Ida's mind a great deal. Her health continued to improve as she studied privately and went to lectures, continuing her own self-education. She seemed healthy and to be enjoying life. However, about five months after her visit to the Zellenkas, she ran into Hans, and this seemed to frighten her a great deal. Hans, too, was so shocked at the accidental meeting that he stepped off the curb in surprise and was run over by a carriage. Fortunately, he was not seriously hurt. While seeing Hans catapulted Ida back into her symptoms, she continued to study and vowed never to marry.[9]

Then, in March 1902, following a two-week bout of facial neuralgia, Ida returned to Freud on April 1—fifteen months after she had walked out on him. But Freud was still more than just a little annoyed at her having abruptly left his analysis and told her frankly that he would not take her on as a patient. Ida took the time during that visit to tell him that Klara Zellenka had died, that her father and Peppina were still involved, that she had seen Hans on the street in Vienna, and that both Peppina and Hans had confessed to sexual improprieties. It appeared that she was happy to report Hans's confession about the incident at the lake, confirming that it was a not a figment of her imagination as everyone had declared.[10]

Freud, still refusing to take her back as a patient, told her that her facial pain came about because she had noted in the newspaper his promotion to associate professor, which he had finally recieved after many years of striving. He went on about her pain:

> It was self-punishment for having slapped Mr. K in the face and transferring her feelings about him onto Freud. But Freud adamantly refused to take Dora back as a patient, declaring that he did not know what kind of help she wanted from him. Instead he "promised to forgive her for her having deprived [him] of the satisfaction of affording her a far more radical cure for her troubles." Dora left and never saw Freud again.[11]

Even though Philipp called on Freud several times, promising him that Ida was going to return to him to complete the analysis, Freud knew this would not happen, even after she did indeed return on that day in April to request his assistance. Freud believed that Ida broke off her analysis as a way of engaging in revenge upon men in general and Freud in particular, as a stand-in for other men in her life. She had been betrayed and injured by the men in her life, and she seemingly could take it out only on Freud. "He felt hurt and wounded by her behavior."[12]

As Steven Marcus writes in "Freud and Dora," even though Ida, by his refusal to see her, considered herself finished with Freud, he certainly was not done with her. He had begun to write up the case study almost before she walked out the door that last day in 1900, and he continued to feel, if not obsessed with her, that he had learned a great deal from her aborted analysis. He clearly wanted to make his emerging knowledge known.[13]

Following this failed treatment of Ida, Freud ruminated for about four years before he made his case study public, even though he had completed it in the three weeks following her departure. Freud initially submitted the manuscript, and it was accepted for publication, in January 1901. However, for unknown reasons (about which there has been much speculation), Freud also offered the manuscript to another publisher, but then pulled it from that publication. He then asked for it back from another publisher and then let it sit for four years unpublished. The manuscript was eventually published in the *Monatsschrift* in 1905.[14]

Why did Freud delay publication when he had several potential publishers and had finished the case study shortly after Ida left analysis? Decker has a few theories and concludes:

> Unconsciously Dora was many things to Freud. She was Dora the servant and childlike wife, over whom he could exercise superiority and a certain amount of control. In this way a threatened physician was able to deal with the challenges presented by an hysterical female patient. She epitomized as well Freud's lack of sympathy for the well-to-do, quasi-functional young women who formed a part of his practice.[15]

Freud felt that Ida's abrupt departure from analysis was the acting out of a revenge fantasy, an emasculating of men, which prevented him from successfully completing the analysis. He seemed singularly unconcerned about the consequences for Ida of the aborted analysis; his ego was his main concern. Freud lived with a great deal of "disappointment" his whole life: disappointed by his father, Jung later in life, and now he was disappointed and frustrated by a seventeen-year-old girl. Freud had "been drawn by Dora's youth and attractiveness, had probed her most secret sexual thoughts and feelings, and out of his inexperience had allowed an antitherapeutic sexual tension to develop."[16]

123

## Part III. Triumph Over Freud

It seems only natural that Ida bolted. Ida's biggest threat in life had been the licentious predator who had invaded her family and the overt sexuality in which her father and his paramour engaged. She didn't need another threat, and in her treatment room, no less. And yet, it was because of her time with Freud that she was able to lead a somewhat normal life.

While Freud dithered about whether to publish the case study of Dora, Ida's life was strange in the New Year. In truth, her symptoms abated, but she was puzzled and confused by what had happened in her analysis with Freud. At the same time as she was trying to recover from her association with Freud and the fantasy world he demanded that she recreate for him, real life was intruding.

It is in this case study of Dora, so famous and so frequently read, even today, that Freud looks his worse. Ida had turned to him for help, and he told her that she must recognize her desire for her molester. Many have written that the case of Dora is remarkable in that is describes a patient's rejection of the physician. Freud was a train wreck in the treatment of Ida, according to Kramer:

> Freud's narcissism is on display at a distressing level. He fails his patient and makes it out that he is the injured party. It is a tribute to Freud's skill at storytelling that this example of blaming the victim stood more or less unchallenged between its appearance in 1905 and the mid–1960s, when Freud's developmental theories and his attitudes toward women came under new scrutiny.[17]

But perhaps Ida got revenge, not only on the Zellenkas by finally calling them out for what they did to her, but also on Freud, because she, spunky as she was and a fighter, went on to have a reasonably good life. Shortly after being rejected by Freud, she met someone, married him, and subsequently had a child she adored.[18]

# CHAPTER 13

# Marriage

What did triumph over Freud look like?

By her own admission, Ida did not appear to want what other women of her time wanted: a husband, a home of her own, or even children. She had mentioned to Freud during her last visit with him that she wanted to continue her "work." What this work entailed is hard to say, other than perhaps her studies, lectures, and museum attendance. She was no doubt diligent in wanting to learn and might have been endeavoring to follow in the footsteps of her brilliant brother. As she told Freud, that was preferable to marrying.[1]

However, something changed her mind about marriage. Maybe she was lonely with her brother gone and her family fairly in tatters. Or maybe she met someone at just the right time. Or perhaps her desire for a child catapulted her into more positive thoughts about marriage. In any event, about a year after her last meeting with Freud, she met someone, became engaged, and married. And Ida loved children. She cared deeply and consistently for the Zellenka children. It has been argued that she had strong maternal feelings. Perhaps it was because her own mother disappointed her so deeply that she wanted to be able to do for another child what had not been done for her. And Freud seemed to believe from what Ida told him in passing that these urges of hers, these maternal cravings, were deeply rooted in Ida.

Freud came to these conclusions after hearing from her about her visit to the Zwinger in Dresden, which was a palatial complex of gardens and artwork. There, she viewed the *Sistine Madonna*, also called the *Madonna di San Sisto* because that is the name of the church where it was first seen in Piacenza, Italy.

This oil painting by Italian artist Raphael was commissioned in 1512 by Pope Julius II for the church of San Sisto, to be its altar-piece. The canvas was one of the last of the Madonna paintings done by Raphael and is a magnificent work. The piece was purchased in 1754 by King Augustus III of Saxony for his collection in Dresden. The painting was very influential in Germany, sparking debate on the questions of art and religion.[2] It seems that Ida was transfixed by the painting, not because of the lessons that could be learned, but because it was a signifier for her of motherhood, and perhaps her desire to bear a child.

Ida was on a trip with a cousin when she visited the Zwinger complex and, as she told Freud, stood before the Madonna for about two hours. Freud asked Ida what it was that so fascinated her about the painting, of the young mother, but she did not know. Freud felt that if the analysis had continued, the issue of mothering and Ida's maternal longing for a child would have been revealed to her.[3]

But to have a child in Vienna and elsewhere in 1903 one had to have a husband. Ida's primary view of marriage came from the lives of three women whose marriages were a disaster: her mother, her aunt Malvine, and Peppina. She may have had other role models where being a wife was something positive, but if so, they were few and far between. Ida's prevailing view of marriage would likely have been what she witnessed in the marriages of those three women. That, coupled with her distrust of men—her father, Hans Zellenka, and Freud—was good enough reason to eschew the marital state.

Still, she did enter into marriage with Ernst Adler on December 16, 1903. It's hard to say what motivated Ida to marry, as little is known of the courtship between them, only that he lived in Leopold-stadt and was an unsuccessful composer and engineer.

Born in 1873 in Budapest, Ernst initially lived with his father and mother, Ignaz and Josephine (von Sonnenthal Adler). An only child, Ernst was a musician by avocation but an engineer by profession. According to Ellis, following the death of his mother in Budapest, he moved to the Vienna home of his maternal uncle, "the celebrated Jewish actor Adolph Ritten von Sonnenthal, a well-regarded comedic and tragic actor."[4]

Like Ernst, Ritten von Sonnenthal was born in Budapest in 1834

The *Dresdner Zwinger* is a palatial complex with gardens in Dresden, Germany, and is one of the most important buildings of the Baroque period in Germany. Along with the Frauenkirche, the Zwinger is the most famous architectural monument of Dresden (Stephan Czuratis [Jazz-Face], Wikimedia Commons).

under the trying circumstances of poverty, which no doubt was similar to how Ernst's mother was raised. As a young boy, Ritten apprenticed as a tailor, but he developed a love of the theater after seeing a performance

Adolf Ritten von Sonnenthal (1834–1909) was a famous Austrian actor. He visited the United States in 1885, and again in 1899 and 1902, achieving great success (Portrait Collection Friedrich Nicolas Manskopf at the library of the Johann Wolfgang Goethe—University Frankfurt am Main, Wikimedia Commons).

## Part III. Triumph Over Freud

by Bogumil Dawison, one of Germany's great actors of his day. Dawison both fostered young Ritten and trained him for the stage. As a professional actor, Ritten was beloved, playing a wide variety of roles. He performed across Germany and Budapest, eventually becoming engaged by Heinrich Laube, the dramatist, novelist, and theater director for the world-renowned Burgtheater in Vienna, where he performed the role of Mortimer in Schiller's *Maria Stuart*.[5]

Adolf Ritten was not handsome, but he excelled in drawing-room comedy and was reputed to be a great interpreter of Shakespeare, Goethe, Schiller, and Ibsen. Among his most impressive roles were Romeo, Hamlet, Macbeth, Wallenstein, and Faust. He became *Oberregisseur* (assistant director) of the Burgtheater in 1884 and its provisional general manager in 1887–88 and 1889–90. Ritten was a practicing Jew and more than once was a target of anti–Semitic attacks; nonetheless, he resisted all attempts made to convert him. The emperor made him a nobleman in 1881, and he made guest appearances as an actor in Russia and the U.S.[6]

And so it was that, prior to marrying Ida, Ernst was likely surrounded by a world of culture, especially of music and theater, as he had been living with his uncle and his father. Marrying Ernst gave Ida access to the glittering world of Viennese theater from an insider's perspective. Always a lover of Vienna's cultural world, Ida would have been fascinated while traversing this rarefied community of theater and music.

They may have met through mutual friends, as Ida had an affinity for Viennese theater and the arts. It would seem likely that Ernst, a would-be musician, frequented the world of his uncle, which intersected with Ida's world. What changed Ida's mind about marrying can only be guessed. Did she feel a kinship with Ernst because of their shared love of the arts? Was it because they were both involved in the Jewish cultural world of Vienna? Or was it a grand passion? Decker asks some of the same questions:

> What happened to change Dora's mind? Did she simply succumb to conventional pressures? Had her parents urged her to wed in spite of her inclinations? Did she experience a romance that momentarily swept all before it? Had she been moved by feelings of wanting a child? There is evidence only to

support the latter, although much else probably played a role. Clearly Dora had found a great emotional satisfaction in mothering the K.'s two children.[7]

Ernst was nine years older than his bride, which was the same age difference as between Ida's mother and father. As her new husband was not successful in his field of engineering or in music, he accepted a position with Ida's father, working in one of his factories.[8]

Freud apparently knew of the marriage between Ida and Ernst and believed it to be good for Ida, basing it on his knowledge of her two dreams. In Ida's first dream, he would recall, she turned away from a man she loved toward her father, which Freud believed signified her movement from health to sickness. Freud believed Ida's second dream signaled her intent to turn away from her father toward health and the realities of life.[9]

About the wedding itself, Decker writes:

> The wedding was celebrated in Vienna's fashionable Reform temple located on Seitenättengasse in the Inner City. Like her mother, Dora married a man nine years older than herself, and like her Aunt Malvine, she chose a man from Hungary. Dora's parents had serious misgivings about her bridegroom, but Otto, true to character, refrained from joining in their negative voices, thus giving the impression—true or not—of solidarity with his sister.[10]

While Ida's parents were not thrilled with Ernst, her father hired him for work in his factories and continued to "indulge his daughter materially." Despite their misgivings about the marriage, the family appeared to have accepted it and even celebrated it. In support of Ernst, Philipp once hired musicians to provide Ernst with the opportunity to hear his musical compositions played by a full orchestra.[11]

Ida also seemed to have an appreciation for her new husband's family (of course, she did not know his parents) and for what he brought to the marriage. Decker writes, "Her husband's family, even before they had moved to Vienna, had become as acculturated a part of the Hungarian secular world as the Czech Jews had of the Viennese."[12]

There being no apparent indication of a wedding trip, immediately following their marriage, the couple moved into Alsergrund, the Ninth District, where both her parents and Freud lived, as well as other prosperous and famous people. Upwardly mobile Jewish physicians, merchants, and factory owners inhabited that neighborhood. It would also later be the area of Vienna where Viktor Frankl, famous author, psychoanalyst, and survivor of the Holocaust, lived. Other famous people lived there as well: Theodor Herzl, the Jewish Austro-Hungarian journalist and father of Zionism; Schubert lived and composed music there; and Beethoven died there at his apartment at Schwarzspanierstrasse 15.[13]

Ida and Ernst settled into married life, living in a building on Julius-Tandler-Platz. The area was a hub for academics, musicians, arts, and science as it was the home of the University of Vienna, the General Hospital (*Allgemeines Krankenhaus*), theaters, concert halls, and parks. Today, the area is a commercial hub in Vienna, nowhere near as elegant a street as it was in Ida's time. The building, however, still exudes a gracious, elegant ambiance.[14]

This is the building where Ida and Ernst Adler started their married life and where their son, Kurt Herbert, was born. The building, on Julius Tandler-Platz, now faces the Franz Josefs train station and shows the grandeur of a bygone age (Papergirl, Wikimedia Commons).

## Chapter 13. Marriage

In the early days of their marriage, Ida seemed to be in good health and spirits, as far as can be determined, and it can be assumed that Ida and Ernst were compatible. They certainly took advantage of the various cultural activities that Vienna had to offer, especially given that Ernst's uncle, the actor, would have introduced them to the world of the arts and especially the theater. And Ida herself had already been enjoying the intellectual and cultural opportunities that Vienna had to offer. They walked the streets surrounding their apartment in the Ninth District, shopping, going to parks, and visiting friends and relatives. By all accounts, Ida and Ernst had much in common: they were both Jews who were more secular than not, having been brought up and assimilated into Western society.

I, too, have walked the streets of the Ninth District on my own pilgrimage to Freud's consulting office. As it is now, the neighborhood in Ida's time consisted of large apartment buildings, certainly more elegant than Leopoldstadt in the Second District, where most of the Jewish residents of Alsergrund lived in Ida's time. The austere buildings of the University of Vienna are there, and of course the Vienna Sigmund Freud Museum is still located at Berggasse 19 where, six days a week, Freud analyzed Ida and other famous people.

The Danube Canal is at Alsergrund's eastern border, and the foothills of the Vienna Woods tiptoe into the Ninth District. Alsergrund is separated by the Danube Canal as it runs from Brigittenau to Leopoldstadt. I can imagine Ida walking the streets of Alsergrund, just as I did, taking in lectures, attending concerts in the Golden Hall in the *Musikverein*, and reading papers in the famous coffee houses of Vienna (such as the *Weiner Kaffeehaus*). Vienna was then, and still is, a fascinating city, and I can easily believe that Ida enjoyed all it had to offer following her marriage to Ernst.

## CHAPTER 14

# Motherhood

While Ida appeared to enjoy marriage and the Viennese life she was living, she awaited the prize that she really valued and sought, motherhood. On February 4, 1905, sixteen months after her marriage, twenty-two-year-old Ida gave birth to Kurt Herbert Adler at home. Decker writes:

> If Dora had indeed married to gratify her maternal longings, her labor and delivery dealt her a grievous blow. After her son was born, she felt she could not undergo the pains of labor again and vowed to have no more children. In more than one way, this was a decisive period in her life. On June 14, 1905, a few months after their infant son's birth, Dora and her husband formally left the Jewish community. The following day they were baptized in the Protestant church.[1]

Kurt himself has this to say about his birth:

> I was born in Vienna, in 1904.... I was a premature child—I think I was a seven-month baby—and I was born on a Sunday night at 11:30 p.m. There is a saying—or was, at least—in Austria, that a child born on a Sunday would be a lucky person. So my mother absolutely wanted a Sunday child, and she made every effort that I would be born on Sunday, the second, and not on Monday, the third, as it appeared I would. I was born at home. It was customary in Europe then that children were born in the home of parents who had an adequate apartment, and not in hospitals. And so it was.[2]

At about the same time that Ida gave birth to Kurt Herbert, Freud finally gave birth to the case study of Dora, which had languished in his filing cabinet for four years following the analysis of Ida.[3] The case study was condemned in its first review as a form of mental masturbation, an immoral misuse of his medical position.[4] But others enthusiastically reviewed the case, and by the mid–1900s, Freud and his case had gained general psychoanalytic acceptance. Little is known of what Ida thought of the case study once it was published, but she did tell several physicians whom she visited that she was the "Dora" of the case, and seemed proud of this fact.

Ida had more important things, however, to think about and take care of than Freud and his case study of her. Even though her pregnancy and delivery had been terrible, she now had a son she adored, and she was, by all accounts, both a devoted and a fierce mother. Ida coddled her son, as she and Ernst were wealthy and had every advantage to pass on to their child.

Ida was aware of the growing anti–Semitism in those years, which is one reason that she, Ernst, and their son, converted to Protestantism, a very common act by Jews during that time. Decker writes about her conversion:

> She had been mistreated socially as a Jew and a woman, her love for her father and Mrs. K. had been rewarded by their sacrificing her for their own ends, she had been used by Mr. K. as a servant, and she lived in an emotional void created by her angry and compulsive mother. If there had ever been a human being who yearned for acceptance, it was Dora.[5]

Ida had an understanding of what was happening in Vienna and in Austria as she was well-read and informed. Prior to meeting Ida, Ernst had been turned down for employment on religious grounds.[6] Ida did not want her son to have any such impediments to a good life, and so she made sure that Kurt was prepared for the future. Especially in light of the rising anti–Semitism, she taught him English, among other languages. In any event, learning English was the custom for middle-class families living in Vienna. According to Kurt, he also learned French when he was five years old, which was the language they all spoke at home. They never spoke German, although they knew it. He also learned Italian.[7]

Despite what must have been going on in Vienna and the rest of Austria, it appears that Kurt had a privileged childhood. In the interview he conducted in July 1985, he has this to say about his early years:

> We stayed in that apartment until 1907 (the apartment on Julius-Tandler-Platz). That means I was two years plus when we moved to the next apartment, in a house in which we remained until 1934. Strangely enough, I remember the moving and the arriving in this apartment. It was a very light apartment, surrounded by gardens and trees, while the other one had been

in the real city, you know, without trees, only with noise, and near a railroad station with steam locomotives which one heard! I don't remember seeing them when I was that young, but I remember the noise.

I started going to school in Vienna when I was about six, and I went to what would be primary or grammar school—! I am really not quite familiar yet, probably never will be, with the way you describe it here—in Vienna. I went to a private school which had five grades. But, being a good student and ahead of my classmates, they made me skip the fifth grade, and I went after four years to the Gymnasium, all within five minutes of my parents' apartment, the schools being next to each other.[8]

Kurt attended preparatory schools in Vienna. As his father was a musician, from a young age Kurt would likely have been given musical instruction as well as instruments. He began piano lessons when he was five years old.

Later in his life, Kurt mentioned in an interview that he "got into the music business when I was 13 years old. I sight-read the score of *Walküre*. I'd never heard it, and the man who heard me told my mother that I'd better go to a good teacher. I regret that I've never conducted that one, and I know it very well."[9] Kurt also described in adult reminiscences, corroborated by his childhood friends, that the Adlers lived a well-to-do but not ostentatious lifestyle. He recounted that his parents, as well as the rest of Ida's family, enjoyed a prosperous life in the period before World War I.[10]

Ida's father was still wealthy, as his factories were successful. Ida continued to attend social events, and, while no longer Jewish, the Adlers still socialized within the confines of the Jewish community. In 1911, when Kurt formally started his education, Vienna was still the intellectual as well as the material capital of Austria. Both its university and its medical faculty had worldwide reputations. From the *1911 Encyclopædia Britannica/Vienna*:

As a general rule, the Viennese are gay, pleasure-loving and genial. The Viennese women are justly celebrated for their beauty and elegance, and dressing as a fine art is cultivated here with almost as great success as in Paris. As a rule, the Viennese are passionately fond of dancing; and the city of Strauss, J.F.K. Lanner (1801–1843) and J. Gung'l (1810–1889) gives name to a "school" of waltz and other dance music. Opera, especially in its lighter form, flourishes, and the actors of Vienna maintain with success a traditional reputation of no mean order. Its chief place in the history of art Vienna owes to its musicians, among whom are counted Haydn, Mozart, Beethoven and Schubert.

## Chapter 14. Motherhood

The Viennese school of painting is of modern origin; but some of its members, for instance, Hans Makart (1840–1884), have acquired a European reputation.[11]

In various publications, Kurt has discussed his parents:

My mother was born Bauer, Ida Bauer, and some of her ancestors came from Czechoslovakia. She grew up in Vienna, and spoke only very little Czech. Her father, Filip Bauer, whom I recall as an especially kind man, was a textile manufacturer. He had factories in Bohemia, which at that time was a part of the Austro-Hungarian monarchy, Austro-Hungarian Empire, if you wish.

My father, Ernst Adler, was born in Budapest, but his parents died, I believe, when he was a baby; I certainly didn't know them. He grew up in Vienna in the house of the famous actor, Adolph Ritter [sic] von Sonnenthal, who was made a nobleman by the Emperor Franz Joseph. He was one of the most famous actors in the Burgtheater, which was the imperial, legitimate theater. Sonnenthal and Kainz, Joseph Kainz, are the names one remembers most from the turn of the century, and slightly before, as the most successful and prominent actors in the capital of Austria. My father tried, from what I've heard, to imitate Sonnenthal, who was a very elegant man, at least as far as clothing goes. I've seen photos of my father in his young years where he wore the same clothes as I have recognized in photos of Sonnenthal.[12]

As Kurt was growing up, he became more and more interested in music, perhaps because of the reputation of his uncle, but also because Ida had exposed him not only to theater and opera but also to music lessons at a very young age. Did Ida foresee that her son could have a brilliant musical career, or was this something that was brought into being by his father, the frustrated and unsuccessful musician? Was Kurt living out his father's dream?

There is no record of his motivation for choosing music as his career, only what Kurt says in his interview—that his parents encouraged him in his exposure to music. As he recounts, however, there was a small problem:

I was about thirteen, fourteen years old, but at that time, I didn't go too often (to the opera).

There was another small problem: my father, who was more or less on the capitalist side, didn't like it too much if I went to this "Social-Democratic" box, you know? But he got used to it, and the more I studied music, the more he realized how good it was for me, how important the attendance of those performances was. He did something else. He was a bridge partner of the then–opera director, Franz Schalk. And Mr. Schalk invited me to attend any rehearsal I wanted to attend. So, if I wanted to, I could start in the morning and stay in the opera house until night.[13]

Life was good for the Adlers. Ida was healthy, it appeared Ida and Ernst were compatible and experienced little to no friction in their marriage, and their son was on his way to an eventful life. Decker explains,

Neither her husband's career nor Dora's way of life was at stake. He had a job with his wealthy father-in-law and did not have to worry about a civil service or professional position. She was not a poor young woman who wanted to rise through marriage or a working-class woman who simply wanted to marry a Christian man she had met at her job.[14]

# CHAPTER 15

# The Bauer Family
# After Freud

From 1880 to 1910, the population of Vienna doubled. This great influx of people created housing shortages, social deprivation, and working-class unrest, which created a social threat, especially to prosperous Jews. Nonetheless, Jews still played a leading role in the artistic and intellectual life of the city, and Vienna was still one of the leading scientific centers of Europe. It was also a city where Adolf Hitler spent his formative years.[1]

In 1912, Ida's son Kurt was seven years old and attending school. His father, Ernst, was working for Ida's father, Philipp, and his mother was taking care of her home, rearing her son, and, one imagines, visiting with her parents and brother and staying involved in the arts. She was also the driving force behind Kurt's education.

In those early months of 1912 when Kurt was in primary school, things went on normally as they had for some time for the Bauer-Adler family. Notwithstanding being Jewish, both Ida and her husband felt that nothing was unavailable to them in Austria, and Ida believed that her son could achieve anything he wanted. As Kurt went through his school years, he continued to have a strong interest in music, which was encouraged at home.

Again, from Kurt's recollections about life with his parents:

Speaking about my father, he was in a position to hire orchestras, and he listened to his not-very-good music by hiring an orchestra to play it. Some of his works were also published, by Doblinger in Vienna, a firm that still exists. I always wanted to find out if there are any plates left, because now even his bad music would interest me.

[My] father was also an admirer of the first record players, which played with a big horn and an incredible weight, and the records also were heavy.

## Part III. Triumph Over Freud

He had an enormous collection of recordings. And he owned what probably was the first portable record player. He had a trunk which he designed built specially so he could take the record player, the horn, and a fairly large number of records along when he traveled. I was terribly impressed—not necessarily favorably, because my mother made fun of my father's addiction to the portable record player.

I should mention something else about him: he was one of the first individuals to own a private car in Vienna, around 1900. Later on, he did not keep cars in Vienna, but rather he kept them at the factories in Bohemia, because he did not wish for me to grow up as a child who had a car at his disposal. That seemed to my parents as something one just didn't do, if one didn't want to be considered nouveau riche or whatever.[2]

Vienna must have been a magical—and musical—place in the early 1900s, especially for Ida and her family. In addition to Kurt's maternal great-uncle, Adolf Ritten von Sonnenthal, Kurt had other relatives in the musical world: one of his father's cousins was the composer and pianist Rudolph Reti. Kurt recalled that as a child he went to Reti's recitals, "sitting impatiently in the first row with white gloves, because a child of my standing and class had to wear white gloves for a recital."[3] Apparently, Kurt hated those white gloves, but one can assume that his parents, particularly Ida, would have wanted the family to bow to the conventions of the day. Kurt explained:

I had also to wear those white gloves when, on Sundays, we rode in a two-horse carriage taking either my grandfather, my mother and me, or my father, my mother and me to the Prater, which was "the thing to do." The Prater is a very beautiful place, and not only the amusement park, which most people know. It has lovely meadows and woodsy parts, and it is not so far from the Danube. We went in this carriage, and I had to have my hands in my lap with the white gloves—and I was annoyed that I couldn't go in dirty clothes to the Prater, where the amusement park was.[4]

Ida's parents, Philipp and Käthe, must have been thrilled with Otto's accomplishments, but also somewhat worried about his professional beliefs, which were not the same as theirs. I would assume they were happy that their daughter had regained some equanimity and peace in her roles as wife and mother. They must also have been pleased with the emerging accomplishments of their grandson, Kurt.[5]

Ida's satisfaction with life would not last forever, however. Into this bright world of adulthood came a number of challenges for both of the Bauer children, Otto and Ida. First, their mother, Käthe, became ill with colon cancer. It can be assumed—and hoped—that Ida helped her mother in her final years, although this is not recorded; nor is it known whether Otto helped to care for her. Käthe died in August of 1912 at fifty years of age.[6] All the Bauers continued to live in the same area in the Ninth District of Vienna.

Shortly thereafter, Philipp Bauer became increasingly and progressively ill from his almost lifelong diagnosis of tuberculosis, although the death certificate would read "degeneration of the prostate." It has been recorded that Ida again took up nursing duties for her father, caring for him tenderly, with the singular devotion that she had exhibited when she was a young girl. Otto also helped to nurse his father—strangely, as he had been more intimate with his mother over the years than with his father, often siding with her when he would side with anyone at all.[7]

It appears that Peppina did not have contact with the Bauers and was not involved with Philipp at this time. We do know that by the time that Philipp died, the Zellenkas had moved to Opernring, part of Vienna's fashionable inner ring road (Ringstrasse), close to the opera house. The Zellenkas were out of the picture around the time that Ida and Otto's parents died and they disappeared from the Bauer-Adler circle, even though they were living in Vienna. By 1913, according to Ellis, Hans and Peppina were still married, despite frequent discussions about divorce. By this time, Hans had been promoted to deputy director of Philipp Haas and Sons.[8]

Philipp died in July of 1913, less than a year after the death of his wife, and just one month before his sixtieth birthday.[9] Kurt has said that his grandfather was an especially kind man, and so was perhaps saddened by his death. Kurt would have turned eight just three months before his grandfather died.[10]

Several notices of Philipp's death appeared in Vienna's *Neue Freie Presse*, and there were also articles about him in various Merano newspapers thanking him for his "continued efforts as a fundraiser for the humanitarian developments there that had continued even after his departure from Meran in 1887."[11]

Following the deaths of her parents, Ida's various symptoms

began to reemerge. As war was on the horizon and her son was becoming more and more independent, there were good reasons for a woman who somatized her feelings to again fall ill.

World War I began on July 28, 1914, after the assassination of Archduke Franz Ferdinand and his wife Sophie, and lasted until November 11, 1918. It pitted Germany, Austria-Hungry, Bulgaria, and the Ottoman Empire against Great Britain, France, Russia, Italy, Romania, Japan, and the United States. While there had been tensions in Europe for a while, it was the assassination that sparked the four-year conflagration.

In his interview, Kurt recalled the assassination:

On June 28th, 1914—I was nine years old—we (my parents and the family of one of the most prominent directors of a main bank in Vienna) were on the Kalmberg in the Kaffeerestaurant for coffee in the afternoon. A military band was playing. Suddenly, the bank director was called to the telephone. An instant later the band stopped playing, and when the bank director came back, he said, "The Crown Prince has been shot in Sarajevo." And of course everybody felt that was not the end of it, and felt what was coming, which was the First World War.
   Speaking about music, it was amazing to the ears of a child that a military band stopped in the middle of the bar.[12]

The war would take a heavy toll on the Bauer-Adler family. Otto entered the war and was decorated for bravery; however, he was also captured and became a prisoner of the Russians for three years, unable to return to his prior life until September 1917. Ernst, Ida's husband, was initially thought to be too old at forty-one to be called into service; yet, a year later in the spring of 1915, he was called up. Unfortunately, Ernst was never the same following the war. He returned handicapped, having suffered from head and ear injuries. As a result, Ernst suffered in a number of ways: his memory was impaired, he had lifelong balance issues, and he seemed to be affected psychologically. Additionally, Philipp's brother, Karl, who had taken over the family business following the death of Philipp, died of heart failure, which left the family enterprise without a leader.[13]

Obviously, Kurt was too young to have any involvement in the war, but, like his mother, he felt the deprivations brought on by it. It must have been frightening for the young man to have his uncle be a prisoner of war and his father a casualty of it. Additionally, there was never enough food to eat, hardly any fuel for those who still had motor vehicles, and the mounting inflation would endure for several years. The end of the war came with the signing of the Treaty of Versailles on June 28, 1919, but there was no end yet to the deprivation.

Still, Kurt continued with both his academic and musical studies. He was fourteen when the war ended and continued his education at the preparatory school. He entered the Vienna Academy of Music in 1922, and from 1923 to 1927, he attended the Vienna Conservatory of Music and the University of Vienna. Kurt made his musical debut in 1925 as an orchestral conductor at the Vienna theaters, which were managed by noted European theatrical producer Max Reinhardt. Kurt continued in that capacity until 1934, while at the same time acting as a coach, accompanist, chorus director, and instructor. From 1934 to 1937, he conducted at opera houses in Germany, Italy, and Czechoslovakia. Eventually, he assisted Arturo Toscanini at the 1936 and 1937 Salzburg Festivals and, during the summers, served as an instructor at the Salzburg Mozarteum.[14]

Although the war ended, Austria and Germany would not be the same, and the affairs of the Bauer-Adler family were changed forever as well. As Ellis writes, "Czechoslovakia was granted independence and responded by nationalizing foreign-owned businesses, including the factories owned by the Bauer family. Much of the Bauer family's wealth was lost." The Zellenkas did not fare any better. Peppina had always received income from the Biedermann Bank in Merano, which survived until 1932, but it was never as profitable as it had been. And while Hans was able to keep his position with Philipp Haas and Sons, Austria was in economic collapse.[15]

Ida's personal situation was not at all good either: her parents were dead, her finances greatly reduced, and her husband was no help to her given that he was now nearly an invalid. Ida needed money—most especially, according to Ellis, to support the musical education of Kurt, "who was proving to be a child prodigy." And so it was that Ida, always the survivor regardless of her situation, rented out rooms to people who wanted to play bridge, which was all the rage with fashionable women in Vienna.[16]

## Part III. Triumph Over Freud

As to how Freud survived in Vienna during and after the war, like everyone else, he had to become accustomed to a different way of life. Decker writes that he took food in lieu of payment and "relied on food packages, money, cigars, and clothing from English and American relatives, wealthy followers, and friends and pupils in Holland and Switzerland. All his old fears and resentments of penury were reawakened."[17]

All was not lost, however. By 1921, things began to improve in Austria. Freud's practice began to pick up again, and he would be even more celebrated than he had been prior to the war. Ida's brother would bring honor to the family because of his political activism and leadership, and, most of all, Ida had great plans for her incredibly talented son.[18]

Ida had her dreams, but she also had her ailments—all while her brother was achieving fame across Europe.

# CHAPTER 16

# The Politics and Power of Otto Bauer

During the years when Ida was seeing Freud, getting married, and having a child, Ida's brother and for many years her close companion was achieving professional success and accolades. To please his father, Otto had achieved a law degree at the University of Vienna and went on to obtain a doctoral degree in law in 1907. Always political, he joined the Social Democratic Party of Austria and founded *Der Kampf,* the theoretical journal of the party. By 1912, he was considered a leading leftist socialist.[1]

When Otto was entering his adult years, following his education, he was fluent in four languages, was a habitual cigarette smoker, and decided to dedicate his life to socialist causes, much to the consternation of his father, who wanted him to enter the manufacturing business.[2]

Otto was apparently influenced in his ideas and ideals by his father's bachelor brother, Karl. According to Decker, this uncle was a favorite of Otto's in much the same way that their aunt Malvine was of his sister. Like Malvine, Karl loved spending time with Philipp and Käthe's children. In his case study of Ida, Freud mentioned Karl, a man he had met and called a hypochondriacal bachelor. Freud felt that Ida's propensity for hysteria might have come from her father's side of the family, as both Karl and Malvine had problems, according to Freud.[3]

Otto's ideas about socialism were enhanced by Karl, but his socialism came much earlier—in Merano. He realized there that the source of his father's prosperity "was the labor of the weavers in the Bauer factories and that only the weavers' work and poverty made it

143

possible for him to dedicate himself to his studies, an opportunity 'forever denied' them."[4]

Otto had sympathy for those less fortunate than him. He felt a need to reverse the injustice that he saw around him all the time. He himself felt the sting of life's unfairness at age seven or eight, when his father became ill and uprooted the family. This had repercussions for Ida, as we saw earlier, but for Otto as well. Otto also seemed to understand that his father's health, or lack thereof, undermined his parents' marriage and created great unhappiness for his mother—that and his affair with Peppina. Otto felt it was these things that brought about his mother's increasingly dysfunctional housecleaning. Otto also felt burned by the injustice of being a Jew. Even though he was not an observant Jew, he chose not to convert and lived openly as a Jew, the repercussions of which were felt both socially and professionally.[5]

Otto was also influenced in his politics and social views by Socialist Party leader Victor Adler (1852–1918), whom he came to worship. Adler had converted from Judaism and appeared to experience self-hatred, which was largely theoretical. He believed that Jews had created their own anti–Semitism because of their fanatical adoption of capitalism. He—and Otto—adopted Marxist views that capitalism would fall and Jews "would at last find acceptance."[6]

Otto made learning, and then politics, his world. He became less involved with his family, especially Ida. And he continued to refuse to take sides in the battles that were ongoing in the Bauer household. Ida and Otto had completely opposite views of their father's affair with Peppina: Ida would complain to Otto about it; Otto professed not to care one way or another what his father was doing, claiming it was not their business.[7]

From 1907 through 1936, Otto would write and publish a number of books. During his university years, it appeared that he did not have much of a social life or love life. Kurt explains that Otto was a Social Democrat—and "incredibly clever and talented."[8] Apparently, he wrote a Napoleonic drama when he was seven years old and, according to Kurt, "it is really quite an opus. I have the manuscript of it."[9]

Kurt spoke very admiringly of his uncle:

After the collapse of the Austro-Hungarian Empire in 1918, he became the first Secretary of Foreign Affairs for the new Austrian Republic. He was furthered by an older Social Democrat with the name of Viktor Adler—no relative. He was the leader of the party; he liked my uncle very much, and it was he who opened the doors for his political career.[10]

According to the lengthy interview that Kurt gave many years after Otto's death, his uncle was a man "with such a memory. He wrote volumes of books and when he quoted, he quoted from memory." He goes on to recall that even when proofreaders would check his books and quotes within the books, there was never an error. Kurt said that his uncle was a genius in the field of politics and social development. "He was brilliant in all respects; there is no other word." Kurt was exposed to his uncle's brilliance at a young age, as Otto and Ida were so close.[11]

Although Jewish (Ida and her family eventually converted to Christianity; Otto did not), both Ida and Otto felt that nothing was unavailable to them in Austria. Otto felt strongly that Jews and Christians would be so intermingled in Europe that there would be no differentiation between the two. According to Decker, "That is why he rejected his sister's limited, and to him, ineffective solution of conversion and instead advocated intermarriage." While Ida had converted and lived as a Christian, as did her son and husband, Otto preferred to live openly as a Jew.[12]

It was not until the death of his parents that Otto married. He was thirty-three at the time and chose a woman ten years older than himself, Helene Landau, who already had three children. Despite his lifelong belief that Jews should intermarry, he did not, Helene also being Jewish. Perhaps he rationalized this decision since he did not have children by Helene, thus avoiding "placing any Jews on earth." Later in life, at the age of forty-five, and still married to Helene, Otto fell in love with another woman who was also Jewish. Hilda Schiller-Marmorek was a beautiful married woman who was ten years younger than him—and, like his wife, a committed socialist. While both Hilda and Otto spoke often of divorcing their current partners to marry each other, that did not happen. Otto ultimately followed in his father's footsteps, taking a younger, beautiful woman as a mistress and remaining married to his older wife.[13]

Strangely, Otto, like his father and sister, also sought the advice of Freud. He visited him for reasons that are not readily known but possibly because of professional unhappiness, as Freud tried to convince Otto to become a university professor. Otto, however, was having none of that; he continued working professionally as a politician. Freud did suggest that if he was trying to make people happy by being a political force and changing the world for the good of the people, it would never work. According to Freud, people don't want to be happy.[14]

Even though neither Otto nor Ida lived near Freud, Freud seemed to have kept track of the Bauer family. Freud knew that Ida had married and had a son, and he knew that Otto was a prolific and respected political writer and steady contributor to the Socialist Party publications. There is some suggestion that Otto's visit, which didn't seem to impact Otto in any discernible way, might have had repercussions for Freud. Decker writes: "Nonetheless it is a distinct possibility that Otto's visit evoked in Freud memories of a long-ago failure and thoughts of the theoretical and technical strides he had made in the intervening time. For it was just in the four previous years that Freud had begun to publish a series of findings that seemed directly linked to Dora's treatment."[15]

In papers Freud had written just prior to World War I, he suggested that he knew he had made mistakes with Ida, and he wrote about the difficulties he encountered with his patient, specifically his lack of understanding of the countertransference. Freud had matured, as had Ida. And perhaps in seeing Otto and talking to him, learning as he must have about his family, he saw that Ida had made progress and appeared to be stable.

# CHAPTER 17

# World War I

In the beginning of 1914, Freud, Ida, and Otto were all maturing and both enduring the hazards and experiencing the happiness of growing older. Freud was more accepting of his "minority status" and had decided to make a virtue out of necessity—meaning that he knew who he was, and he had a modicum of professional success and a somewhat happy family situation. While Freud considered himself German in all aspects of his life, he understood that he was also a Jew.[1]

For her part, Ida continued to try to be part of the majority; she had converted to Christianity and had enough money to enjoy all the accoutrements of wealth and privilege. She had arrived after striving for social acceptance "at the highest possible level," all the while abandoning the intellectual pursuits of her earlier years. By the age of thirty-two, Ida had abandoned her previous avant-garde literary and artistic interests, apparently without remorse. She was now interested in decorating and attending the opera. Along with her husband, they encouraged their son's musical aptitude. Ida had great hopes for her son.[2]

Otto was professionally successful and politically savvy. He founded *Der Kampf*, the theoretical journal of the Socialist Party in 1907, and from 1907 to 1914 he was secretary of the party. He was viewed as successor to his mentor, Viktor Adler, as party leader.

All three, Freud, Ida, and Otto, were enjoying the fruits of their labor, but by August 1914, the clouds of war would envelope all three.

The possibility of war had been apparent for some time. What would be known as the Great War began because of a complicated set of factors; primarily, however, the worldwide conflagration began because of an assassination. On June 28, 1914, a great friend of Kaiser Wilhelm of Germany, Austrian Archduke Franz Ferdinand, along with his wife, Sophie, were on a state visit to Sarajevo in Bosnia—which had been annexed by Austria-Hungary. The couple were scheduled to inspect the imperial armed forces in Bosnia-Herzegovina. As they were touring in an open carriage, with little or no security, someone threw a bomb at their car, which rolled off the back of the car. This shook them up but did not hurt or injure them; it did, however, wound an army officer and some bystanders. As they continued touring, they apparently took a wrong turn somewhere near Gavrilo Princip, a nineteen-year-old dissident and member of the nationalist Young Bosnia movement. Armed with weapons supplied by a Serbian terrorist organization and awaiting his chance, Princip fired at point-blank range, fatally wounding both the archduke and his wife. Princip then attempted to turn the gun on himself but was restrained by onlookers until the police arrived. The assassinated royal couple were rushed to hospital, where both died within an hour. Austria-Hungary had no choice but to retaliate in response to such an aggressive and egregious crime, so with Germany's support, they declared war on Serbia on July 28, 1914.[3]

Following this, on August 1, Germany declared war on Russia, Serbia's ally. Russia then invaded France, via Belgium, which forced Britain to enter the conflagration, declaring war on Germany. Over the next four years, others would become involved—Italy, Japan, the Middle East, and the United States. More than twenty million soldiers died, and twenty-one million more were wounded, while millions of people fell victim to the influenza pandemic of 1918 that the war helped to spread.[4]

In his interview with Timothy Pfaff, Kurt Adler has spoken about this period:

> As a child I was brought up as a typical bourgeois child, where money was available (which I did not know), but also as a child who had an insight into the ideals and philosophy of the Social Democrats who took over in 1918. Took over in Austria, I should say—as well as in Germany.
>
> In 1918 my father was still in the Austrian army, although he was an invalid because he had a very bad ear problem, which was caused by coming back to Vienna from the Polish front too late for an operation. He lost his hearing in the left ear, and also it affected his entire nervous system in a very adverse

way. But he was still in the Ministry of War, active in the army, until 1918. My mother and I were in Czechoslovakia, which at that time was still Bohemia, at the house of a friend of the family whose name was Dr. Richard Strauss, but not the composer: he was also a manufacturer, textile manufacturer.[5]

Having lost her father the year before, Ida would now lose her brother, with whom she was still extremely close, perhaps closer to him than to anyone. Otto was off to war. He was decorated for bravery and then captured and sent to a Russian prison, not to return until September 1917. And her husband, who for some time had been kept out of the war, was finally called up. Decker writes: "Dora's husband, at forty-one, was not called up for a year, but in late spring of 1915, he too went off." Ernst would return a changed man, permanently disabled from head and ear injuries that affected his sense of balance and his memory.[6]

As if that were not enough, Philipp's older brother Karl, whom Otto thought of as a mentor in his earlier years, died of heart failure. Since he had been the head of the family firm upon the death of Philipp, Karl's death meant that the business was without leadership. And it was that business, which had been so successful under Philipp's leadership—and Karl's—that allowed the Adler family to live the lifestyle to which they, and Ida, had become accustomed.[7]

Freud, too, would have a difficult time during the war years, as his sons were serving in the Austro-Hungarian army. And, like the Bauers, Freud depended on international support for his lifestyle and his professional livelihood. The war ended those connections, and he began to suffer financially as well as emotionally—like Ida and Ernst. Freud also became increasingly less healthy, suffering from diarrhea, constant fatigue, and a chronic mild depression.[8]

Nonetheless, Freud was still productive in the period leading up to the war and during it. He continued his infighting with members of various international psychoanalytic societies. By 1914, Freud was up to his old tricks again: he would take on mentees and receive professional accolades and then would throw them off, which he was ready to do with Carl Jung, as well as other professional colleagues whom he considered to be his patients.[9]

During the war years and for some time following the war, Freud was fearful about the political fate of his profession of psychoanalysis. As Kramer writes, "He favored organization over their members and systems of thought over fellow feeling."[10] And personally, Freud worried about his family as well. While he was very productive in terms of writing papers, he also expressed feelings of helplessness, fearing impoverishment and death.[11]

Overall, Ida and her son fared better than Freud, Ernst, and Otto. Decker explains about the terrible winter of 1917 that Austria endured, as did Ida and Freud to some degree. The hardships of food scarcity, mounting inflation, lack of fuel, and a thriving black market created an immense weariness.[12] However, Ida was better off than most. Because of the friend Kurt mentioned in his reminiscence of the war years, true to form, Ida was able to capitalize on social contacts and draw on their inherited resources. "They spent part of the summer of 1918 on vacation in Bohemia, at the home of a friend of the family, and that fall were able to afford music lesions for their talented son with the president—the first oboist—of the Vienna Philharmonic."[13]

The war eventually ended in November 1918, with Austria becoming a third-rate, land-locked, small, and inconsequential nation. Due to the war, new countries were formed and preexisting countries enlarged at the expense of Austria. South Tyrol was given to Italy, and Austria was "deprived of the provinces that had made it an industrial and agricultural force. The Bauer factories were now on foreign soil in Czechoslovakia, and the family lost its wealth."[14]

The famous Viennese coffeehouses now served ersatz coffee and artificial beer and chocolate. And according to Decker, if you could get bread and potatoes, they were rotten. Milk, meat, soap, fuel, and paper were not to be had at all. Families had to wear coats and hats indoors during the winter months to keep warm. Both Ida and Freud's family had a bit more than most, but still, they had lost much. Ida's inheritance disappeared almost overnight, and "by 1923, the Austrian currency had completely collapsed."[15]

Ida—and Freud—survived. By 1921, things in Austria improved somewhat, but Ida was faced with the recognition that she and her family had lost the industries that provided them with wealth and status. Almost all Ida had now were big dreams for her son—but Ida was always able to dream big and to survive. She also "believed that the political prominence of her brother in the new Austrian Republic would prove valuable to her family."[16]

Ida was nothing if not a striver and an achiever, especially as she could see that her son might achieve greatness now that he had a focus. As Kurt has recounted:

> I took conducting classes at the Vienna Conservatory under Rudolf Nilius, an Austrian conductor, who gave the students the opportunity to lead the orchestra, which was quite large. At the Academy, the teacher of the conducting class was a Dutchman who never let the students conduct. Since I felt that this was very important for the development of a young, aspiring musician and conductor, I joined the Conservatory, and there took orchestration and score-reading as well.
>
> I also attended opera classes at the Conservatory. Unforgettable to me was an opera class given by the famous Danish tenor Erik Schmedes, who was singing all the important Heldentenor roles at the opera. He taught mainly by demonstrating. When it came to the Bridal Chamber Scene in Lohengrin, he would pick out a student (usually a pretty student) and act it with this girl. I learned then, already, how the personality and the appearance of the singer had to be respected. Speaking about Lohengrin, I remember how Schmedes taught the Gral narrative.[17]

While life was somewhat manageable for the Bauer-Adler family following the war, given that they had friends to help them, the start of the new decade would bring insurmountable challenges.

# PART IV

## *The Aftermath*

No one who, like me, conjures up the most evil of those half-tamed demons that inhabit the human breast, and seeks to wrestle with them, can expect to come through the struggle unscathed.

—Sigmund Freud

# CHAPTER 18

# The New World Order

The situation in Vienna in 1922 was not at all good for Austria, and it soon became clear that it was not boding well for Ida and her family. During the war Ida lost her money, as her father's factories were shut down, but because of friends and her brother's connections, she managed to hold onto her social and economic position. While it was not what she had previously enjoyed, she still had some semblance of status.

Ida and son Kurt had spent some of those years living in Czechoslovakia at the home of friends. But Ida began to see that Jews were afraid in this new world order and must have wondered what it meant for her.

Ida was not afraid, as she and her family had converted to Christianity, which she had done to protect her family, especially her son, from the consequences of Austrian-German anti–Semitism. Yet she could not shelter herself or her family from the rampant violence in Vienna in those years following the war.[1]

Austria, a landlocked country, was in turmoil. Street gangs roamed the city. Harassment of Jews was common. Street clashes were not infrequent, so just shopping or walking around town was problematic. Schoolboys who looked Jewish were beaten up by gangs of young boys.[2]

The government and the people of Austria, including Ida, did not know how to move forward. The country was now under democratic rule instituted by a new constitution. Otto Bauer, Ida's beloved brother, who had spent three years in a Russian prison camp, had returned to Austria in 1917. Then, following the death of Viktor Adler in 1918, Otto had become the leader of the Austrian Social Democrats. From November 1918 to July 1919, the Austrian Social

Democrats formed a coalition government with the Christian Social Party, and Otto Bauer was appointed Minister of Foreign Affairs. He had proposed that nation-states be created, and he was one of the principal advocates of Austrian *Anshluss* (unification) with Germany. As a foreign minister of the new government, Otto signed a secret agreement with Germany to solidify unification. However, this was rejected by the Allies, as the treaty of Versailles expressly prohibited the union of Austria and Germany.[3] Ultimately, he would resign his post in protest but would nonetheless remain a leader of the country for decades.[4]

While things were difficult for Ida and her family, she did find some bright spots in her life. Certainly, one of those bright spots and very comforting to Ida was the knowledge that Otto was always there. She had always been proud of him and his illustrious career, and they still were very close, almost as close as they had been when they were children. She felt that she could depend on her older brother to help her, and, due to his high-ranking position, he somehow was able to make life a little easier for her. No doubt he was one of the few men that she felt she could trust, having found that her father, Hans Zellenka, a number of physicians over the years, and even Freud had let her down, betrayed her, ruined her. Otto never let her down.

Still, while she was happy with her relationship with her brother, she was unsettled by her son. In the years after the war, Kurt was beginning to live his own life. By 1922, at seventeen years of age, he had just graduated from Gymnasium. He was unsure what he wanted to do next, and this worried Ida. She had high standards for him and had been prepping him for years to be successful and accomplished, like her brother. Kurt has said, "My mother was so ambitious that the best grade was never good enough for her. So I really had to work in the early years at *Gymnasium*."[5]

Ida was afraid that after all her hard work raising Kurt, all the money spent on education, music lessons, and other accoutrements of fine living, he would just float around and not make something of himself. Using her brother as a role model for her son probably did not go over very well with the young man. He had been unhappy about a number of things within his family for some time. He felt his parents did not provide him with what he thought was due him. Decker writes that Kurt "was raised austerely. Growing up, he had next to no money at his disposal." He possibly did not understand or know of the financial ruin that was facing the Adler family.[6]

In later years, he would talk about his childhood and his feelings of not ever having enough. It has been said that perhaps his temper and his cantankerous nature, which were feared but respected in the world of opera, originated in those early years. In Kurt's defense, by the time he was seventeen, there had been a war, his father was ill and unable to work, his grandparents had died, his family wealth had disappeared, and his mother was relegated to opening up her house to bridge players in order to make money for the family. At his age, he just wanted to meet girls and party—of course.

Ultimately, however, things finally resolved for Kurt, and he began making decisions that were in line with his mother's thinking and her desires for her son. He decided to enter the Vienna Academy of Music in 1922 and then the University of Vienna the following year. Ida was indeed happy about Kurt entering university and pursuing his own interests, but she was not too happy about his leaving the nest to live a life of his own. And she was unhappy about a lot of other things.[7]

Whenever Ida became unhappy or things did not go her way, she became symptomatic. Now with Kurt about to leave home—and her—she began to manifest several symptoms. One of Ida's more troubling physical symptoms at the time was a hearing problem.

She had been seeing an ear, nose, and throat specialist who treated her for an inner ear disturbance. But she had other physical symptoms as well. Because she smoked, she had coughing fits. She walked with a limp in her right leg, which she had had since she was seeing Freud. Also, she and Ernst had little or no contact—and they certainly did not enjoy a robust sexual life. And even if they had wanted to have sex, she probably would not have been able to enjoy it or endure it as she had premenstrual issues every month, vaginal discharge, and constant constipation, like her mother before her. Ernst seemed to care little about Ida's problems.[8] He apparently had enough of his own woes to deal with. And to make matters worse, she suspected that Ernst was unfaithful to her, without any real evidence. She could not bring herself to divorce him, however, like Peppina and Hans.

Now, with her husband uninvolved in her life and her son off on his own, Ida's illnesses resurfaced. She was seeing a physician who had diagnosed one of her conditions as Ménière's disease, an inner ear issue, which produced dizziness. This condition was keeping her bedridden. Ménière's disease is a disorder of the inner ear that can lead to hearing loss as well as dizzy spells; it mostly affects only one ear. She also heard continual noises in her ear that prevented her from sleeping. Her ear, nose, and throat specialist suggested that she see a physician by the name of Felix Deutsch. Although Freud had lost touch with Ida and Otto, it was through Deutsch, a psychoanalytic personal physician, that Freud was able to keep up with the goings-on of the Bauer-Adler family.[9]

Born in Vienna in 1884, Felix Deutsch was educated at the University of Vienna and held Zionist convictions. He graduated from medical school in 1908, having studied internal medicine. He met Helene Deutsch, the famous psychoanalyst, in Munich in 1911. They were married shortly thereafter and remained married for fifty-two years. Dr. Deutsch likely became interested in psychosomatic medicine because of his wife and because he was Freud's personal physician for a short period. He would become a leading expert in the emerging field of psychosomatic illness.[10]

As to his famous wife, from whom he perhaps gained some of his psychoanalytic theories, Helene Rosenbach Deutsch was a Polish-American psychoanalyst and colleague of Freud. Her concern and theoretical interests were the psychology of women. Following a youthful affair with socialist leader Herman Lieberman, Helene married Felix Deutsch in 1912. After some miscarriages, she gave birth to a son, Martin. In 1935, she fled Germany, immigrating to Cambridge, Massachusetts. Her husband and son joined her a year later, and she worked there as a well-regarded psychoanalyst up until her death in 1982.[11]

When she was referred to Deutsch, Ida knew that she was going to be seeing a preeminent physician of internal medicine, someone with connections to Freud and with a strong background in psycho-analysis. Apparently, one of the first things she confided to Deutsch was that she had been Freud's patient—that she was the famous Dora.

It was in the late fall of 1922 that, as Deutsch writes, "an oto-laryngologist asked my opinion about a patient of his, a married woman, forty-two years old, who for some time had been bedridden with marked symptoms of Ménière's syndrome."[12]

Ida's initial appointment with her otolaryngologist took place with Ernst present, but he "left the room shortly after he had listened to her complaints, and did not return." Ida gave a recitation of her complaints, which included migraines, and then went on a "tirade," according to Deutsch, about her husband's indifference to her suf-fering and her unfortunate marital life. She then discussed the long-ing she felt for her son, who had begun to neglect her. Ida recounted how one night when Kurt was out carousing, she waited for him throughout the entire night. This led her to continue speaking about her difficulties with her husband and how she could not have another pregnancy because she could "not endure the labor pains."[13]

It was to Deutsch that she began to talk about her unfaithful husband and denounced men as selfish, demanding, and unforgiving; she was quite open about the fact that she did not like men. She also relayed to him the saga that she had discussed with Freud. Deutsch felt that her primary symptom, ringing in the ear, was connected to her relationship with her son. When he said that she was continually "listening for his return from his nightly excursions, she appeared ready to accept it and asked for another consultation with me."[14]

At the next consultation with Deutsch, Ida discussed her dislike for her mother and her disgust with marital life, her premenstrual pains, and a vaginal discharge after menstruation. She discussed with Deutsch her "unhappy childhood because of her mother's exag-gerated cleanliness, her annoying washing compulsions, and her lack of affection for her." She also spoke with pride of her brother's career and her fear that her son would never measure up to Otto. At the end of this consultation, she told Deutsch that she felt bet-ter, thanked him profusely, and left. Her brother, however, called him several times to express his satisfaction with her recovery and how difficult it was to get along with her "because she distrusted people and attempted to turn them against each other."[15]

Decker writes about Ida's meetings with Deutsch:

> When Deutsch revisited Dora's home, he found her out of bed; she declared that her dizziness and tinnitus were gone. She thanked him "eloquently" and said she would send for him once more if she got sick; however, she never called again. Shortly after Deutsch's visit, Otto telephoned him several times, "expressing his satisfaction with her speedy recovery. He was greatly concerned about her continual suffering and her discord with ... her husband...." Otto requested an office appointment with Deutsch, who declined in view of Dora's improvement.[16]

In summing up his meetings with Ida, and then writing about her in an article, it is interesting that Deutsch openly disparages Ida, questioning her ability to be happy and suggesting she possibly brought about her husband's eventual early death because of her paranoid behavior. (The article was written in 1957 after the death of Ida's husband, Ernst, although at the time of seeing him, her husband was still alive. Deutsch also mentioned Ida's death in New York.) There are many pieces of information and conclusions he makes in the article that do not line up with what other writers have said about Ida: that she was self-absorbed and had a "propensity to use her sensory perceptions in her hysterical symptoms."[17]

Deutsch closes his article by saying that Ida's death was a blessing to those who were close to her: "She had been as my informant phrased it, one of the most repulsive hysterics he had ever met."[18]

Interestingly, scholars will continue to debate whether Deutsch and Freud were right in their analysis of Ida. Deutsch's article is an attempt to exonerate Freud, as Decker argues, "for overlooking the transference," as he blamed Ida for her own continued illness.[19]

Incidentally, it was during the time when Deutsch was Freud's physician that Freud was secretly dealing with a growth in his mouth. The side effects of smoking finally caught up with him. He was operated on more than once, and his cancer was thoroughly excised. According to Decker, he was fitted with a large prosthesis to replace the parts of his right palate and upper and lower jawbone that had been removed by the surgeries.[20]

## Part IV. The Aftermath

At this time when Ida was still plagued by symptoms and unhappy at home, Kurt made his musical debut in 1925 as an orchestral conductor at the Vienna theaters managed by noted European theatrical producer Max Reinhardt. Now Ida was able to find great solace, not only in the achievements of Otto but also those of her son, Kurt.[21]

# CHAPTER 19

# The Nazi Period

Bridge was all the rage between the two world wars. While her husband was sinking into invalidism and her son was making his way across Europe as a prominent musician, Ida used the card game to try and pull herself together. To do this, she partnered with Peppina Zellenka, of all people.[1] It was the fashion in Vienna in 1930 to play bridge, and every Viennese coffeehouse wanted to hire a female bridge teacher. Traditionally, bridge was a card game played by men in their clubs, but it was now no longer the purview of men exclusively. Women were taking to the game in droves, opening up opportunities for excellent bridge players like Ida and Peppina, her former nemesis.[2]

Invention was always Ida's trump card—to use a bridge term. She often turned adversity into something positive, although with a lot of struggle. Perhaps she took up bridge initially because her husband had been an excellent player and his enthusiasm for the card game rubbed off on her. It's possible she watched him play for years and thus became familiar with the rules. Because money was in short supply for Ida and other Viennese people after the war and prior to the start of the second one, she was always looking for ways to take care of her family. At one point, she made extra money by renting a room in her house where people could come to play the popular card game. She also helped out at a bridge club in Vienna and joined private bridge circles where women could be taught by other women who had mastered the card game—as she herself had done.[3]

An offshoot of whist, a British card game, bridge came into its own in the 1930s, both in Europe and the United States. The game has more rules and regulations than any other pastime other than, possibly, chess. Two international clubs set up the agenda and the rules for playing bridge: the Portland Club of London and the Whist Club of New York. With the rise of duplicate and tournament bridge in the 1930s and 1940s, the American Contract Bridge League and the European Bridge League became the predominant rulemakers.[4]

Bridge became so famous in Vienna that there is even a hand named after it: the Vienna coup. According to the *Encyclopaedia Britannica*, "The characteristic of the Vienna coup is that a high card must be played early, apparently establishing a card in an opponent's hand but actually subjecting him to a squeeze that could not have been effected had the high card remained unplayed."[5]

Ida was in her element. She was good at the game, so good that she taught the game to others—even Peppina, her partner in her bridge-teaching enterprise. Peppina, now in her fifties, had somehow stayed in contact with Ida and maintained friendly terms with her. After Hans died in 1928, Peppina took up the bridge craze and joined Ida. Bridge filled the hole in Ida's life for some time. As Decker writes, "At least for a while Dora found a rewarding outlet for her intelligence. She also had something tangible to fill her hours, because by 1930, her son was no longer at home."[6]

But the situation in Austria was getting perilous, and as Vienna's fortunes fell, so did Ida's. While she might have had a small inheritance from her parents, she was mostly lucky that there were still some women with enough money to continue taking bridge lessons.

It was during this time that Ida experienced a setback. On December 28, 1932, not unexpectedly, Ernst Adler died of coronary disease. At the time of his father's death, Kurt, who had recently married, was conducting the Volksoper in Vienna.[7] Upon learning of the death of his father, Kurt came to Ida's side.

As Kurt tells it:

> I had already been on an engagement in the opera houses in Germany at that time, and he, on Christmas Day, 1932, had a heart attack, after having been examined three weeks earlier and declared in perfect health. Did I say he was fifty-two years old? He never had been sick with the heart; his only trouble was his ear. There were two Christmas holidays, the 25th and the 26th of December, in Catholic countries like Austria, and we couldn't find a heart specialist. Everybody was out of town; only the old family doctor was available. My father spent a horrible night, which I will never forget; he was in

incredible pain, from the 27th to the 28th of December. And on the 28th, we finally had a specialist at the house. In the morning he said, "I don't think he can survive this." He came back in the afternoon around five o'clock, and said, "Well, since he pulled through so well until now, I think we made it." At eight-thirty in the evening he died, in his sleep, a few hours later.[8]

In the aftermath of Ernst's death, Ida herself began to have heart problems in the form of palpitations, which could have been due either to her cigarette smoking or to a psychosomatic response to her husband's death. In any event, she became frightened of the palpitations and fearful of dying herself. Life became quite intolerable for Ida in the aftermath of Ernst's death. On one hand, it is surprising that she reacted so strongly, as he was a husband she did not seem to love and with whom she had not had conjugal relations for many years. Yet, on the other hand, as Decker explains, she was a woman who somatized her emotions, so if she was feeling regret or sadness, it came out in symptoms. Decker also explains that Ida became difficult, using her ailments and her grief to gain sympathy from whomever would listen to her.[9]

Ida continued going from one doctor to another, having one gynecologic operation after another, as attempts to "clean herself," which of course goes back to her mother and her cult of cleanliness.[10]

To add to Ida's woes—and Europe's—Hitler came to power in Germany in January 1933. This emerging situation was fraught with peril not only for Ida, whose concern was primarily financial, but also for Otto. The rise of Hitler signaled the potential demise of the democratic state, of which Otto was a proponent and prime mover. Otto "had spent his life trying to oblige his relatives, avoid confrontation, and keep the peace at all cost," according to Decker. He had lived a life of appeasement within his family. Now, he saw this quality affecting not only those closest to him, but his country as well.[11]

Democracy, as envisioned by Otto Bauer, was doomed to fail due to political rather than economic factors, which were dire but eclipsed by what was going on in politics: a weak parliament, ossification and bureaucratization of political parties, the personal charisma of authoritarian politicians, and even the Catholic Church, which was much more involved in national and international politics than it ought to have been.[12] All of this brought about instability in Vienna and for Ida—again.

It is clear that Otto had his own troubles. The change in the government and the political climate caused Otto to flee, first to Czechoslovakia. As a consequence, he was not readily available to Ida for the support and comfort he normally offered her. Even if he had been beside Ida, however, there was not much he could do to help her; he was barely able to take care of himself. Decker writes of Otto and his behavior at that time, "Like Hamlet, he knew what ought to be done; but also like Hamlet, he could not bring himself to do it."[13]

Decker concludes that Otto, from a very young age, around the time he was ten, worried about internecine strife, spending his life trying to oblige relatives and keep the peace at all costs. It had always been Otto's fate to try and hold not only a family together, but as he entered politics, to keep a nation together, all of which started in childhood: Otto's self-involved parents had set the stage for the Herculean task of making sure that Otto could hold everything together.[14]

Surprisingly, the Jews of Austria were not worried about Hitler initially, even though the Nazis were destroying books, censoring the press, overlooking terrorism perpetrated against Jews, and firing Jews from government jobs. Freud, for one, although he felt that the climate was not good, nonetheless held on to an optimism that would not serve him well ultimately.[15]

During the next few years, things began to change drastically as Austria's independence began to fade. In July 1936, the chancellor of Austria, Kurt von Schuschnigg, made a pact with Germany in the hopes of appeasing Hitler. He allowed the outlawed Austrian Nazi party to become members of his cabinet and let them go about their business.[16] Nevertheless, von Schuschnigg would not be able to hold on to Austria's autonomy as Hitler's troops crossed the border into Austria and German bombers raided the skies over Austria's cities, including Vienna. Then on March 14, 1938, Hitler entered Vienna, receiving a rapturous hero's welcome. The general population of Vienna waved swastika flags to welcome Austria's son back home as Nazi Germany annexed Austria and removed its chancellor from office.[17]

Many of the city's Jews began to try to emigrate from Austria. To do so, they had to stand in long lines, night and day, at the Sankt Margarethen police station to obtain visas and any other documentation that would be necessary for them to leave the country. In addition, they had to pay an exit fee and register all their immovable and most of their movable property, which was then confiscated.[18]

Then, toward the end of 1938, an event took place that was to signal a turning point for Jews in Austria and other German-speaking

**During the Second World War, Hitler spoke to hundreds of thousands of Austrian citizens gathered in the Heldenplatz in Vienna to hear his declaration of annexation, March 15, 1938 (photograph by Heinrich Hoffmann, National Archives).**

countries. Over two days, November 9–10, Nazi leaders unleashed a series of pogroms against the Jewish population of Germany and recently incorporated territories, which was called Kristallnacht, or the Night of Broken Glass. The synagogue in Vienna was burnt down and people were pulled from their homes, spit upon, and made to clean up the streets. Mobs attacked Jewish people, and many would be ultimately rounded up and sent to "work camps" later.[19]

And what of Ida during all of this? As horrible as this must have been for her and her family to witness, she nonetheless felt safe, unlike Freud, as they were no longer Jewish, having converted to Christianity when her son was born.

And what of Freud? As far as he was concerned, he would not be affected as much as other Jewish physicians and academics because he was famous and had important connections—or so he thought. Nevertheless, his home was indeed entered by the Nazis. At one point, his son was imprisoned for a day; afterwards, he was continually harassed by the Gestapo. Freud finally saw the handwriting on the wall and tried to get a visa, which the German authorities were not inclined to give him. In fact, they refused to give him and his family passports. Freud had not been entirely sure he wanted to leave Vienna, but his influential friends, especially Ernest Jones, urged him to move to England. The Nazis again came to his apartment, this time taking away his daughter, Anna. She spent a day in prison, and it was only through Freud's famous friends that she was not sent to a concentration camp.[20]

Freud was now thoroughly convinced that he needed to leave Vienna, and so it was that he and his family left Austria on June 6, 1938. It was due to those influential friends of Freud's that he, his wife, and daughter were provided with visas, tickets, money, and passports. He also found support from the United Kingdom and was able to emigrate there. However, other members of his family, including his sisters, were left in Austria and perished in the Holocaust.[21]

## CHAPTER 20

# Kurt in the United States

While all hell was breaking out in Europe, Kurt was still playing music and interacting with some of Europe's greatest musicians:
Richard Strauss, for one; and others such as Leo Blech; Otto Klem-
perer; Bruno Walter. At some point during his career in Europe as a
musician while he was playing the piano and the violin, he was asked
if he ever thought about conducting, which he had not. However,
he did get his chance in December at Christmastime. As he tells it,
"While I was in Kaiserslautern, which was four seasons, I conducted
both opera and operetta" during the years 1928 to 1932.[1]

Kurt was also working for Otto Preminger, the famous movie
director, and traveling all over Austria, as well as being somewhat
settled in Kaiserslautern. He was not only playing and conducting,
but was also engaged in administrative duties. Kurt was supposed
to go on tour in 1932, following those four years in Kaiserslautern.
"That was at a time when Germany already was threatened by the
Nazi movement. As an Austrian citizen, I needed a permit to work,
which expired in the summer of '32. I was told that I couldn't get
it extended." Kurt returned to Vienna and worked both in Italy and
Austria.[2]

Between 1933 and 1934, while Kurt was conducting at the
Vienna Volksoper, he was likely able to visit with his mother as well
as his uncle, Otto, who was by then having his own problems. In 1933
when Hitler came to power and Kurt was making music, Otto was
still an official of the Austrian government. In this same year, Engelbert Dollfuss, with help from the Christian Social Party, created
an authoritarian dictatorship in Austria. Decker writes that Otto
knew what had to be done, knew what he had to do, but could not.
By 1934, Otto was living in exile, having fled into Czechoslovakia

on February 13, leaving Ida completely alone. He and other Austrian socialists set up headquarters in exile.[3]

Soon, the Nazis attempted a takeover of the Austrian government. The takeover was unsuccessful, but Dollfuss ended up being killed during the attempted coup. As Decker explains, "It failed, but Dollfuss was killed.... The new chancellor was Kurt von Schuschnigg, a studious, distant thirty-four-year-old lawyer who continued to govern an independent Austria under emergency decrees."[4]

Ida, living in Vienna alone and under Nazi regime, did not feel that she or her son were safe, regardless of having converted to Christianity, which would be undone by the Nazi Nuremberg Laws of 1936. In them, it was declared that anyone with even one single Jewish grandparent was a Jew. With Otto and Kurt no longer in Vienna, Ida was very lonely. She could still travel to Czechoslovakia to visit Otto, but he would be too busy to have much of a visit. And from 1935 to 1938, Kurt was traveling and performing, only to come back to Vienna briefly.[5]

One spring day in Salzburg in 1937 when Kurt was sitting in the library, he was asked if he spoke English, which he did. He was told that there was a woman from Chicago who had fired several musical coaches, and Kurt was asked if he would be willing to be her coach. Kurt asked, "What for? She will fire me, too." But he did make the appointment to see her, and as he described, "there was a very tall lady." She was not identified by name, but she had a brother and other friends from the United States, all of whom wanted Kurt to come with them back to the States. He declined, as he had other commitments in Salzburg, Reichenberg, and Berlin. At some point, however, this still-unnamed woman wrote to Kurt saying that it looked like war in Berlin. "Wouldn't you like to come to the States now?" But Kurt was still not ready. Kurt had an American friend, however, who was acquainted with the United States secretary of state, Cordell Hull. Hull told Kurt's friend that he had a voucher for him to come to the States whenever he was ready—regardless of quota. Kurt's American friend was Janet Fairbank.[6]

During this time, Kurt was married to a woman he had met when he was in Kaiserslautern during his last season. Gertrud Moellnitz, called Trudl, was a mezzo-soprano. "She was an excellent actress, with a faulty vocal technique, fabulously good-looking and very successful. She got letters all the time asking her for dates."[7]

Kurt recalls:

Then we got married. She came to Vienna after we both left Kaiserslautern. She was from Leipzig, in Germany. We were married in 1932. She performed, also, in various special music theater groups in Vienna, and a talent scout for Warner Brothers saw her and wanted her to come to Hollywood. She learned English, and when the time came that a decision had to be made, I opposed her going to Hollywood.

Well, when I decided to go to Chicago she opposed leaving Europe, and so she didn't go with me. But we met again after the war, and now my present wife, and she and her husband, and I we're all very good friends. She visited us here, and we visited her in Hamburg, where she lived.[8]

The breakup of his marriage to Trudl, his first wife, whom he married in Europe, took place while Kurt was in Chicago, having left her—and his marriage. There was no divorce, as Trudl obtained an annulment; thus, Kurt would be able to say that he was married only twice. (But as we shall see, he actually had three wives.)[9]

This annulment between Kurt and Trudl dissolved their marriage in 1938. In 1940 in Chicago, he married Diantha Warfel, an American writer, often considered his first wife. They were married for twenty-three years, from 1940 until 1963, and from this marriage, they had two children.

In his interview with Timothy Pfaff, he spoke of this marriage:

Diantha and I met in a very strange way. For a while, I conducted an amateur orchestra in this very wealthy suburb of Chicago. The Chicago Musician's Union didn't like my working with amateurs. At one rehearsal, there was a young girl present who was a friend of the girl who managed the orchestra. She was a student, no less.

When the union forced me to give up conducting this orchestra, not so long thereafter, Diantha wrote me a note, saying that she was glad to hear that I had to give up the rehearsal, because I was the only one who took them seriously. The members of the orchestra wanted, really, not only to play their instruments, but to play around, and my efforts were too sincere for that. The letter was so fascinating that I called her. But she had never time, and I had never time, so our dates were very scarce. Frequently I had to drive to rehearsals with a chorus, which I directed outside of Chicago; so she rode with me to the rehearsals.

## Part IV. The Aftermath

And then, in the summer—it was 1940—while I was training the new
Chicago Opera Chorus (which was a daily rehearsal time of seven hours),
I decided to take off a few weeks in July. I wanted to go to the mountains.
Actually, I had asked Diantha earlier if we shouldn't get married, but she had
said no. When I asked her to go with me to the mountains, she said, "Well,
I'm sorry, my parents would never agree that I go with you without being
married." So we got married quickly and went to Estes Park, and Grand Lake,
and other places in the Rockies—on honeymoon.[10]

Kurt felt himself to be very lucky: "The circles in which I moved
in Chicago were rather high-level financial circles."[11] These friends in
high places helped Kurt not only professionally but also personally.
They were able to bring his mother to the United States, as things
were getting very difficult for Ida in Vienna.

While all this love-making, music-making, and marriage was
taking place with Kurt in the United States, back in Austria, Ida was
somehow able to distract herself from her bodily concerns. According to Decker, "In those times, it was through pride in the sure progress of her son's career" that she was able to forget her somewhat
imagined ills.[12] The city of Vienna exploded with signs and symbols
of Nazism. Huge swastikas appeared on house walls. Mobs roamed
the streets. If someone even looked Jewish, they were tormented. As
Decker writes:

> Even before the German Nazis entered the city, local Nazis and impulsive
> mobs unconnected with National Socialism began to molest and beat Jews
> and plunder and destroy business and residential Jewish property. Soon cus-
> tomers of Jewish merchants and wholesalers, and clients of Jewish doctors,
> dentists, and lawyers, stopped worrying about paying their bills.[13]
> And the police looked away.

Ida's most severe torment began on May 20, 1938, as that was
when Ida's citizenship was torn away from her and she was declared
a Jew. She watched as Jews—people she knew, prominent Viennese—
were carted off to concentration camps. She now realized that she
must leave Austria.

So began the trek from one office to another gathering forms—a
passport, especially. And one can assume that while Ida was preparing to leave her homeland, Kurt was in the United States working with his wealthy and famous contacts, trying to get his mother

to the States. At the same time, Otto, who now resided in Paris, was trying to get his sister to France. Ida was fifty-six years old and alone, but she was determined and "dedicated herself to survival."[14]

And then Ida received the worst possible news.

# Chapter 21

# Ida's Escape

At the start of the New Year in 1938, both Ida's brother and her son had either left Vienna or were preparing to do so, each for reasons of their own. Her parents and husband were deceased. Ida was no doubt desolate. She loved her son, adored him in fact, and depended upon her brother. And things in Vienna were becoming increasingly complicated.

At the time, there were more than 170,000 Jews living in Vienna, as well as some 80,000 people, like Ida, of mixed Jewish-Christian background; in other words, converts from Judaism. Approximately ten percent of the city's inhabitants were Jewish in one form or another. Vienna was, and had been for some time, an important center of Jewish culture and education, with Viennese Jews well-integrated into urban society and culture as physicians, academics, writers, and artists—the cultural elite, if you will.[1]

On the surface, the city of Vienna remained the same as always in those early days of 1938. But almost daily, events happened, one after the other it seemed, that would change not only Vienna, but Austria as well.

Hitler was pushing for Austria to agree to a union with Germany. Austria, surrounded by fascist countries, was having difficulty avoiding economic and political upheaval. In a vain attempt to avoid a takeover of Austria by German forces, the chancellor of Austria, Kurt von Schuschnigg, met with Hitler on February 12, 1938, in *der Fuhrer*'s Berghof residence in the Bavarian Alps. Hitler presented the chancellor with an ultimatum: hand over Austria to the Nazis or else. According to several accounts, Hitler was abusive and threatening to von Schuschnigg, who had no choice but to capitulate to Hitler's demands.[2]

172

Unsurprisingly, the handover of Austria to Hitler created an upheaval in the Austrian government, with von Schuschnigg trying desperately to hold onto power by reorganizing his cabinet to include former and potential adversaries and allies. In the meantime, Hitler made a speech before the Reichstag, broadcast by the Austrian radio network, suggesting that all ten million Germans, living in different countries and areas, should be part of the Reich. Austrians were divided by his speech, but that did not matter to Hitler. Von Schuschnigg was forced to resign on March 11. The next day, German troops flooded into Austria and were greeted by delirious crowds of Austrians. Austria was now incorporated into Nazi Germany. This became known as the *Anschluss*.[3]

Immediately, the Nazis applied German anti–Jewish legislation to Vienna and the Austrian hinterland. Nonetheless, Ida felt safe as she was not technically Jewish and had important friends, although many of them were leaving the country as fast as they could.[4]

With all this political upheaval, Ida was now experiencing her own personal upheaval as well; she was forced to say good-bye to both her son and her brother. According to Decker:

> He [Kurt] had been coaching a young American soprano, daughter of an influential lawyer. Right before the *Anschluss*, she had gotten her father to get a visa for her teacher from the secretary of state, Cordell Hull. Dora's son arrived in the Midwest early in 1938 and became the conductor of an opera company. Two years later he married again and in 1941 became a naturalized citizen. Otto remained in Czechoslovakia for several weeks, watching helplessly, assessing his own safety and the future of his host country. In May he wisely concluded that he should leave, and he flew to France.[5]

Unfortunately, Ida's feelings of safety did not last for very long after the *Anschluss*. Her son was now living in the United States, her brother had left Czechoslovakia for Paris, and even Freud was gone—not that Ida knew or cared. Not only that, but she was soon declared a Jew by the Nazi regime, and her citizenship and her right to vote were revoked by the German Nuremberg racial laws, which had been introduced into Austria. She watched in horror as hundreds of Jews were sent to the camps—even the wealthiest and most influential families in the Jewish community. She finally realized that she, too, would have to leave Austria. The process of acquiring the

Immediately after the *Anschluss*, Vienna's Jews were forced by the local population to clean the city's pavements. Here, Austrian Nazis and local residents look on as Jews are forced to get on their hands and knees and scrub the pavement, March 1938–April 1938, Vienna, Austria (United States Holocaust Memorial Museum, National Archives).

necessary papers to emigrate out of German-led countries, however, was torturous for Jews, and it was no less so for Ida.

During the time when Ida was trying to get out of Austria, traversing from one office to another to get her papers in order, some 1,800 Jewish men were sent from Vienna to Dachau. Hitler's May 24 order called for the immediate capture of criminal and other Jews; in other words, to the Nazi regime, this meant the entire Jewish population of Vienna. Families were separated, men were broken down physically and spiritually, and Nazism was already in the early stages of genocide, according to Illana Fritz Offenberger. Vienna's Jews were now more vulnerable and increasingly more willing to cooperate with the German regime, just for the chance to escape the terrors of the Third Reich.[6]

It was amidst this horror going on all around her that Ida began her journey out of Austria—and it was not easy. Again, Decker writes:

> Dora began the weary trek that all potential Jewish emigrants faced by going to pick up the necessary forms, but she had to do so at a special office for so-called "racial Jews"—that is, Christians or those without religious affiliation who were defined as Jewish according to the Nuremberg Laws. Although the emigration process contained many enervating detours, the basic steps in getting a passport were to procure the correct forms and then clear the police, the economic and financial authorities, and finally, the Gestapo. If the would-be émigrés were successful, they got passports for a very short while. Along the way they lost most of their property.[7]

Daily life for Vienna Jews continued to be awful. People were arbitrarily interrogated; they were afraid to converse in public, and if they met people on the street, they were too fearful to stop and talk to them.

It is estimated that approximately 201,000 people living in Austria in 1938 were Jewish, many residing in the capital. According to the Austrian Academy of Sciences, during the years 1938–1939, the Jewish population in the Austrian provinces was expelled and forced to relocate to Vienna, following which the local Jewish community organizations were successively abolished. A first major wave of escape and emigration began with 91,530 individuals considered to be Jewish by Nazi definition, who remained in Vienna. Thus, Vienna had the highest number of Jews of any city in the entire German Reich. And it was from Vienna that most Jews were deported. The majority of deportations—about 45,527 women, men, and children—took place from Vienna's *Aspangbahnhof*, the Aspang railway station, in forty-five transports to ghettos and extermination sites in the East.[8]

During the early spring of 1938 and for several years after, both Otto and Kurt made attempts to get Ida out of Austria. They each, in their own way, probably tried many avenues to help Ida escape the frightful situation she found herself in. Ida was the most desperate she had ever been, with real and imminent danger all around her. Ida surely must have thought that life could not get any worse, but she was wrong.

Otto died of heart failure in a small Paris hotel on July 4, 1938, four months after Austria had become part of the Third Reich. He was fifty-seven years old and living in a modest furnished apartment on the *Rue Turgot*. Ewa Czerwińska-Schupp writes:

> His close friend and long-time editorial assistant of Vienna's *Arbeiter-Zeitung*, Otto Leichter, who was called to Bauer's death bed by his wife Helena, wrote, "There was no doubt to anyone who was able to spend Bauer's last months with him that he died of a broken heart in the truest and saddest sense." Bauer passed away believing that he was responsible for the defeat of the party and unhappy about his forced emigration and separation from his native country. He was also distressed over the fate of his comrades and the new party, the Revolutionary Socialists of Austria, after Hitler's *Anschluss*.[9]

Otto had always had a somewhat troubled personal life. While his parents were alive, he did not marry. At the time of his death, he was married to Helene Gumplowicz-Landau, whom he met at the Café Central in Vienna when she was still married to the lawyer Max Landau. She was ten years Otto's senior and a published author, having written many works in economics. She was also an influential figure in the Polish Social Democratic Party of Galicia, a "territorial organization." "Her open but critical mind and vivid temperament put a spell on Bauer—he married her in 1920. The couple had no children but their choice turned out to be right for both. In spite of Bauer's many affairs, she remained his closest partner in intellectual work and party activism until the end of his life."[10]

Ida may have learned of her brother's death from his sister-in-law. According to Decker, "If she did get the news of his stately funeral, attended by socialist leaders from all over Europe, with orations by the highest dignitaries, such as Léon Blum, the former French prime minister, she might have drawn a bit of comfort."[11]

But she was also still struggling to escape Austria. Since Ida frequently took on the ailments of the people she loved when they died—especially as she did for her husband—she might have begun having palpitations again. Regardless, she had an increasingly urgent need to get out of the country as the situation for Jews was becoming more and more difficult.

Come the New Year in 1939, Ida was still in Vienna, unfortunately. The Nazis continued rounding up Jews, Ida among them, from certain apartment houses. "Jews living in 'Aryan'–owned apartments were evicted, and Jewish owners had to take in the evicted Jews." By the mandate of the regime, Ida even had to change her name to one more Jewish: Sara. Finally, with her name changed on official records, she managed to obtain a visa to France. That notwithstanding, life was very difficult for her, both because she was Jewish and because of the known activities of her deceased brother.[12]

To emigrate to Paris where friends of her brother's would help her, Ida was forced to hide for some time in seventy-year-old Peppina's home in Vienna while she waited to receive her visa and other necessary papers. Thanks to support from political allies of her brother, both in France and America, she eventually obtained permission to travel to Paris in 1939. During her travels, Ida had the misfortune of developing typhoid.

Ultimately, Ida had to flee Paris ahead of the German occupation of *that* city, which took place in June of 1940. She then traveled through the South of France to Casablanca in Morocco. It was not until September 1941, according to Ellis, that she finally traveled to America on board the SS *Serpa Pinto* to be reunited with her son.[13]

Like so many before her, fifty-eight-year-old Ida landed at Ellis Island and would now be attempting to make a new life for herself in a foreign country. Fortunately, in addition to being fluent in French, German, and Italian, Ida could also speak English. According to her great-granddaughter in her novel, *Ida*, Kurt was conducting in Chicago at the time of her arrival in America and could not meet her, so he sent a friend in his place—Martin Magner.[14]

As it turned out, Martin Magner, Ida's first contact in the United States, was a German. He had been befriended by Kurt, as they had both worked in Prague together directing operas. George Bernard Shaw was a fan of Magner and, ironically, Sigmund Freud had offered to train him as a lay psychoanalyst on the strength of a play he wrote about a psychiatrist. In 1936, Magner immigrated to the United States and settled in Chicago, where Kurt was also working in the theater. Magner did radio work for a while, and then eventually television, working as a producer and director for twenty-five years, first for NBC and then from 1950 to 1965 for CBS in New York. His work included pioneering shows like *Studio One, The Goldbergs, Lamp unto My Feet,* and *Robert Montgomery Presents.*[15] So even though Kurt was not there to greet his mother, Ida was in good company.

# CHAPTER 22

# The Aftermath

After passing through Ellis Island, Ida took the train from New York City to Chicago to be reunited with her son—finally, after years on the road. Once in Chicago and together with her son, she met his second wife, Diantha, an American writer who was born in Indianapolis. Unbeknownst to Ida, Diantha was pregnant with their first child at that time.

Born in 1917, Diantha Warfel graduated from the University of Chicago, after which she studied nursing at Presbyterian Hospital in Chicago. She was an avid fencing enthusiast, winning several medals in Illinois. She and Kurt married on July 7, 1940, and ultimately had two children, Kristan and Ronald. Eventually, the family left Chicago and moved to San Francisco, where Kurt became general director of the San Francisco Opera. Diantha won the Boys' Life Dodd-Mead Writing Award for her fencing book entitled *On Guard!*, which was published in 1961.[1]

Not surprisingly, Ida was a difficult mother-in-law. She confused and annoyed her daughter-in-law and was not much help in the raising of her new grandchild. She apparently tried to fit in, but it was difficult for her, and even the arrival of her first grandchild was not something that thrilled Ida.

Once Kurt and his family left Chicago for San Francisco, Ida returned to New York, where she lived as a subtenant with a socialist comrade. According to Friedrich Adler (a friend of Otto Bauer, not a relative), she worked at a factory.[2]

Gaetano Merola, then general director of the San Francisco Opera, had heard of Kurt Herbert Adler. It would appear that he was quite an admirer: over the telephone, he invited Kurt to be the chorus director for the San Francisco Opera in 1943. So while Ida lived and worked in New York, her son was making a name for himself in San Francisco.

Living in the United States was difficult for Ida. Because of her personality and disposition, she did not get along well with people. Ida also continued to suffer from her various complaints, eventually succumbing to the same illness that killed her mother: colon cancer. Decker writes of her time in the United States:

> It is likely that Dora did not live with her son in the Midwest and later on the West Coast where he again went to work with an opera company but instead resided in New York. By now almost sixty, she lived out the war years unhappily with many of her familiar physical problems. Then her constipation worsened. Did Dora suspect that she was suffering from her mother's mortal illness? Did she avoid seeking medical advice in order not to hear the dreaded diagnosis? By the time her cancer of the colon was diagnosed it was too late for a successful operation. Judging by her reactions to previous stressful periods she had endured, it is likely that her anxiety at this juncture was great. In 1945 her son accepted an engagement in New York, probably to be near his mother. Dora died the same year in Manhattan's Mount Sinai Hospital.[3]

In his interview with Pfaff, Kurt recalls his mother's final days.

> My mother came to the United States in 1938. When I left, she was still in Vienna, but going to France. Leon Blum, the famous socialist Prime Minister of France, had been a close friend of my uncle's. My uncle had been asked by the Czech government, where he lived from 1933 to '38, to leave Czechoslovakia, because the situation with Germany and Czechoslovakia had become very ticklish. So he went to Paris and died there suddenly; he was born in 1873 and died in Paris in the summer of 1938. Leon Blum insisted that my mother come to Paris, which she finally did after I had left. He arranged for her to leave the night before the Germans occupied Paris, for the south of France. She spent quite a few difficult years there, and finally came here via Casablanca, where she was interned in a hospital and came down with cholera, had Arabian male nurses, and had her visa expire. I succeeded in having it renewed because the foreign office in Washington was well-acquainted with my uncle and certainly wanted to open the doors for his sister, after he had died. So she came to this country—I forget the exact years. She lived first in Chicago with me, and then moved to New York, where I also moved. She died of cancer in 1943. Sixty-three years old at the time.
>
> I was here, but only for a short part of the year. In 1942 it was at the suggestion of my predecessor, Maestro Merola, that I moved from Chicago to New York. So in 1945 I returned from here to New York instead of Chicago; my mother was already there. She died in our apartment after having been

operated on, but it was too late, and I think probably the knowledge of how to handle cancer operations wasn't quite advanced enough.[4]

And what of the rest of the characters in the "Dora" saga?

Peppina and Hans Zellenka's son, Otto, renounced the Jewish faith in 1924. But like Ida, this did not protect him from the anti–Semitism of the Nazis. According to Ellis, Otto was "pensioned off from his job as part of the purging of Jews from government positions, despite being only forty-six years old. He left Austria in 1939, sailing to New York, where he lived in Manhattan."[5]

As for Peppina, she was one of a few Jews who managed to stay in Vienna in the same place as she had lived with Hans—Opernring 15. Ellis continues:

> Toward the end of 1939, Jews in Vienna began to be forcibly moved from their homes into shared apartments. We assume that Peppina's move in August 1939 to Gonzagagasse in the First District (Innere Stadt) was part of that process. From May 1942 onward, all Jews in Vienna were forcibly resettled in the Second, Ninth, and Twentieth Districts to facilitate later deportation. In August 1942 Peppina moved once again, this time to Glockengasse in the Second District, where her lover Philipp Bauer and the young Sigmund Freud had both grown up. By this time, Peppina would have worn the yellow star on her clothing at all times.[6]

Unfortunately, that was not the end of it for Peppina. At seventy-two years of age, she was deported to Theresienstadt Ghetto, the concentration camp near Prague, and admitted into the camp under the name of Bettina Zellenka. The Nazis called this camp a Home for the Aged, for wealthier Jews—in other words a model ghetto. It's possible that Peppina paid for the opportunity to live there, but in all probability, she, like other new arrivals, was robbed and then moved into shameful living conditions and put to work.[7]

Ellis continues: "When Theresienstadt was liberated by the Soviet Army in May 1945, Peppina Zellenka was among the 17,000 people found alive. She was seventy-five years old, one of just 169 survivors from the 1,300 Jews deported from Vienna on September 24/25, 1942. She had survived Theresienstadt for thirty months."[8]

Peppina lived for a short while in the Hotel Pension Kumbichl, dying on January 16, 1949, at the age of seventy-nine. The cause of death was heart failure, influenza, and bronchial pneumonia. She was buried in the Jewish cemetery in Innsbruck next to her husband, Hans.[9]

As for Ida's son, Ida would have been thrilled to know that Kurt became one of the most famous impresarios in the United States. In the years following his move to San Francisco, Kurt took on more and more administrative details as Merola's health and energy diminished. While Adler was not the board's natural choice to replace Merola at the time of his death in 1953, after three months of acting as the company's artistic director and with the help of its president, Robert Watt Miller, Adler was confirmed as general director. Like his mother, he was never considered an easy person to get along with. Nonetheless, he would go on to win fame as the autocratic director of the San Francisco Opera Company, where he introduced to the American public famous European musicians such as Birgit Nilsson, Renata Tebaldi, and Leontyne Price. He would eventually record albums with Luciano Pavarotti and Placido Domingo.

Katharina Adler, great-granddaughter of Ida Bauer Adler, who has written a fictional account of her famous relative's life, entitled *Ida* (photo by Christoph Adler, courtesy Katharina Adler).

Kurt divorced his second wife, Diantha, in 1963. He married Nancy Goodhue Miller of San Francisco on August 23, 1965. He was sixty years old at the time, and his wife was twenty-three years old. They had two children: Sabrina, born in 1980, and Curtis Roman, born in 1983. Kurt died of a heart attack at his home in Ross, California, on February 9, 1988. He was survived by his wife, Nancy Miller; two daughters, Kristin Krueger and Sabrina; two sons, Ronald and Curtis Roman; and two grandchildren.[10]

Ida has survived to this day—as Dora. In recent years, feminism has taken on Freud's handling of Ida. Several leading feminist scholars, including Toril Moi and Hélène Cixous, would see Dora, as written up by Freud, as a symbol of silent revolt against male power over women's bodies and women's language. Conversely, Catherine Clément argued that as a silent hysteric who abandoned treatment, she was less a feminine role mode than Anna O., who went on to become a famous social worker. These are only two of the many interpretations of Dora's fragment of an analysis. Over the years, feminist theory has delved into the study of Freud and Dora, in essence creating an academic subfield on her life and analysis. This renewed interest in Freud's case history of Dora stems from feminist questioning of psychoanalysis.[11]

# CHAPTER 23

# The Scholarship

The critical response to the Dora case study was not universally positive during Freud's lifetime. As Ernest Jones recalled, it was deemed "mental masturbation, an immoral misuse of his medical degree." Yet it led Jones to his own calling to the study of psychoanalysis. Carl Jung, who would become one of Freud's mentees (only to be rejected later), thought the study of Dora was masterful.[1]

By the middle of the twentieth century, the work had become overwhelmingly accepted, with Ida's cough and her mutism signaling internal conflicts and desires.[2] Later, admiration for the technical expertise shown in the work was taken up by Jacques Lacan. Erik Erikson expanded upon the issue of Ida's positive response to Herr Zellenka's advances. Then feminist critics took up the banner from Erikson, claiming that Freud was openly insensitive to the young patient's abhorrence of what was happening to her, both Hans Zellenka's advances and her father's dismissal/allowance of them. Some feminists accused Freud of phallocentrism and considered the case study a perfect illustration of patriarchy in general but especially within the medical profession.[3]

Janet Malcolm, who has written extensively about psychiatry and psychoanalysis, was somewhat sympathetic to Freud, but in general felt that the tone he used with his young patient was inappropriate. And she concluded, even as Freud did, that both countertransference and transference needed to have much more attention than it did in the early years of psychoanalysis.[4] Sadly, Ida was a sacrificial lamb to psychoanalytic theory.

While Ida died in 1945 and Freud in 1939, their lives go on, for better or worse, because of the intense interest in the Dora case study, which is his longest, and is part and parcel of the psychoanalytic canon. With so many mistakes made, it is a wonder that the case survived. Just one of the many mistakes is his having imputed bisexuality to his young patient. As mentioned in an earlier chapter, since Freud potentially had an affair with his sister-in-law, it can perhaps be argued that he projected some of his own issues (the countertransference, unacknowledged at the time) onto Ida Bauer. And it has been argued by Shengold Leonard that the subject of her alleged bisexuality might have come out of the rupture in his relationship with Fliess, Freud's greatest intimacy with another man in his adult life—again, the countertransference. It was during Freud and Fliess's final meeting, at Achensee, that "turned out to be a climax in their personal and theoretical entanglement over bisexuality."[5]

Leonard also remarked on Freud's bullying that was exhibited in the case study:

> Dora's case history exemplifies a remarkable amount of coercion. A male adult forced himself upon a young female who afterward was forced by her father into therapy sessions where the therapist elected to force or "direct" her associations, the pursuit of his own theories perforce interfering with his free-floating attention. Freud built gratuitous reconstructions, projecting onto the young Dora his own excitability and wishes for her excitation and corralling her desires within the orbit of his knowledge and ambitions.[6]

While Leonard was mulling over his ideas in 1990, the published books and articles on the subject continue to this day, and Daniela Finzi still calls the Dora case study one of the most important and interesting studies that Sigmund Freud ever conducted and described. In the preface of her book, she calls it "a watershed in the history of psychoanalysis," even though it was considered a failed study by Freud himself. She also describes how important the issues of sexuality were and are today as the driving engine of psychoneurosis and neurosis in general, as described by Freud.[7] And Hélène Cixous believed Ida was a victim of men's power—even as she both rejected that power and rejected someone else's interpretation of her own body, symptoms and all.[8]

Clément and Cixous had a lively debate about Dora, which is described with clarity in Gilman:

> In her debate with Cixous in *The Newly-Born Woman*, Catherine Clément was more skeptical about the ultimate power of hysteria as a form of

feminine subversion. She maintained that the hysteric is unable to communicate because she is outside of reality and culture—that, in Lacanian terms, her expression remains in the Imaginary, outside the Symbolic. Thus "hysterical symptoms, which are metaphorically inscribed on the body, are ephemeral and enigmatic. They constitute a language only by analogy." Hysterics should be classed not with feminist heroines, but with deviants and marginals who actually reinforce the social structure by their preordained place on the margin. Indeed, their roles are ultimately conservative: "Every hysteric ends up inuring others to her symptoms, and the family closes round her again, whether she is curable or incurable." With regard to Dora, Clément is cool and level-headed: "You love Dora, but to me she never seemed a revolutionary character."[9] In order to affect the symbolic order, or the material world, she argues, the hysteric must somehow break through her private language and act. Thus for Clément, the "successful hysteric" is one, like Anna O./Bertha Pappenheim, who becomes a writer, social worker, and feminist leader.[10]

As we can see, not all feminists agree that young Dora, as portrayed by Freud in his case study, should be viewed as a feminist icon.

Even practicing physicians, not just psychoanalysts, have been interested in the Dora case. *The Lancet*, a premier medical journal, wrote about Dora. Boyce wrote that if Freud submitted his famous case to a medical journal, a reputable one such as *The Lancet*, it wouldn't even get past a first read. Case studies with only one person's issues illustrated, he writes, are "regarded with suspicion." Also, there was a five-year gap between the end of the treatment and the publication of the case study. Still, the most striking aspect of the case, Boyce writes, is that "Freud's Dora, one of the seminal documents of psychoanalysis, is a thorough report of a negative result."[11]

Boyce concedes that while the case would at some level not be worthy of publishing in *The Lancet*, on another level, it was to his credit to admit defeat and to see what this failure meant. "Perhaps this frankness, persistence, and ability to cope with setbacks by learning from failure is one of the reasons psychoanalysis is still going strong," he concludes.[12]

Not all of Freud's patients fared as poorly as Ida Bauer did. Take for instance the case of one of his last living patients, Margarethe Walter. In his analysis of Margarethe, he did much better than he did with Ida. And as Linda Oland Danil argues, although Freud often seemed to disparage women, within the confines of the Margarethe

Walter session, he emphasized that Margarethe should follow her own desires, to the exclusion of what her father dictated.

Apparently, Margarethe saw Freud when she was roughly the same age as Ida—eighteen years of age. Unlike with Ida, Freud dismissed her father and believed Margarethe about all aspects of her life. He wanted her to know that he listened to her fully and saw her as a person in her own right, not as an appendage of men. Margarethe herself said, "Sigmund Freud was [the] first person in my life who really listened to me emphatically, who wanted to find out and learn something about me, the one who truly listened. He looked at me without interruption, he looked at *me*, and his active empathy surrounded and contained me."[13] This was in sharp contrast to how he treated Ida—but then, Margarethe came to Freud toward the end of his career, while Ida came at the beginning.

Regardless of Freud's many missteps and the distrust he sometimes engendered, the gossip that endured, the tattered friendships that he seemed unable to sustain, his legacy remains intact. For all his eccentricities and failings, Freud was seen as a superstar in many ways in Europe and even on his visit to the United States. When he finally left Austria for London, following the interrogation of his daughter by the Gestapo, he made his way—on the Orient Express— and his reputation preceded him. He was interviewed by the BBC and wined and dined by the Hogarth Press, which had been Freud's British publishers. Of course, the publishers were Virginia and Leonard Woolf. As Louis Menard recounts in a *New Yorker* article, Woolf wrote in her diary, "A screwed up shrunk very old man: with a monkey's light eyes, paralyzed spasmodic movements, inarticulate: but alert."[14] So much for stardom. However, upon reflection, Leonard wrote in his autobiography that he felt a great gentleness in Freud as well as great strength. "A formidable man."[15]

Although he died at his house in Hampstead on September 23, 1939, three weeks after the start of the Second World War, his legacy continues to thrive, particularly in America. Many in America were taken with the cardinal Freudian principle that "sources of our feelings are hidden from us, that what we say about them when we walk into the therapist office cannot be what is really going on."[16]

## Part IV. The Aftermath

Numerous books have been written about Freud since his death. Even literary scholars began to review and analyze texts using psychoanalysis. But over the years, there have been dissenting views on how important Freud is or was, how useful psychoanalysis is or was in therapeutic settings or in analyzing literary texts. As I mentioned above, Freud's legacy was in dispute; he was hammered by feminist scholars who took the side of Dora. His cocaine use was also questioned.

Additionally, many drugs put out by the pharmaceutical industry made analysis somewhat redundant since it is both costly and involved hours, months, and years "on the couch." In the late twentieth century, psychoanalysts were sometimes viewed as tricksters who provided nothing of value for the patients.

Freud's legacy has gone up and gone down, then back up again, and recently he has been seen as a literary lion rather than a medical one. His case studies are viewed as literature, and although his science is not universally recognized as having value, his skill in producing narratives continue to earn praise and applause. And it is the Dora case study that seems to be his highest literary offering.

Perhaps the legacy we should be talking about and thinking about is that of Ida Bauer Adler. Students read the case study in college and therapists study Freud's account of her seductions and traumas and learn about the beginnings of transference and countertransference from the Dora case, but Ida herself was a surprisingly resourceful woman. Was she flawed? Yes—but how hard she tried to overcome her awful familial situation. What I think of as the great tragedy of Ida's life is not so much what happened to her during her life, but what happened after. Ida remained Dora—a fictive character without any personhood, which is basically what feminists have argued all along: Dora may have lost her voice, but Ida gained hers. The real woman of the case study was able to leave the cloak of muteness behind her through her marriage, her motherhood, her professional life, and her relationships—with her brother and, yes, even with Peppina.

At the conclusion of the case study, Freud explains that Dora's leaving him was an act of revenge. He wrote:

## Chapter 23. The Scholarship

I knew Dora would not come back again. Her breaking off so unexpectedly, just when my hopes of a successful termination of the treatment were at their highest, and her thus bringing those hopes to nothing—this was an unmistakable act of vengeance on her part. Her purpose of self-injury also profited by this action. No one who, like me, conjures up the most evil of those half-tamed demons that inhabit the human breast, and seeks to wrestle with them, can expect to come through the struggle unscathed. Might I perhaps have kept the girl under my treatment if I myself had acted a part, if I had exaggerated the importance to me of her staying on, and had shown a warm personal interest in her—a course which, even after allowing for my position as her physician, would have been tantamount to providing her with a substitute for the affection she longed for? I do not know.[17]

But maybe this was not all about vengeance. Maybe Ida Bauer, even as a seventeen-year-old, knew how to take care of herself amidst her many travails and symptoms. She never really became well; she suffered for years. But she was able to accomplish a great deal given a chaotic family life and a dire social setting in increasingly anti–Semitic Vienna. She married, had a child, and maintained some relationships. Was she difficult? Probably, but given the cards she was dealt, she was able to make a full life for herself.

# Epilogue

What is the significance of the story of "Dora"?

Although no longer considered an illness, hysteria was predominantly diagnosed as a condition that afflicted women, not men. This was a common interpretation of women's psychological impairment until well into the mid-twentieth century and one recognized as early as ancient Greece. In this "female" condition, the patient developed a multiplicity of symptoms, from fainting and heart palpitations to limb malfunction. According to Sigmund Freud, who studied it exhaustively, it stemmed from sexual experiences generally in childhood that had a traumatic effect.[1]

Freud was a pioneer in psychoanalysis and hysteria. His most prominent case was that of the young woman he called Dora, and while that case study was deemed a failure by Freud, it is still after many decades premier in the annals of case studies, women's psychology, psychoanalysis, and trauma brought on by sexual misconduct of one kind or another.

The significance of the Dora case revolves around the importance of "talk therapy," the use of dreams in analysis, the concepts of transference and countertransference, and the narrative structure of the patient's history. The case effectively introduces the notion of family therapy as well, unheard of in the Vienna of Ida's time, that when one in a family is psychologically ill, the entire family is also. You could say that psychoanalysis was built upon the dysfunction of a young girl and her struggle against powerlessness brought upon by male dominance and maladjustments of the social order.[2]

We know today how family relationships negatively or positively impact the children of the family. The notion of the "identified patient," who in Freud's case study, would have been Dora, extends to the interactions among all family members. According to Pamela Broderick and Christina Weston in *Psychotherapy Rounds*,

> ... although one family member may be the "symptom bearer," the whole family is in distress. Interventions in family therapy are geared toward the family as a unit with the perspective that some individual symptoms are products of relationship struggles within this unit. These individual symptoms are viewed as arising from and being complicated by the family system matrix. Family therapy is considered more of an orientation than a specific type of therapy.[3]

Freud did not analyze Ida with the rest of the family in mind. He seemed to admire the father, had disdain for the mother, and ignored the brother. And he did not recognize that the father, who brought his daughter to the analyst, lied about her situation. He never changed his opinion of Philipp during the course of his work with Ida. In addition to all this, Freud's clinical ability "left much to be desired."[4]

Strangely, Ida Bauer, with her unbelievable desire and need for self-determination, managed to save herself, against all odds. She renounced Freud by aborting her analysis. In leaving Freud, she left not only her therapist, but her father as well.

As Decker points out, reading the Dora case study was at one time, for psychoanalytic students, a way to examine not only the genius that was Freud, but also his limitations. "Freud," Decker writes, "was blind to his own impulses and reactions." Today therapists and analysts realize that the sexual impulses they may have are an occupational hazard and something to use to the patients' benefit—not something to hide from.[5]

Since hysteria is no longer a diagnosis that men tack onto women, we might say that Dora has done us a great service. The Dora case study, illuminating as it did Freud's inadequacies, especially in dealing with a troubled, adolescent female, provided a way out of that type of treatment. In its place now, however, we have anorexia nervosa, bulimia, borderline personality disorder—all conditions leveled at females. The distress of anorexia, which has supplanted the symptoms that beset Ida, still has its roots in familial denial and sexual misunderstandings.

# Epilogue

Without help, young women like Ida who have been traumatized by family or society have difficulty completing the tasks that make for a meaningful adulthood. Ida as an example of a young girl trying to overcoming the vicissitudes of trauma did, on the surface, gain some mastery over her life; however, she was plagued with physical symptoms for most of her life and never did seem to understand that some of her issues were due more to her inability to handle herself and her relationships than with the society and culture within which she lived. Because of this, her problems followed her into marriage and motherhood and complicated her situation during the Nazi occupation.

Even though we have made great advancements in the treatment of people with mental conditions through the use of drugs, talk therapy, cognitive therapy, and other modalities, there is still a stigma—subtle perhaps, but a stigma nonetheless—attached to mental illness, which can be seen in the lack of parity in fees and insurance coverage. And while there have been many changes in mental health care, some studies argue that up to one in five children experience mental health problems. Although there have been many changes and a great deal of progress, it is unclear, according to William Bor and his colleagues, whether the rates of internalizing and externalizing problems have changed in young people.[6]

A recent literature search by Bor and colleagues included studies on toddlers, children, and adolescents (2,349 abstracts in total reviewed). Their findings indicate that recent generations of adolescent girls are at greater risk of internalizing problems and show that there are "gender difference in rates of depression and anxiety disorders with women more likely to experience these disorders than men."[7]

This epidemic of relational and psychological issues still being seen in adolescent girls—those around the age of Ida—says something about our inability or physicians' inability to help young women, as they were unable to do in Ida's Vienna. So the story of Dora, as outlined in Freud's case study, can be seen as a gift. Jean-Michel Rabaté argues that "using *Dora* as a fictional name for Ida Bauer may prove to have been Freud's most lasting stroke of genius." In transforming his patient into the Greek word meaning "gifts," he provides us with a story that is as useful today as it was then. Using a child as *bride* or *bribe* is as dreadful a parental activity today as it was then. Ida was given to Hans Zellenka to compensate for her father's affair with Peppina Zellenka.[8]

Ida Bauer was indeed a gift. The case study even today is poignant, but Ida's life affirms that the human spirit can survive and transcend. Ida did have a problematic life and she lived in a problematic time, but she was able to survive. Life should be about more than survival, but in Ida's case, the fact that she did is amazing.

# Chronology

| 1853 | Birth of Philipp Bauer, father of Ida, on August 14 in Pollerskirchewn, Úsobí, Czechia (Czech Republic) (Freiberg, Moravia). |
|------|------|
| 1856 | Birth of Malwine Friedmann (Bauer), favorite paternal aunt of Ida's, on January 6, in Pollerskirchen, Úsobí, Czechia (Czech Republic). |
|      | Birth of Sigmund Freud, May 9, Příbor, Moravian-Silesian Region, Czech Republic, named Sigismund Schlomo Freud. |
| 1859 | New regulations establish full freedom of trade; Vienna's economy grows rapidly, and with it the city's population. |
| 1860 | Freud's family moves to Vienna and settles in Leopoldstadt. |
| 1861 | Birth of Katharina Bauer (Gerber), mother of Ida, on October 18, Königinhof, Dvůr Králové nad Labem, Czechia (Czech Republic). |
|      | Birth of Martha Bernays, July 26, in Hamburg, Germany; future wife of Sigmund Freud. |
| 1873 | Birth of Ernst Adler, husband of Ida, on February 12, in Budapest. |
|      | Freud graduates summa cum laude, Leopoldstädter Kommunal-Real-und Obergymansium, Vienna, Austria. |
|      | Freud enters Vienna University to study medicine. |
| 1875 | Freud changes first name from Sigismund to Sigmund. |
| 1880 | Josef Breuer works with Bertha Pappenheim (Anna O.) until 1882; Freud very interested in Breuer's work. |

# Chronology

| 1881 | Birth of Otto Bauer, brother of Ida, September 5, in Vienna in Leopoldstadt. |
| | Freud qualifies as a doctor of medicine. |
| 1882 | Bauer family moves to Berggasse 32, in the Ninth District, a few doors from Freud's eventual office and apartment at Berggasse 19. |
| | Freud meets and shortly becomes engaged to Martha Bernays. |
| | Birth of Ida Bauer (Freud's Dora), November 1. |
| 1884 | Freud begins study of physical and psychological effects of cocaine. |
| 1885 | Freud travels in October to Paris to study with Jean-Martin Charcot; he works with the famous neurologist until February 1886. |
| 1886 | Freud opens private practice in Vienna in April, specializing in nervous disorders. |
| 1887 | Freud marries Martha Bernays. |
| | Freud takes on Mathilde Schleicher, a 27-year-old musician with nervous disorder, as a patient. |
| | Philipp Bauer's first encounter with Freud. |
| 1888 | The Bauer family moves to Tyrol area due to Philipp's tuberculosis and failing health. |
| | The Pappenheim case study is written up by Freud and Breuer. |
| 1889 | The marriage of Hans and Peppina Zellenka in Merano; Ida is 7 years old. |
| 1890 | Mathilde Schleicher dies, September 24. |
| 1891 | Freud moves into Berggasse 19. |
| 1892 | Freud treats "Elizabeth von R." (Ilona Weiss) in what he described as his first full-length analysis of hysteria. |
| 1894 | Ida definitively diagnosed with hysterical symptoms. |
| | Philipp recovers from blindness; moves into his syphilis tertiary stage. |
| 1895 | First use of the term "psychoanalysis" by Freud, in *Zur Ätiologie der Hysterie*. |
| 1895 | Anna O. case study is published in *Studies in Hysteria*. |

| | |
|---|---|
| **1898** | Ida first visits Freud at fifteen years of age. |
| **1899** | February–March, Ida returns alone to Vienna, shortly after the death of her aunt Malvine Friedmann (Bauer), April 7, at the age of 43, in Vienna. |
| | Bauers move to Reichenberg, near one of Philipp's plants; Philipp appears to be recovered from his illnesses. |
| **1900** | Bauers move back to Vienna. |
| | Freud begins analysis of "Dora" (Ida Bauer), in October. |
| | Ida leaves analysis abruptly on December 31. |
| **1901** | Freud begins writing up case study of Dora, titling it *Traum und Hysterie* (Dreams and Hysteria; draft sent to journal but rejected because of sexual content). |
| **1902** | Ida returns to Freud, her last visit, in April. |
| | Freud is appointed Professor Extraordinarius, University of Vienna, Vienna, Austria, after three failed attempts. |
| **1903** | Ida marries Ernst Adler, a frustrated violinist. |
| **1905** | After much deliberation and thought, Freud publishes the Dora case study. |
| | Kurt Herbert Adler, son of Ida Bauer, born on February 4 (will become head of the San Francisco Opera). |
| | Freud publishes "Bruchstück einer Hysterie-Analyse" (Dora case study), *Monatsschrift für Psychiatrie und Neurologie* 18:285–310. |
| **1907** | Otto Bauer receives a degree in law from the University of Vienna. |
| **1912** | Death of Ida's mother, Katharina "Käthe" Bauer (Gerber), on August 12, at the age of 50, probably in Vienna. |
| **1913** | Death of Ida's father, Philipp Bauer, on July 3, at the age of 59, in Vienna. |
| **1914** | First World War begins in July. |
| **1919** | Signing of the Treaty of Versailles, ending the war. |
| **1921** | Things turn around for Ida and her family. |

# Chronology

| | |
|---|---|
| **1922** | Kurt is 17 years old and in university. |
| | Ida visits Felix Deutsch. |
| **1923** | Freud is diagnosed with cancer of jaw and palate. |
| **1925** | Kurt makes his debut as conductor, travels to Germany and Italy. |
| **1932** | Death of Ernst Adler, on December 28, at the age of 59, in Vienna. |
| **1933** | Public burning of books by the Nazis on May 10 in Berlin, Germany; included were books by Freud. |
| **1936** | Kurt assists Toscanini at the Salzburg Festival. |
| **1938** | Hitler invades Austria, March 12 (the *Anschluss*). |
| | Kurt emigrates to U.S. |
| | May 20, German Nuremberg racial laws of 1935 introduced into Austria. |
| | Ida is declared a Jew. |
| | Ida arrives in Paris. |
| | Death of Ida's brother, Otto, on July 5, at the age of 56, in Paris (before Ida's arrival). |
| | Daughter of Sigmund Freud, Anna, is arrested and interrogated by the Gestapo; Freud, Martha, and Anna escape to London. |
| | Kristallnacht, November. |
| **1939** | Death of Sigmund Freud, on September 23, at the age of 83, in London. |
| **1941** | Ida sails into NYC; is reunited with son, Kurt. |
| **1945** | Death of Ida Bauer Adler, at the age of 63, in New York City. |
| **1988** | Death of Ida's son, Kurt Herbert Adler, on February 9, at the age of 83, in San Francisco, California. |

# Chapter Notes

## Preface

1. Appignanesi and Forrester, *Freud's Women*, 146–70. This discusses Freud's case concerning the young woman whose symptoms emanated from her highly dysfunctional and sexually exploitive family.

2. Freud, *Dora*, 1–122. Freud's first version of his case study about Dora, as mentioned in the text, was titled *Dreams and Hysteria*. Much about the case is explained by James Strachey in the editor's note to Freud's "Fragment of an Analysis of a Case of Hysteria."

3. Sheila Kohler, "Nabokov's Lolita and Freud's Dora." Kohler writes about both writers needing to hide the identity of the people who will be in the case history and the novel. Nabokov, according to Kohler, seems to be influenced by Freud's case study.

4. Freud, *Dora*, 138. This edition of Freud's case study of Dora includes an introduction by the editor, Philip Rieff, an American sociologist and cultural critic. Rieff taught sociology at the University of Pennsylvania from 1961 until 1992 and has authored a number of books on Sigmund Freud and his legacy.

5. Rieff, introduction to *Dora*, 12. Rieff's introduction provides the reader with an overview of Dora's case and Freud's interpretations.

6. Freud, *Dora*, 142n2.

7. Sealey, "Strange Case," 36–50. Sealey argues that the long case history served as an exemplar in psychoanalysis and medicine. She examines how it came to be used by Freud and how his case studies became institutionalized.

8. *Ibid.*, 40. In this article, the author argues that the Dora case needed to be longer than usual because it was "internally complex enough to warrant such a long description"; *Ibid.*, 38.

9. Rieff, introduction to *Dora*, 10.

10. Moi, "Representations of Patriarchy," 60–74. This journal article examines works on feminist theory and women's writing on the intersections of literature, philosophy, and aesthetics.

11. Decker, *Freud, Dora, and Vienna*, 106. Decker has written the definitive book on Ida Bauer, Freud, and Vienna during Freud and Ida's lifetime. Much of what I learned about Ida Bauer first came from Decker's work.

12. Ellis, Raitmayr, and Herbst, "The Ks," 8. This is one of the few works that examines both Peppina and Hans Zellenka, who, if it weren't for their interactions with Freud and especially with the Bauers, would not even be a footnote in history.

13. *Ibid.*, 9. Ida was aware that everyone in Merano talked about the liaison between Peppina Zellenka and Philipp Bauer. Ellis writes, "The affair that ensued was conducted with little attempt at concealment."

14. Freud, *Dora*, 81–132. The first dream, which is short, is told by Ida and analyzed by Freud. Here, he notes that the dream-thoughts behind the dream included a reference to "my treatment"; *Ibid.*, 113–32. The second dream was recounted to Freud a few weeks after the first dream. "And when it had been dealt with the analysis was broken off," Freud writes. One can assume that this second dream was the straw that broke the camel's back, since it led to Ida's leaving analysis with Freud.

15. Decker, *Freud, Dora, and Vienna*, 152. Through my personal correspondence with Katharina Adler, Ida's great-granddaughter and the author of *Ida*, a fictive account of her great-grandmother's life, Adler affirms that Ida was aware of the growing anti–Semitism in the early 1900s. This is why she, her husband, and her son converted to Protestantism, a very common act by Jews during that time.

16. Thorell, "Teenager and the Analyst," 158–65; Thorell, "A Psychoanalytic Study of Narrativity," 16–27.

## Introduction

1. Bloom, "Freud." Bloom has called Freud the greatest modern writer because of his great storytelling abilities.

2. Dimsdale, "Conversion Disorder." The word *hysteria* originates from the Greek word for uterus, and the condition was thought to occur mainly in women.

3. Freud and Breuer, *Studies on Hysteria*, 1–376. These two physicians worked closely together for several years. In this work, they describe the symptoms of hysteria and illustrate the case studies of a number of patients with whom Breuer had worked.

4. Philip Rieff, introduction to *Dora*, 7.

5. "Virtual Jewish World: Vienna, Austria," Jewish Virtual Library, https://www.jewishvirtuallibrary.org/vienna-austria-jewish-history-tour. Judaism was in its ascendancy in Vienna during the early years of Ida Bauer's life, with Jews creating a number of institutions including hospitals, *Gymnasia*, and places of worship.

6. Decker, *Freud, Dora, and Vienna*, 33.

7. Billig, "Freud and Dora," 8. Billig wrote that when Ida and Freud came together, he was depressed and unsuccessful and she was depressed and unhappy. They made a strange pair, as she felt alienated from her family and from the culture she grew up in, and he felt a bitter sense of rejection from mainstream society.

8. Ellis, Raitmayr, and Herbst, "The Ks," 10. In one of the few published articles about "the Ks," the name Freud gave to Herr and Frau Zellenka, Ellis and colleagues described the couple who befriended the Bauer family while both families were living in Merano—and who caused such havoc for Ida Bauer.

9. Kohler, "Nabokov's Lolita and Freud's Dora." In this fictionalized version of Ida's and Freud's relationship, Kohler suggests that although Freud accused Ida of denial, perhaps it was Freud who was in denial.

10. Adler, *Ida*, 1–456. Ms. Adler's novel has been published in German and Spanish.

## Chapter 1

1. Lackey, "Secret Austro-Hungarian Plan," 149–59. This altercation had no direct bearing on Ida's life but is representative of the chaotic times in Vienna and central Europe at the time of her birth.

2. Barron et al., "Sigmund Freud," 143. In this article, the authors examine the secrets that Freud held dear. The article focuses on two aspects of his work: 1) the development of his theory and technique with regard to holding secrets and 2) his motivation to unveil those secrets.

3. Carnochan, *Looking for Ground*, 45. In his earliest work with patients, Freud would begin with a hypnotic induction placing patients in a trance to see if they could recall where their symptoms were coming from.

4. Barron et al., "Sigmund Freud," 152.

5. *Ibid.*, 153.

6. "Sigmund Freud," Encyclopedia Britannica, https://www.britannica.com/biography/Sigmund-Freud. Although Freud had two older half-brothers, his strongest, if also most ambivalent, attachment seems to have been to a nephew, John, one year his senior, who provided his model of friendship. He later hated him as a rival, a situation which Freud reproduced often at later stages of his life. Freud's father was authoritarian, while his mother was possessed of a softer personality. Perhaps this is why he gravitated to his older nephew as a release from his father.

7. Freud Museum, "Sigmund Freud Chronology." The Freud Museum in Vienna is located on Berggasse 19, in the actual consulting room and apartment building where Freud lived and worked.

8. Bloom, *Western Canon*, 345–66. Freud is quoted as saying that psychology is a Shakespearean invention.

9. "Freud-Bernays, Martha (1861–1951)," Encyclopedia Britannica. Martha came from a distinguished Hebrew family. She was the daughter of Berman Bernays, a merchant, and his wife, Emmeline Philipp Bernays. The intelligent, well-educated Emmeline shared her husband's Jewish orthodoxy, as did Martha. Martha was also intelligent without pretensions, svelte, attractively pale, and gracious. She had a warm personality and many friends, as well as male admirers; "Sigmund Freud," Encyclopedia Britannica, https://www.britannica.com/biography/Sigmund-Freud. Martha and Freud would have six children, one of whom was Anna Freud, a noted psychoanalyst in her own right.

10. Freud Museum, "Sigmund Freud Chronology."

11. *Ibid.*

12. Webster, "Freud, Charcot and Hysteria." Charcot was one of the earliest influencers of Freud, as Freud was impressed by Charcot's work on traumatic hysteria. Freud came to understand that one of the principal forms of neurosis came about when a traumatic experience led to the processing of unconscious symptom formation.

13. Kumar et al., "Jean-Martin Charcot," 47. As a practicing neurologist, Charcot saw a range of patients with neurologic conditions. He is credited with first seeing the correlations between the clinical features of multiple sclerosis (MS) and pathological changes noted postmortem. Hunter, "Hysteria, Psychoanalysis, and Feminism," 466. This is the story of Bertha Pappenheim and her analysis with Josef Breuer, who suppressed her identity, as we came to know from her biography from later sources. She came from a prestigious family and was considered attractive and highly intelligent, but she suffered from hysteria.

14. *Ibid.*

15. Borch-Jacobsen, "Mathilde Schleicher (1862–1890)." Freud would write that Mathilde came from a distinguished family but was prone to nervous illnesses.

16. *Ibid.*

17. *Ibid.*

18. Borch-Jacobsen, "Bertha Pappenheim (1859–1936)." Sigmund Pappenheim had inherited a grain trading company and was considered a millionaire. Bertha's mother, Recha Goldschmidt, came from an old Frankfurt family which counted among its members the poet Heinrich Heine. The Pappenheims were strictly Orthodox, and Bertha received the traditional education of a *höhere Tochter* (girl of the upper middle class waiting to be sent on the "marriage market").

19. Robert Kaplan, "O Anna," 62. Kaplan tells the remarkable story of Anna O. and her recovery from multiple symptoms brought on by the death of her father. She was committed to a number of mental institutions but would go on to live a meaningful and important life.

20. Davis, "Freud's Dora," 1. In the case study and other places, Freud discusses his difficulty in choosing a name, as he wanted to provide Ida Bauer with anonymity. He called her Dora after his daughter Rosa's maid and also after Josef Breuer's daughter Dora.

21. Appignanesi and Forrester, *Freud's Women*, 171–72. This book describes Freud's relationship with women—patients, relatives, friends—and establishes Freud's views on femininity.

22. "Sigmund Freud," Encyclopedia Britannica, https://www.britannica.com/biography/Sigmund-Freud. Fliess and Freud maintained a close fifteen-year relationship, with Fliess providing invaluable insight into Freud's theories. It has been argued that Freud's notions of sexuality, particularly that of infants, could be attributed to his relationship with and discussions with Fliess; Freud, *Interpretation of Dreams*. It is here that Freud introduces his theory of the unconscious with respect to dream interpretation. He revised the book at least eight times, which indicates his changing views of dreams and the unconscious.

23. Gay, *Freud*, 103. This biography traces Freud's life and education. This exhaustive work is admiring of Freud and his legacy and, as Gay indicates, has left open some issues where evidence is too fragmentary to permit accurate conclusions, such as the question of whether

Freud had a love affair with his wife's sister.

## Chapter 2

1. Cole, "Men's Mother Complex."
2. *Ibid.*
3. "The Famous Break Up of Sigmund Freud and Carl Jung Explained in a New Animated Video," Open Culture, http://www.openculture.com/2018/06/famous-break-sigmund-freud-carl-jung-explained-new-animated-video.html.
4. Josh Jones, "Young Dr. Freud."
5. Ernest Jones, *Life and Work*, 32–33.
6. Josh Jones, "Young Dr. Freud."
7. "The Baby Born with Her Head Inside Her Amniotic Sac: Incredible Photos Capture the 1-in-80,000 'Bubble Birth' of Miracle Girl," Daily Mail Online, November 12, 2020; Charles Dickens, *David Copperfield* (CreateSpace Independent Publishing Platform, 2015).
8. Gay, *Freud*, 11, 503–5.
9. Stevens, *Sigmund Freud*, 144–46.
10. Ernest Jones, *Life and Work*, 421.
11. Jensen, *Streifzüge durch das Leben*, 21.
12. "Pappenheim Bertha (1859–1936)," Encyclopedia.com, https://www.encyclopedia.com/women/encyclopedias-almanacs-transcripts-and-maps/pappenheim-bertha-1859-1936.
13. Shapiro, *Jewish 100*, 276.
14. Darling, "Jan 29 Anna Freud."
15. *Ibid.*

## Chapter 3

1. "Filipp Bauer," Geni, https://www.geni.com/people/Filipp-Bauer/6000000010132981567. In most accounts that describe Ida's father, his name is spelled "Philipp," which is the way I chose to spell it; Decker, *Freud, Dora, and Vienna*, 42. Pollerskirchen was a small market town in the Bohemian-Moravian hills, where Jews had resided for generations among the Czech Catholics.
2. Decker, *Freud, Dora, and Vienna*, 42.
3. "Jakob Bauer," Geni, https://www.geni.com/people/Jacob-Bauer/6000000010132848169. Acccording to this source, Jakob had two wives, but it appears that Babette was the mother of all of Philipp's siblings; Decker, *Freud, Dora, and Vienna*, 42. Ida's aunt Malvine, with whom Ida spent much time growing up, was a woman with many physical and psychological issues—issues that Freud felt Ida copied.
4. Decker, *Freud, Dora, and Vienna*, 42.
5. "Bohemia, Czech Republic," Encyclopedia Judaica, https://www.jewishvirtuallibrary.org/bohemia. Bohemia was once a duchy of Great Moravia, then later an independent principality, then a kingdom in the Holy Roman Empire, and ultimately a part of the Habsburg Monarchy and the Austrian Empire. Prague was and is its main and most famous city and was a haven for the Jewish population that had settled there as early as the tenth century.
6. "Bohemia and Moravia," Yivo Encyclopedia of Jews in Eastern Europe, https://yivoencyclopedia.org/article.aspx/Bohemia_and_Moravia.
7. Decker, *Freud, Dora, and Vienna*, 18. Joseph II's edict had a definite effect on Bohemian Jews, as it marked them off as different from most other Jews in the Habsburg Empire.
8. *Ibid.*, 18, 19. While there were advantages for the Jews from Joseph II's edict, there were also concerns, such as heavy and harassing taxation.
9. "Austria Virtual Jewish History Tour," Jewish Virtual Library, https://www.jewishvirtuallibrary.org/austria-virtual-jewish-history-tour, accessed August 30, 2020.
10. Decker, *Freud, Dora, and Vienna*, 47. The area where the Bauer family came from was home to linen weavers at least since the sixteenth or seventeenth century.
11. *Ibid.*, 42.
12. *Ibid.*, 22–24. Most Jews coming to the city, wealthy or not, first resided in Leopoldstadt, which was where they would find friends and relatives who could provide a place to stay and a sense of familiarity and orientation; "Leopoldstadt

district, Vienna, Austria," Encyclopedia Britannica, https://www.britannica.com/place/Leopoldstadt, accessed August 30, 2020. District 2, in Vienna, Leopoldstadt, was an area allotted to Jews in 1622. Until the Nazi regime, Jews resided and worked there, only leaving in 1938 when driven out.

13. Decker, *Freud, Dora, and Vienna*, 14. At the time of the Bauers' arrival, the Second District was an area that was more ghetto than village.

14. *Ibid.*, 22. Leopoldstadt, located on the other side of the Danube Canal, was a mixed residential and business area, with houses, shops, doctors' offices, and entertainment.

15. Grabinsky, "The Ghost Architect of Vienna," *Tablet*, November 9, 2017, 3. The Island of Matzo, as the Second District was called, has been the center of Jewish life since the days of the seventeenth-century ghetto. Most of Vienna's Jews still live there today.

16. Czernin, "Vienna Prater," https://www.dascapri.at/en/stories/vienna-prater/, accessed August 20, 2020. At one time the Prater was reserved as a hunting area for royalty; however, since 1775, the Prater has belonged to the people, with its recreational areas, beer gardens, coffeehouses, and bocce courts. It is home to the famous Vienna Riesenrad.

17. Decker, *Freud, Dora, and Vienna*, 24. While they would not stay within the Jewish "ghetto" of Leopoldstadt, the Bauers (and Philipp's wife's family) still would "cluster" together in the more fashionable sections of Vienna.

18. *Ibid.*, 43.

19. *Ibid.*

20. Mandal, "Cause and Transmission of Syphilis," 3.

21. "Bernhard Gerber," Geni, https://www.geni.com/people/Bernhard-Gerber/6000000016237776796, accessed December 26, 2018.

22. Decker, *Freud, Dora, and Vienna*, 15. Ida's mother was born in northern Czechoslovakia about 25 miles from the Polish border. It is likely that her family came to Vienna in the 1860s.

23. Freud, *Dora*, 34. Perhaps the need to clean and keep order was because

Käthe was a child of elderly parents. Also, since she moved from what she apparently considered her beloved country village to the big city of Vienna, she may have felt somewhat unsettled. She also was dealing with her husband's illnesses, especially his syphilis.

24. *Ibid.*

25. "Encyclopedia Judaica: Textiles," Jewish Virtual Library, https://www.jewishvirtuallibrary.org/textiles, accessed December 25, 2018.

26. *Ibid.*

27. *Ibid.*

28. Weinzierl, "Jewish Middle Class."

29. Beckermann, ed., *Die Mazzesinsel*, 33–35.

30. Decker, *Freud, Dora, and Vienna*, 51–53.

31. "Hoffnung auf sozialistische Revolution," Austria-Forum, https://austria-forum.org/af/Wissenssammlungen/Essays/Politik/Otto_Bauer_sozialistische_Revolution, accessed August 10, 2020; Decker, *Freud, Dora, and Vienna*, 43.

32. *Ibid.*, 14.

33. *Ibid.*

34. Mahony, *Freud's Dora*, 5. Here, Mahony claims that this case study is *not* a model of treatment but a remarkable exhibition of the rejection of a patient by a clinician, an inkblot test of Freud's misapprehensions about female sexuality and adolescence.

35. *Ibid.*, 3, 4.

36. Decker, *Freud, Dora, and Vienna*, 40.

37. Mahony, *Freud's Dora*, 3.

38. Freud, *Dora*, 36. Freud recounts that Ida went through the usual infectious diseases of childhood without suffering any damage. She told him that Otto was the first to start an illness, then she would follow suit.

39. Decker, *Freud, Dora, and Vienna*, 44.

40. *Ibid.* At this time, Merano was a health resort for older, ailing, and wealthy Jewish families. And it was here that the Bauer family would encounter Herr K. and his wife, Frau K., so called by Freud in his case study. The ensuing relationship with this couple, the Zellenkas, and their

two children would cause the tattered Bauer family to completely unravel.

## Chapter 4

1. Decker, *Freud, Dora, and Vienna*, 47.

2. *Ibid.*, 44.

3. "Merano City Guide 2020," https://www.kundenbereich.it/media/33a95195-e9f8-4097-8d62-be91447c46c7/nocache/cityguide2020-part1.pdf, 14, 16, accessed September 1, 2020. Today, Merano (Italian; Meran, German) is still viewed as a salubrious spa town for the wealthy, who take to the waters for their curative effects.

4. "Virtual Jewish World: Merano, Italy," Jewish Virtual Library, https://www.jewishvirtuallibrary.org/merano-italy-jewish-history-tour, accessed May 4, 2019. The history of the Jewish community in Merano dates to the first half of the eighteenth century, when the Tyrol region belonged to Austria.

5. *Ibid.* It was the Königswarter family who, through their donation to the Jewish community of Merano, established a sanatorium for poor Jews suffering from tuberculosis (1873), two cemeteries in Bolzano and Merano, and the first synagogue.

6. "The History of the Jewish Community in Merano: The Jewish Sanatorium in Meran," Comunita Ebraica di Merano, http://www.meranoebraica.it/en/node/12, accessed September 1, 2020. The Jewish community had a wish to help other people, which was the underlying rationale for turning a villa into a sanatorium for poor Jewish patients.

7. "History," Meranerland.org, https://www.meranerland.org/en/highlights/history/, accessed September 1, 2020. Merano has a long history as a health resort and was considered one of the first tourism strongholds of the era of the Habsburgs. Many famous people came to Merano for their health. In addition to Kafka, Freud and his family also came here.

8. Ellis, Raitmayr, and Herbst, "The Ks," 4.

9. "Virtual Jewish World: Merano, Italy," Jewish Virtual Library, https://www.jewishvirtuallibrary.org/merano-italy-jewish-history-tour, accessed August 28, 2020. The Jewish community, although small, runs the cultural center and library in Merano for Jews and non-Jews alike, to improve the knowledge of the Jewish community in Merano.

10. *Ibid.*

11. "The History of the Jewish Community in Merano," Judische Gemeinde Meran, http://www.meranoebraica.it/en/node/12, accessed December 11, 2020.

12. Decker, *Freud, Dora, and Vienna*, 44.

13. *Ibid.*, 45.

14. *Ibid.*, 55.

15. *Ibid.*, 6.

16. Zadoff, *Next Year in Marienbad*, 26–30. Dr. Zadoff's research and teaching have focused on Jewish history, culture, and Holocaust studies.

17. Adler, *Ida*, 1–456. Katharina Adler (b. Munich, 1980) is the great-granddaughter of Ida Adler, whose name before her marriage to the not-very-successful composer Ernst Adler was Ida Bauer. Adler's novel is written in German.

18. Decker, *Freud, Dora, and Vienna*, 43.

19. Freud, *Dora*, 35.

20. *Ibid.*

21. *Ibid.*, 36, 37.

22. Tolmach Lakoff and Coyne, *Father Knows Best*, chap. 2.

23. Freud, *Dora*, 34.

24. Decker, *Freud, Dora, and Vienna*, 53, 54.

25. Freud, *Dora*, 34.

26. Decker, *Freud, Dora, and Vienna*, 53.

27. Masadilová, "Františkovy Lázně (Franzensbad)." Františkovy Lázně is surrounded by vast green spaces of parks and forests that are the pride of the town and provide visitors (and patients) with an indispensable repose.

28. Decker, *Freud, Dora, and Vienna*, 56. Decker writes that it was a cousin, Elsa Foges, who remembered Otto as a "boy genius."

29. *Ibid.*, 53.

30. *Ibid.*, 57.

31. *Ibid.*, 58.

32. *Ibid.*
33. *Ibid.*

## Chapter 5

1. Decker, *Freud, Dora, and Vienna*, 65.
2. Ellis, Raitmayr, and Herbst, "The Ks," 1–26. This is one of the few articles that fully detail the life of both Hans and his wife, Peppina.
3. "History: Jew's Lane—Christian's Lane," Judisches Museum Hohenems, https://www.jm-hohenems.at/en/jewish-quarter/history, accessed November 4, 2020.
4. "Austria: Hohenems," *JGuideEurope*, https://jguideeurope.org/en/region/austria/hohenems/, accessed November 5, 2020.
5. Ellis, Raitmayr, and Herbst, "The Ks," 2, 3.
6. *Ibid.*, 3.
7. *Ibid.*, 4. Merano became one of the area's most prestigious health resorts, due in part to the Biedermann Bank, which became the heart of its financial and cultural development.
8. *Ibid.*, 3, 4.
9. *Ibid.* It is unclear whether Isidor, Peppina's father, had any banking experience, but the Biedermann relatives did not want to leave everything to him. A younger Jewish banker, Friedrich Stransky, was brought in to work alongside Isidor. It is also unclear if this was a problem for Isidor, but Stransky enhanced the holdings of the entire Biedermann family by his astute banking knowledge. Additionally, he cemented his value to the family by marrying Peppina's mother's sister, Rosine Biedermann, who came from Hohenems.
10. Freud, *Dora*, 34. Here, Freud discusses Philipp Bauer's sister, Malvine, whom Freud had met, possibly in Merano as well as in Vienna. In the Dora case study, Freud makes assumptions about her without having seen her in a diagnostic setting. He also calls her Philipp's older sister, but, according to other authors, she was his younger sister.
11. Decker, *Freud, Dora, and Vienna*, 50.

12. *Ibid.*; Ellis, Raitmayr, and Herbst, "The Ks," 4.
13. *Ibid.*
14. *Ibid.*, 5. The Leopoldstadter Tempel, where Hans's parents were married, was an imposing synagogue that stood in the Leopoldstadt District until its destruction by National Socialists in 1938.
15. Ellis, Raitmayr, and Herbst, "The Ks," 5; Sig et al., "Medicinal Leech Therapy," 337–43. In Austria, during the time that Hans's father was involved in selling leeches, leech therapy was an important primary treatment for a number of conditions; today, treatment with leeches is complementary and/or integrative.
16. Ellis, Raitmayr, and Herbst, "The Ks," 5. Hans Zellenka, who was not considered a very nice person, was much more successful than his father. This was probably due to the discipline and enterprise of his mother.
17. *Ibid.*, 6. In 1867, the company's founder, the original Philipp Haas, was awarded the Edward the Great Cross of the Order of Franz Josef for achievements that included building homes for the company's workers and creating a pension fund for retired workers.
18. *Ibid.* Hans was not the ineffective shopkeeper that Freud describes him as being in the case study of Dora; he was ambitious and worked for an up-and-coming influential company.
19. *Ibid.*; "Otto Zellenka," Geni, https://www.geni.com/people/Otto-zellenka/6000000053832859020, accessed September 1, 2020.
20. Ellis, Raitmayr, and Herbst, "The Ks," 8.
21. Decker, *Freud, Dora, and Vienna*, 65.
22. Ellis, Raitmayr, and Herbst, "The Ks," 8.
23. "Königswarter Foundation," Judische Gemeinde Meran, http://www.meranoebraica.it/en/node/9, accessed May 3, 2020.
24. Ellis, Raitmayr, and Herbst, "The Ks," 8.
25. *Ibid.*, 9.
26. *Ibid.*

27. Freud, *Dora*, 33; Ellis, Raitmayr, and Herbst, "The Ks," 10.
28. Decker, *Freud, Dora, and Vienna*, 69.
29. *Ibid.*, 68, 69.
30. *Ibid.*, 69.
31. *Ibid.*

## Chapter 6

1. Decker, *Freud, Dora, and Vienna*, 69.
2. Ellis, Raitmayr, and Herbst, "The Ks," 11.
3. Decker, *Freud, Dora, and Vienna*, 70.
4. *Ibid.*, 77.
5. *Ibid.*
6. *Ibid.*
7. *Ibid.*, 76.
8. *Ibid.*, 78.
9. Gilman, "Electrotherapy and Mental Illness," 347.
10. Decker, *Freud, Dora, and Vienna*, image between 178–179.
11. *Ibid.*, 12.
12. *Ibid.*, 13.
13. Ellis, Raitmayr, and Herbst, "The Ks," 11.
14. Decker, *Freud, Dora, and Vienna*, 4.
15. Pass Freidenreich, "Jewish Women Physicians," 79–105.
16. Makari, *Revolution in Mind*, 134–35.
17. Rieff, introduction to *Dora*, 10.
18. Barron et al., "Sigmund Freud," 145.

## Chapter 7

1. Decker, *Freud, Dora, and Vienna*, 57.
2. Adler (great-granddaughter of Ida Bauer Adler), correspondence with the author, April 2020. Ms. Adler's own book, *Ida*, written about her famous relative, is a fictional account of "Dora's" life.
3. Blum, "Anti-Semitism in the Freud Case Histories," 83.
4. Decker, *Freud, Dora, and Vienna*, 57.
5. Weinzierl, "Jewish Middle Class," 12. In 1878, the Ministry of Culture and Education permitted women to take the school-leaving examination but did not allow the marks of this examination to be entered in a student's report card, which was mandatory for access to the universities. In 1896, the ministry allowed girls, once they turned age eighteen, to take their final examination at certain boys' secondary schools, but it retained the restrictions on the posting of grades.
6. Decker, *Freud, Dora, and Vienna*, 75.
7. *Ibid.*
8. *Ibid.*, 76.
9. *Ibid.*; Paolo Mantegazza, an Italian neurologist, physiologist, and anthropologist, wrote notable books on sexology, which Ida read under the direction of Peppina. His position was a liberal one. He became the object of fierce attacks because of the extent to which he practiced vivisection.
10. Freud, *Dora*, 52.
11. *Ibid.*, 48.
12. Ellis, Raitmayr, and Herbst, "The Ks," 9.
13. *Ibid.*, 8.
14. *Ibid.*, 9.
15. *Ibid.*, 10.
16. Freud, *Dora*, 49.
17. Decker, *Freud, Dora, and Vienna*, 48.
18. *Ibid.*
19. Ellis, Raitmayr, and Herbst, "The Ks," 11, 12.
20. Decker, *Freud, Dora, and Vienna*, 80.
21. *Ibid.*, 81–83. The Secessionists were a feature of the cultural life of upper-middle class citizens of Vienna at the time. The formation of the Vienna Secession in 1897 marked the beginning of modern art in Austria. Their work illustrated the new instinctual and cultural flowering of Vienna.
22. *Ibid.*, 83–84.
23. *Ibid.*, 84, 85.
24. Freud, *Dora*, 38.
25. M. Guy Thompson, *Truth About Freud's Technique*, 93.
26. Freud, *Dora*, 41, 42.
27. Billig, "Freud and Dora," 8.

## Chapter 8

1. Appignanesi and Forrester, *Freud's Women*, 146.
2. *Ibid.*, 150.
3. Freud, "L'hérédité et l'étiologie des névroses," 161–69; Élisabeth Roudinesco and Michel Plon, *Dictionnaire de la psychanalyse*, 1216.
4. Freud, *Interpretation of Dreams*, 262.
5. Tutter, "Sex, Subtext, *Ur*-text," 523–48
6. Freud, *Dora*, 41, 42.
7. Appignanesi and Forrester, *Freud's Women*, 149.
8. *Ibid.*, 150.
9. *Ibid.*
10. Freud, *Dora*, 42.
11. *Ibid.*
12. *Ibid.*
13. M. Guy Thompson, *Truth About Freud's Technique*, 97.
14. *Ibid.*, 98.
15. Freud, *Dora*, 38.
16. *Ibid.*, 45.
17. *Ibid.*, 46. Freud goes on to explain that this was a riddle which her memories were unable to solve. She forgot where her sexual knowledge came from.
18. Tolmach Lakoff and Coyne, *Father Knows Best*, 113.
19. Freud, *Dora*, 80, 81.
20. *Ibid.*, 39.

## Chapter 9

1. Rudnytsky, foreword to *Freud and the Dora Case*, xii. This, as we shall see later, contributed to Freud's blindness about the countertransference involved in his treatment of Ida, which he did not fully recognize until sometime after the aborted analysis.
2. Ralph Blumenthal, "Hotel Log Hints at Illicit Desire That Dr. Freud Didn't Repress," *New York Times*, December 24, 2006, https://www.nytimes.com/2006/12/24/world/europe/24freud.html, accessed September 20, 2020.
3. "Bernays-Freud, Minna (1865–1941)," Encyclopedia.com, https://www.encyclopedia.com/psychology/dictionaries-thesauruses-pictures-and-press-releases/bernays-freud-minna-1865-1941, accessed September 20, 2020.
4. *Ibid.*
5. Gay, "Sigmund and Minna?"
6. *Ibid.*
7. Maciejewski, "Minna Bernays as 'Mrs. Freud': 5–21. Once this article was published, it was a sensation, and other rumors spread: that Minna was pregnant and had an abortion. None of this is verified; Hirschmüller, "Evidence for a Sexual Relationship Between Sigmund Freud and Minna Bernays?" *American Imago* 64, no. 1 (2007): 125–29, DOI:10.1353/aim.2007.0013.
8. Gay, "Sigmund and Minna?" 134.
9. Galef and Galef, "Freud's Wife," 514. This is an extensive description of the relationship between Freud and his wife—the good and the bad—as well as Freud's relationship with Minna and the possibility of sexual involvement between the two. The authors suggest, however, that Freud had sublimated his sexual desires early in his life.
10. Decker, *Freud, Dora, and Vienna*, 202.
11. Freud, *Dora*, 81. This was recounted by Dora in the case study.
12. *Ibid.*, 82.
13. *Ibid.*, 83–85.
14. Romano, *Freud and the Dora Case*, 53–54.
15. *Ibid.*
16. Freud, *Dora*, 83.
17. Decker, *Freud, Dora, and Vienna*, 114.
18. *Ibid.*
19. Freud, *Dora*, 96.
20. Decker, *Freud, Dora, and Vienna*, 114.
21. *Ibid.*, 118.

## Chapter 10

1. Freud, *Dora*, 114. The dream is recounted in full in the case study and is much more involved and detailed than the first dream.
2. *Ibid.*, 114–15.
3. *Ibid.*
4. *Ibid.*, 116. The young man in this passage probably sent the book to Ida to keep his existence present in her mind,

as he saw himself a potential suitor for her hand—once his financial position improved.

5. The *Sistine Madonna*, also called the *Madonna di San Sisto*, shows the Madonna holding the Christ Child. It was commissioned by Pope Julius II and painted by Raphael in 1512. The painting was moved to Dresden in 1754.

6. Freud, *Dora*, 117.

7. *Ibid.*, 118.

8. *Ibid.*, 118, 119.

9. *Ibid.*, 119.

10. *Ibid.*, 120.

11. *Ibid.*

12. Leckie, *Culture and Adultery*, 254. Leckie expands upon the importance of the letter Ida received in the dream telling of her father's death, which would then allow her to "read whatever she wanted." In fact, the author goes on, the reading of the encyclopedia is also a way of determining for herself, through letters and books: "Is this geneaology of women's writing one way that Dora might rewrite ... her history?"

13. Heller, *Freud A to Z*, 84.

14. *Ibid.*, 84–85.

15. *Ibid.*, 86.

16. Decker, *Freud, Dora, and Vienna*, 96.

17. Adler, email to the author, April 26, 2020.

18. Freud, "Sigmund Freud Papers: Interviews and Recollections, 1914–1998," Set A, 1914–1988; Interviews and; Foges, Elsa January 7, 1953

19. Boyce, "Art of Medicine," 949.

20. Freud, "The Unconscious," 59–78.

## Chapter 11

1. Ouweneel, *Freudian Fadeout*, 42.

2. Kramer, *Freud: Inventor*, 80, 81.

3. *Ibid.*, 81.

4. Decker, *Freud, Dora, and Vienna*, 89, 90.

5. Heller, *Freud A to Z*, 5.

6. *Ibid.*, 7.

7. *Ibid.*, 8.

8. Decker, *Freud, Dora, and Vienna*, 90, 91.

9. Kramer, *Freud: Inventor*, 83.

10. Decker, *Freud, Dora, and Vienna*, 91.

11. Heller, *Freud A to Z*, 41.

12. *Ibid.*, 40, 41.

13. *Ibid.*, 88.

14. Kramer, *Freud: Inventor*, 100.

15. *Ibid.*, 101.

16. Heller, *Freud A to Z*, 88.

17. Freud, *Dora*, 135.

18. Kuriloff, "What's Going On with Dora?" 73.

19. *Ibid.*

## Chapter 12

1. Decker, *Freud, Dora, and Vienna*, 148. Philipp wanted Freud "to bring Dora to reason."

2. Freud, *Dora*, 34.

3. *Ibid.*

4. Decker, *Freud, Dora, and Vienna*, 50.

5. *Ibid.*, 55, 56.

6. *Ibid.*, 149.

7. Ellis, Raitmayr, and Herbst, "The Ks," 12. I would assume that Ida was deeply saddened by the loss of Klara, whom she had spent a great deal of time with, serving as the child's babysitter, when they were in Merano.

8. *Ibid.*, 149, 150.

9. *Ibid.*, 150.

10. *Ibid.*

11. *Ibid.*

12. Marcus, "Freud and Dora," 398, 399.

13. *Ibid.*, 399.

14. Decker, *Freud, Dora, and Vienna*, 146.

15. *Ibid.*

16. *Ibid.*, 147.

17. *Ibid.*

18. Kramer, *Freud: Inventor*, 102.

## Chapter 13

1. Decker, *Freud, Dora, and Vienna*, 151.

2. Vincent Finnan, "The Sistine Madonna," Italian Renaissance Art.

3. Decker, *Freud, Dora, and Vienna*, 151; Freud, *Dora*, 116.

4. "Ing. Ernst Adler," Geni, https://www.geni.com/people/Ing-Ernst-

Adler/6000000016255032507; Ellis, Raitmayr, and Herbst, "The Ks," 13.

5. "1911 Encyclopædia Britannica/Sonnenthal, Adolf von," transcription of the 1911 *Encyclopædia Britannica* article, on Wikisource.org, https://en.wikisource.org/wiki/1911_Encyclop%C3%A6dia_Britannica/Sonnenthal,_Adolf_von, accessed December 2, 2020.

6. "Sonnenthal, Adolf Ritten Von," Encylopedia.com, https://www.encyclopedia.com/religion/encyclopedias-almanacs-transcripts-and-maps/sonnenthal-adolf-ritter-von, accessed December 2, 2020.

7. Decker, *Freud, Dora, and Vienna*, 151.

8. Mahony, *Freud's Dora*, 14.

9. Freud, *Dora*, 118.

10. Decker, *Freud, Dora, and Vienna*, 151, 152.

11. *Ibid.*, 152.

12. *Ibid.*, 153.

13. Mark Brownlow, "On the Trail of Famous Viennese," Visiting Vienna, 2005–2020, https://www.visitingvienna.com/famous-people/.

14. Pam Cooper-White, "Where 'Dora' Walked," Vienna Blog, February 3, 2014, https://pcooperwhite.wordpress.com/2014/02/03/where-dora-walked/.

## Chapter 14

1. Decker, *Freud, Dora, and Vienna*, 152.

2. Pfaff, "Kurt Herbert Adler," 1.

3. Freud, *Dora*, 119.

4. Ernest Jones, *Life and Work*, 383. Jones, the eminent biographer of Freud, had little positive to say about the case study. An English physician, he became a psychoanalyst upon reading and reviewing the Dora case study.

5. Decker, *Freud, Dora, and Vienna*, 155.

6. *Ibid.*

7. Pfaff, "Kurt Herbert Adler," 2, 3.

8. *Ibid.*, 1, 2.

9. "Administrator/Conductor Kurt Herbert Adler: A Conversation with Bruce Duffie," http://www.bruceduffie.com/khadler.html, October 11, 1986.

10. Ellis, Raitmayr, and Herbst, "The Ks," 13.

11. "Vienna," transcription of the 1911 *Encyclopædia Britannica* article, on Wikisource.org, https://en.wikisource.org/wiki/1911_Encyclop%C3%A6dia_Britannica/Vienna.

12. Pfaff, "Kurt Herbert Adler," 13.

13. *Ibid.*, 4, 5.

14. Decker, *Freud, Dora, and Vienna*, 154.

## Chapter 15

1. Bourne, *Who's Who*, 17.

2. Pfaff, "Kurt Herbert Adler," 7, 8.

3. *Ibid.*, 8.

4. *Ibid.*, 9.

5. Decker, *Freud, Dora, and Vienna*, 159.

6. *Ibid.*

7. *Ibid.*

8. Ellis, Raitmayr, and Herbst, "The Ks," 13.

9. Decker, *Freud, Dora, and Vienna*, 158, 159.

10. Pfaff, "Kurt Herbert Adler," 3.

11. Ellis, Raitmayr, and Herbst, "The Ks," 13.

12. Pfaff, "Kurt Herbert Adler," 8, 9.

13. Decker, *Freud, Dora, and Vienna*, 165.

14. "Adler, Kurt Herbert," Social Networks and Archival Context (SNAC), https://snaccooperative.org/ark:/99166/w6c85nvz.

15. Ellis, Raitmayr, and Herbst, "The Ks," 14.

16. *Ibid.*

17. Decker, *Freud, Dora, and Vienna*, 167.

18. *Ibid.*

## Chapter 16

1. Bourne, *Who's Who*, 17; Pfaff, "Kurt Herbert Adler," 7, 8.

2. Decker, *Freud, Dora, and Vienna*, 58.

3. Freud, *Dora*, 34.

4. Decker, *Freud, Dora, and Vienna*, 58.

5. *Ibid.*

6. *Ibid.*, 59.

7. *Ibid.*, 61.
8. Pfaff, "Kurt Herbert Adler," 3.
9. *Ibid.*
10. *Ibid.*
11. *Ibid.*, 4.
12. Decker, *Freud, Dora, and Vienna*, 157, 158.
13. "Adler, Kurt Herbert," Social Networks and Archival Context (SNAC), https://snaccooperative.org/ark:/99166/w6c85nvz.
14. Decker, *Freud, Dora, and Vienna*, 158–60.
15. *Ibid.*, 161.

## Chapter 17

1. Decker, *Freud, Dora, and Vienna*, 164.
2. *Ibid.*, 165.
3. Annette McDermott, "Did Franz Ferdinand's Assassination Cause World War I?," History, https://www.history.com/news/did-franz-ferdinands-assassination-cause-world-war-i.
4. *Ibid.*
5. Pfaff, "Kurt Herbert Adler," 9.
6. Decker, *Freud, Dora, and Vienna*, 165.
7. *Ibid.*
8. *Ibid.*
9. Kramer, *Freud: Inventor*, 147.
10. *Ibid.*, 149.
11. *Ibid.*, 150.
12. Decker, *Freud, Dora, and Vienna*, 165.
13. *Ibid.*, 166.
14. *Ibid.*
15. *Ibid.*, 166, 167.
16. *Ibid.*, 167.
17. Pfaff, "Kurt Herbert Adler," 12.

## Chapter 18

1. Decker, *Freud, Dora, and Vienna*, 170.
2. *Ibid.*
3. Bourne, *Who's Who*, 17.
4. "Otto Bauer," Encyclopaedia Britannica, https://www.britannica.com/biography/Otto-Bauer.
5. Pfaff, "Kurt Herbert Adler," 13.
6. Decker, *Freud, Dora, and Vienna*, 170.

7. Pfaff, "Kurt Herbert Adler," 13; Decker, *Freud, Dora, and Vienna*, 171.
8. Decker, *Freud, Dora, and Vienna*, 171.
9. *Ibid.*
10. "Deutsch, Felix (1884–1964)," Encyclopedia.com, https://www.encyclopedia.com/psychology/dictionaries-thesauruses-pictures-and-press-releases/deutsch-felix-1884-1964.
11. "Female Psychology—Helene Deutsch 1884–1982," American Psychoanalytic Association, https://web.archive.org/web/20120722204459/http://apsa.org/About_Psychoanalysis/Noted_Psychoanalysts.aspx#deutsch, accessed October 18, 2014.
12. Deutsch, "Footnote to Freud's Fragment," 159–167.
13. *Ibid.*
14. *Ibid.*, 163; Decker, *Freud, Dora, and Vienna*, 171, 172.
15. Deutsch, "Footnote," 163.
16. Decker, *Freud, Dora, and Vienna*, 172.
17. *Ibid.*
18. Deutsch, "Footnote," 167.
19. Decker, *Freud, Dora, and Vienna*, 170, 172.
20. *Ibid.*, 174.
21. "Adler, Kurt Herbert," Social Networks and Archival Context (SNAC), https://snaccooperative.org/ark:/99166/w6c85nvz; Pfaff, "Kurt Herbert Adler," 12.

## Chapter 19

1. Ellis, Raitmayr, and Herbst, "The Ks," 14.
2. Decker, *Freud, Dora, and Vienna*, 175.
3. Ellis, Raitmayr, and Herbst, "The Ks," 14.
4. "Laws of Bridge," *Encyclopedia Britannica*, https://www.britannica.com/topic/bridge-card-game/Laws-of-bridge.
5. "The Vienna Coup," *Encyclopedia Britannica*, https://www.britannica.com/topic/bridge-card-game/The-Whitfeld-six#ref256399.
6. Decker, *Freud, Dora, and Vienna*, 175.
7. "Gertrude Trude Adler (Moellnitz),"

Geni, https://www.geni.com/people/ Gertrude-Trude-Adler/6000000026165610074; "Ing. Ernst Adler," Geni, https://www.geni.com/people/Ing-Ernst-Adler/6000000016255032507; Decker, *Freud, Dora, and Vienna*, 175.

8. Pfaff, "Kurt Herbert Adler," 117, 118.

9. Decker, *Freud, Dora, and Vienna*, 175.

10. *Ibid.*

11. *Ibid.*

12. *Ibid.*, 177.

13. Czerwińska-Schupp, *Otto Bauer (1881–1938)*, 88.

14. Decker, 177.

15. *Ibid.*

16. *Ibid.*, 178.

17. *Ibid.*, 181.

18. Chas Early, "March 14, 1938: Hitler Receives a Hero's Welcome on His Return to Vienna," British Telecom, March 8, 2018, https://home.bt.com/news/on-this-day/march-14-1938-hitler-receives-a-heros-welcome-on-his-return-to-vienna-11363967774018.

19. "Vienna," United States Holocaust Memorial Museum, https://encyclopedia.ushmm.org/content/en/article/vienna.

20. "History Stories," History, https://www.history.com/news/kristallnacht-photos-pogrom-1938-hitler.

21. Decker, *Freud, Dora, and Vienna*, 183.

## Chapter 20

1. Pfaff, "Kurt Herbert Adler," 27, 28.

2. *Ibid.*, 36.

3. Decker, *Freud, Dora, and Vienna*, 177–79.

4. *Ibid.*, 180.

5. *Ibid.*

6. Pfaff, "Kurt Herbert Adler," 40–42.

7. *Ibid.*, 48.

8. *Ibid.*

9. *Ibid.*

10. *Ibid.*, 53.

11. *Ibid.*, 57.

12. Decker, *Freud, Dora, and Vienna*, 180.

13. *Ibid.*, 182.

14. *Ibid.*, 186.

## Chapter 21

1. "Vienna," United States Holocaust Memorial Museum, https://encyclopedia.ushmm.org/content/en/article/vienna.

2. Hibbert, *Benito Mussolini*, 115; Rees, *The Holocaust*, 111–12.

3. "Vienna," United States Holocaust Memorial Museum, https://encyclopedia.ushmm.org/content/en/article/vienna.

4. *Ibid.*

5. Decker, *Freud, Dora, and Vienna*, 184.

6. Offenberger, *Jews of Nazi Vienna*, 99–127.

7. Decker, *Freud, Dora, and Vienna*, 185–86.

8. "Deportations from Viennas [*sic*] Nordbahnhof, 1938–1945," ÖAW, https://www.oeaw.ac.at/en/ikt/research/sites-of-memory-spaces-of-memory/deportations-from-viennas-nordbahnhof-1938-1945.

9. Czerwińska-Schupp, *Otto Bauer*, 1.

10. *Ibid.*, 14.

11. Decker, *Freud, Dora, and Vienna*, 187.

12. *Ibid.*, 188.

13. Ellis, Raitmayr, and Herbst, "The Ks," 16, 17.

14. Adler, *Ida*, trans. Jamie Lee Searle (Rowholt e-book, 2018), https://rowohlt-theaterverlag.de/fm90/592/Adler_IDA_sample%20translation.pdf.

15. "Martin Magner: Celebrated Theater, Radio and Television Director," *Variety*, January 30, 2002, https://variety.com/2002/scene/people-news/martin-magner-1117860017/.

## Chapter 22

1. Donald Eugene Thompson, *Indiana Authors*.

2. "Friedrich Adler Papers," International Institute for Social History, http://hdl.handle.net/10622/ARCH00135.

3. Decker, *Freud, Dora, and Vienna*, 189.

4. Pfaff, "Kurt Herbert Adler," 18.

5. Ellis, Raitmayr, and Herbst, "The Ks," 16.

6. *Ibid.*, 17.

7. *Ibid.*

8. *Ibid.*, 18.

9. *Ibid.*, 18, 19.

10. Janos Gereben, "Kurt Herbert Adler: Biography," archived from the original on June 30, 2007, http://www.mrichter.com/opera/files/adler.htm, retrieved August 11, 2007.

11. Patricia Kristof Moy, "Remembering Kurt Herbert Adler," San Francisco Classical Voice, 2005, archived from the original on September 27, 2007, https://web.archive.org/web/200709272 05400/http:/www.sfcv.org/arts_revs/ad lertribute_4_12_05.php, retrieved August 11, 2007.

## *Chapter 23*

1. Ernest Jones, *Life and Work*, 383.

2. Gay, *Freud*, 761.

3. Fenichel, *Psychoanalytic Theory of Neurosis*, 221–24.

4. Malcolm, *Psychoanalysis: The Impossible Profession*, 96.

5. Leonard, *Freud's Dora*, 12.

6. *Ibid.*, 143.

7. Finzi and Westerink, eds., *Dora, Hysteria and Gender*, muse.jhu.edu/book/61919.

8. Burd, "Portrait of Dora," 2–32, DOI: 10.2307/465136.

9. Cixous and Clément, *Newly-Born Woman*, 154.

10. Gilman et al., *Hysteria Beyond Freud*, 332–33.

11. Boyce, "Art of Medicine," 948–49.

12. *Ibid.*

13. Linda Roland Danil, "A Few Remarks on Freud and Women," https://versobooks.com/blogs/4022-a-few-remarks-on-freud-and-women.

14. Louis Menand, "Why Freud Survives," *New Yorker*, August 28, 2017, https://www.newyorker.com/magazine/2017/08/28/why-freud-survives.

15. *Ibid.*

16. *Ibid.*

17. Freud, *Dora*, 131.

## *Epilogue*

1. Freud and Breuer, *Studies on Hysteria*, 4, 5; Cohut, "Controversy of 'Female Hysteria,'" https://www.medicalnewstodaylcom/articles/the-controversy-of-female-hysteria, accessed January 20, 2021.

2. Bogousslavsky, ed., "Hysteria," 109.

3. Broderick and Weston, "Family Therapy."

4. Sachs, "Reflections on Freud's Dora Case," 49.

5. Decker, *Freud, Dora, and Vienna*, 191.

6. Bor et al., "Are Child and Adolescent Mental Health Problems Increasing in the 21st Century?" 606–16.

7. *Ibid.*, 613.

8. Rabaté, "Dora's Gift," 92.

# Bibliography

Adler, Katharina. *Ida*. Berlin: Rowohlt Verlag GmbH; 1st edition (July 24, 2018).

Appignanesi, Lisa, and John Forrester. "Early Friends, Early Cases, Early Followers." In *Freud's Women: Family, Patients, Followers*. New York: Basic Books, 1991.

_____. *Freud's Women: Family, Patients, Followers*. New York: Basic Books, 2005.

Barron, James W., Ralph Beaumont, Gary N. Goldsmith, Michael I. Good, Robert L. Pyles, Ana-Maria Rizzuto, and Henry F. Smith. "Sigmund Freud: The Secrets of Nature and the Nature of Secrets." *International Review of Psycho-Analysis* 18, no. 2 (1991): 143–63.

Beckermann, Ruth. *Die Mazzesinsel: Juden in der Wiener Leopoldstadt 1918–1938*. Hamburg: Löcker, 1984.

Benvenuto, Sergio. "Hysteria, Again: Dora Flees ... Is There Anything Left to Say About Hysterics?" *Journal of European Psychoanalysis* 21 (2005): 3–32.

Bernheimer, C., and C. Kahane, eds. *In Dora's Case: Freud—Hysteria—Feminism*. New York: Columbia University Press, 1985.

Billig, Michael. "Freud and Dora: Repressing an Oppressed Identity." MS, pp. 1–22, https:// academia.edu/2543725. *Theory, Culture, & Society* 14, no. 3 (1997): 29–55.

_____. *Freudian Repression: Conversation Creating the Unconscious*. Cambridge: Cambridge University, 1999.

Bloom, Harold. "Freud, the Greatest Modern Writer." *New York Times*, March 23, 1986. https://www.nytimes.com/1986/03/23/books/freud-the-greatest-modern-writer.html. Accessed August 2020.

_____. *The Western Canon: The Books and School of the Ages*. Boston: Houghton Mifflin Harcourt, 1994.

Blum, Harold P. "Anti-Semitism in the Freud Case Histories: A Prologue to the Psychoanalysis of Social Prejudice and Racism." *Psyche* 63, no. 3 (2009): 256–80.

Bogousslavsky, J., ed. "Hysteria: The Rise of an Enigma." *Frontiers of Neurology and Neuroscience* 35 (2014): 109–25.

Bor, William, Angela J. Dean, Jacob Najman, and Reza Hayatbakhsh. "Are Child and Adolescent Mental Health Problems Increasing in the 21st Century? A Systematic Review." *Australian New Zealand Journal of Psychiatry* 48, no. 7 (2014): 606–16.

Borch-Jacobsen, Mikkel. "Bertha Pappenheim (1859–1936)." *Psychology Today*, January 29, 2012. https://www.psychologytoday.com/us/blog/freuds-patients-serial/201201/bertha-pappenheim-1859-1936. Accessed August 2020.

_____. "Mathilde Schleicher (1862–1890)." *Psychology Today*, March 4, 2012. https://www.psychologytoday.com/us/blog/freuds-patients-serial/201203/mathilde-schleicher-1862-1890. Accessed August 2020.

Bourne, J.M. *Who's Who in World War One*. New York: Taylor and Francis e-library, 2002. Accessed via Google Books, February 21, 2011.

Boyce, Niall. "The Art of Medicine: Dora in the 21st Century." *Lancet* 386 (2015): 948–49. DOI:10.1016/S0140-6736(15)00111-7.

Broderick, Pamela, and Christina Weston. "Family Therapy with a Depressed Adolescent."

# Bibliography

https://www.ncbi.nlm.nih.gov/pmc/articles/PMC2719446/pdf/PE_6_01_32.pdf. Accessed January 30, 2021.

Burd, Sarah. "Portrait of Dora." Translated by Hélène Cisoux. *Diacritics* 13, no. 1 (1983): 2–32.

Carnochan, Peter G.M. *Looking for Ground: Countertransference and the Problem of Value in Psychoanalysis.* Hillsdale, NJ: Analytic, 2001.

Cherry, Kendra. "Anna O's Life and Impact on Psychology." VeryWellMind. https://www.verywellmind.com/who-was-anna-o-279585. Accessed August 2020.

Cixous, Hélène. "Portrait of Dora." *Diacritics* 13, no. 1 (1983): 2–32.

_____, and Catherine Clément. *Newly Born Woman.* Translated by Betsy Wing. Twin Cities: University of Minnesota Press, 1986.

Cohut, Maria. "The Controversy of 'Female Hysteria.'" *Medical News Today.* https://www.medicalnewstoday.com/articles/the-controversy-of-female-hysteria. Accessed January 20, 2021.

Cole, Richard. "Men's Mother Complex—Rape of the Heart." St. Pancras Relationship Counselling (blog). https://www.relatenow.co.uk/content/mens-mother-complex-rape-heart. Accessed August 2020.

Czernin, Lucia. "Vienna Prater." Das Capri Ihr Weiner Hotel. https://www.dascapri.at/en/stories/vienna-prater/. Accessed August 20, 2020.

Czerwińska-Schupp, Ewa. *Otto Bauer (1881–1938): Thinker and Politician.* Translated by Maciej Żurowski. Boston: Brill, 2017.

Darling, Laura. "Jan 29 Anna Freud Part II." *Making Queer History.* https://www.makingqueerhistory.com/articles/2019/1/29/anna-freud-part-ii. Accessed August 2020.

Davis, Doug. "Freud's Dora: A Victorian Fable." Haverford College. http://ww3.haverford.edu/psychology/ddavis/fdora.html. Accessed August 2020.

Decker, Hannah S. "The Choice of a Name: 'Dora' and Freud's Relationship with Breuer." *Journal of the American Psychoanalytic Association* 30, no. 1 (1982): 113–136.

_____. *Freud, Dora, and Vienna 1900.* New York: Free Press, 1991.

Deutsch, Felix. "A Footnote to Freud's Fragment of an Analysis of a Case of Hysteria." *Psychoanalytic Quarterly* 25 (1957): 159–67.

Dimsdale, Joel E. "Conversion Disorder." *Merck Manual,* July 2018. https://www.merckmanuals.com/home/mental-health-disorders/somatic-symptom-and-related-disorders/conversion-disorder. Accessed August 2020.

Ellis, Andrew W., Oliver Raitmayr, and Christian Herbst. "The Ks: The Other Couple in the Case of Freud's 'Dora.'" *Journal of Austrian Studies* 48, no. 4 (Winter 2015): 1–26.

Erikson, E.H. "Reality and Actuality: An Address." In *In Dora's Case: Freud—Hysteria—Feminism,* ed. C. Bernheimer and C. Kahane, 44–55. New York: Columbia University Press, 1985 (1961).

Fenichel, Otto. *The Psychoanalytic Theory of Neurosis.* New York: W.W. Norton, 1946.

Finzi, Daniela, and Herman Westerink, eds. *Dora, Hysteria and Gender: Reconsidering Freud's Case Study.* Leuven, Belgium: Leuven University Press: 2018.

Freud Museum. "Sigmund Freud Chronology: 1887–1888." Accessed September 24, 2021.

Freud, Sigmund. *Dora: An Analysis of a Case of Hysteria.* New York: Collier/Macmillan, 1963.

_____. *Dream Psychology: Psychoanalysis for Beginners.* Hamburg: Classic, 1921.

_____. "Fragment of an Analysis of a Case of Hysteria." In *The Standard Edition of the Complete Psychological Works of Sigmund Freud,* vol. 7: *A Case of Hysteria, Three Essays on Sexuality and Other Works,* 1–122. Available at https://www.sas.upenn.edu/~cavitch/pdf-library/Freud_SE_Dora_complete.pdf.

_____. "L'hérédité et l'étiologie des névroses." *Revue neurologique* 4, no. 6 (1986): 161–69.

_____. *The Interpretation of Dreams.* New York: Macmillan, 1913.

_____. "Sigmund Freud Papers: Interviews and Recollections, 1914–1998; Set A,

# Bibliography

1914–1998; Interviews and; Foges, Elsa, 1953; Jan. 7, 1953." Manuscripts. Library of Congress. https://www.loc.gov/item/mss3999001463/.
_____. "The Unconscious." In *General Psychological Theory: Papers on Metapsychology.* New York: Collier/Macmillan, 1963, 59–78, 116–50.
Freud, Sigmund, and Josef Breuer. *Studies on Hysteria.* Translated by James Strachey. New York: Basic Books, 1980.
Fritz Offenberger, Illana. "Turning Point: From Vienna to Dachau." In *The Jews of Nazi Vienna, 1938–1945.* London: Palgrave Macmillan, 2017.
Galef, David, and Harold R. Galef. "Freud's Wife." *Journal of the American Academy of Psychoanalysis and Dynamic Psychiatry* 32, no. 3 (2004).
Gay, Peter. *Freud: A Life for Our Time.* New York: W.W. Norton, 1988.
_____. "Sigmund and Minna? The Biographer as Voyeur." *New York Times,* https://movies2.nytimes.com/books/98/10/25/specials/gay-minna.html, accessed November 17, 2020.
Gilman, Sander L. "Electrotherapy and Mental Illness: Then and Now." *History of Psychiatry* 19, no. 3 (2008): 347.
Gilman, Sander L., Helen King, Roy Porter, G.S. Rousseau, and Elaine Showalter. *Hysteria Beyond Freud.* Berkeley: University of California Press, 1993. http://ark.cdlib.org/ark:/13030/ft0p3003d3/. Accessed August 2020.
Grabinsky, Alan. "The Ghost Architect of Vienna." *Tablet,* November 9, 2017.
Green, D. *Freud Versus Dora and the Transparent Model of the Case Study.* Jerusalem: Modan, 1998.
Heller, Sharon. *Freud A to Z.* Hoboken, New Jersey: Wiley, 2005.
Hibbert, Christopher. *Benito Mussolini: A Biography.* London: Reprint Society, 1962.
Hirschmüller, Albrecht. "Evidence for a Sexual Relationship Between Sigmund Freud and Minna Bernays?" *American Imago* 64, no. 1 (2007).
Howes, Ryan. "A Client's Guide to Transference." *Psychology Today,* June 18, 2012. https://www.psychologytoday.com/us/blog/in-therapy/201206/clients-guide-transference. Accessed August 2020.
Hunter, Diane. "Hysteria, Psychoanalysis, and Feminism: The Case of Anna O." *Feminist Studies* 9, no. 3 (1983): 464–488.
Jensen, Ellen M. *Streifzüge durch das Leben von Anna O./Bertha Pappenheim: Ein Fall für die Psychiatrie—Ein Leben für die Philanthropie.* Translated by the author. Frankfurt am Main: ZTV Verlag, 1984.
Jones, Ernest. *Life and Work of Sigmund Freud.* New York: Basic Books, 1961.
Jones, Josh. "Young Dr. Freud: A Film by David Grubin." *PBS Newshour.* https://www.pbs.org/youngdrfreud/pages/family_father.htm.
Kaplan, Marion. "Bertha Pappenheim (1859–1936)." Jewish Women's Archive. https://jwa.org/encyclopedia/article/pappenheim-bertha. Accessed August 2020.
Kaplan, Robert. "O Anna: Being Bertha Pappenheim—Historiography and Biography." *Australasian Psychiatry* 12, no. 1 (2004): 62. DOI:10.1046/j.1039–8562.2003.02062.x.
Kohler, Sheila. *Dreaming for Freud: A Novel.* New York: Penguin, 2014.
_____. "Nabokov's Lolita and Freud's Dora." *Psychology Today,* September 11, 2014. https://www.psychologytoday.com/us/blog/dreaming-freud/201409/nabokovs-lolita-and-freuds-dora. Accessed September 24, 2021.
Kramer, Peter D. *Freud: Inventor of the Modern Mind.* New York: Harper Perennial, 2006.
Kumar, David R., Florence Aslinia, Steven H. Yale, and Joseph J. Mazza. "Jean-Martin Charcot: The Father of Neurology." *Clinical Medicine & Research* 9, no. 1 (2011): 47.
Kuriloff, Emily A. "What's Going On with Dora? An Interpersonal Perspective." In *Freud and Dora: 100 Years Later,* ed. Susan S. Levine. Boca Raton, FL: Routledge, 2005.
Lackey, Scott W. "A Secret Austro-Hungarian Plan to Intervene in the 1884 Timok Uprising in Serbia." *Austrian History Yearbook* 23 (1992): 149–59. DOI:10.1017/S0067237800002940.

# Bibliography

Leckie, Barbara. *Culture and Adultery: The Novel, the Newspaper, and the Law, 1857–1914*. Philadelphia: University of Pennsylvania Press, 1999.

Leonard, Shengold. *Freud's Dora*. New Haven, CT: Yale University Press, 1990.

Maciejejewski, Franz. "Minna Bernays as 'Mrs. Freud': What Sort of Relationship Did Sigmund Freud Have with His Sister-in-Law?" *American Imago* 65, no. 1 (2008).

Mahony, J. Patrick. *Freud's Dora: A Psychoanalytic, Historical, and Textual Study*. New Haven, CT: Yale University Press, 1996.

Makari, George. *Revolution in Mind: The Creation of Psychoanalysis*. New York: Harper Perennial, 2010.

Malcolm, Janet. *Psychoanalysis. The Impossible Profession*. New York: Alfred A. Knopf, 1988.

Mandal, Ananya. "Cause and Transmission of Syphilis." *News Medical Life Sciences* 2. https://www.news-medical.net/health/What-is-Syphilis.aspx. Accessed September 24, 2021.

Marcus, Steven. "Freud and Dora: Story, History, Case History." *Psychoanalysis and Contemporary Science* 5 (1976): 398, 399.

_____. *Freud and the Culture of Psychoanalysis*. New York: W.W. Norton, 1987.

Masadilová, Alena. "Františkovy Lázně (Franzensbad)." Mgr. Alena Masadilová business web site. https://www.visit2prague.cz/tours/spas/item/132-frantiskovy-lazne-franzensbad. Accessed January 20, 2020.

Masson, Jeffrey Moussaieff. *Against Therapy*. Chapter 2: Dora and Freud. New York: Atheneum, 1988.

McCaffrey, Phillip. *Freud and Dora: The Artful Dream*. New Brunswick, NJ: Rutgers University Press, 1985.

Moi, Toril. "Representations of Patriarchy: Sexuality and Epistemology in Freud's Dora." *Feminist Review* 9, no. 1 (1981): 60–74.

Morrissey, Kim. *Dora: A Case of Hysteria*. London: Nick Hern, 1995.

Muslin, Hyman, and Merton Gill. "Transference in the Dora Case." *Journal of the American Psychoanalytic Association* 26, no. 2 (1978): 311–29.

Offenberger, Illana Fritz. *The Jews of Nazi Vienna, 1938–1945*. London: Palgrave Macmillan, 2017.

Ouweneel, Arij. *Freudian Fadeout: The Failings of Psychoanalysis in Film Criticism*. Jefferson, NC: McFarland, 2012.

Pass Freidenreich, Harriet. "Jewish Women Physicians in Central Europe in the Early Twentieth Century." *Contemporary Jewry* 17 (1996): 79–105. https://doi.org/10.1007/BF02965407. Accessed August 2020.

Pfaff, Timothy. "Kurt Herbert Adler and the San Francisco Opera: The Life and Career of Kurt Herbert Adler." Interview with Kurt Herbert Adler. The Bancroft Library, 1985. https://digitalassets.lib.berkeley.edu/rohoia/ucb/text/adlersfcaopera01adlerich.pdf.

Rabaté, Jean-Michel. "Dora's Gift, or, Lacan's Homage to Dora." In *Freud and Dora: 100 Years Later. Psychoanalytic Inquiry* 25, no. 1 (2005): 84–93.

Rabinbach, Anson. *The Crisis of Austrian Socialism: From Red Vienna to Civil War, 1927–1934*. Chicago: University of Chicago Press, 1984.

Ramas, Maria. "Freud's Dora, Dora's Hysteria: The Negation of a Woman's Rebellion." *Feminist Studies* 5, no. 3 (Autumn 1980): 472–510.

Rees, Laurence. *The Holocaust: A New History*. New York: Penguin Viking, 2017.

Rieff, Philip. Introduction to *Dora: An Analysis of a Case of Hysteria*, by Sigmund Freud. New York: Collier/Macmillan, 1963.

Roazen, Paul. *Meeting Freud's Family*. Amherst: University of Massachusetts Press, 1993.

Rogow, Arnold. "A Further Note to Freud's 'Fragment of an Analysis of a Case of Hysteria.'" *Journal of the American Psychoanalytic Association* 26 (1978): 311–330.

Romano, Cesare. "The Dream of the Burning House." In *Freud and the Dora Case: A Promise Betrayed* by Cesare Romano. Abingdon-on-Thames: Routledge, 2015.

Roudinesco, Élisabeth, and Michael Plon. *Dictionnaire de la Psychanalyse*. Paris: Fayard, 2011.

# Bibliography

Rudnytsky, Peter L. Foreword to *Freud and the Dora Case: A Promise Betrayed,* by Cesare Romano, xi–xvi. Abingdon-on-Thames: Routledge, 2015.

Sabbatini, Renato M.E. "The History of Shock Therapy in Psychiatry." http://www.cerebromente.org.br/n04/historia/shock_i.htm. Accessed August 2020.

Sachs, David M. "Reflections on Freud's Dora Case After 48 Years." In *Freud and Dora: 100 Years Later. Psychoanalytic Inquiry* 25, no. 1 (2005): 45–53.

Sealey, Anne. "The Strange Case of the Freudian Case History: The Role of Long Case Histories in the Development of Psychoanalysis." *History of the Human Sciences* 24, no. 1 (2011): 36–50.

Shapiro, Michael. *The Jewish 100: A Ranking of the Most Influential Jews of All Time.* New York: Citadel, 1994.

Sig, Ali K., Mustafa Guney, Aylin Uskudar Guclu, and Erkan Ozmen. "Medicinal Leech Therapy: An Overall Perspective." *Integrative Medicine Research* 6, no. 4 (2017): 337–43.

Stevens, Richard. *Sigmund Freud: Examining the Essence of His Contribution.* London: Red Globe, 2008.

Thompson, Donald Eugene. *Indiana Authors and Their Books, 1917–1966.* Bloomington: Indiana University Press, 1974. http://webapp1.dlib.indiana.edu/inauthors/view?docId=encyclopedia/VAA5365-02.xml;chunk.id=ina-v2-entry-0011;toc.depth=1;toc.id=ina-v2-entry-0011;brand=ia-books;doc.view=0;query=&text1=ollah&field1=text&hit.rank. Accessed June 2020.

Thompson, M. Guy. *The Truth About Freud's Technique: The Encounter with the Real.* New York: New York University Press, 1994.

Thorell, Marge. "A Psychoanalytic Study of Narrativity: An Analysis of Academic Discourse in College English." Unpublished doctoral dissertation. University of Pennsylvania, 1987.

_____. "The Teenager and the Analyst: Dora and Freud." *Schuylkill Valley Journal* 50 (Spring 2020): 158–65.

Tolmach Lakoff, Robin, and James C. Coyne. *Father Knows Best: The Use and Abuse of Power in Freud's Case of Dora.* New York: Teachers College Press, 1993.

Toril, Moi. "Representations of Patriarchy: Sexuality and Epistemology in Freud's Dora." *Feminist Review* 9 (1981): 60–74.

Tutter, Adele. "Sex, Subtext, *Ur*-text: Freud, Dora and the Suggestive Text." Abstract, *International Journal of Psychoanalysis* 101, no. 3 (2020): 523–48. DOI: 10.1080/00207578.2020.1726712.

Webster, Richard. "Freud, Charcot and Hysteria: Lost in the Labyrinth." http://www.richardwebster.net/freudandcharcot.html. Accessed June 2020.

Weinzierl, Erika. "The Jewish Middle Class in Vienna in the Late Nineteenth and Early Twentieth Centuries." Working paper. University of Minnesota, Center for Austrian Studies. http://hdl.handle.net/11299/60664. Retrieved from the University of Minnesota Digital Conservancy, 2003.

Yuknavitch, Lidia. *Dora: A Headcase.* Portland, OR: Hawthorne, 2012.

Zadoff, Mirjam. *Next Year in Marienbad: The Lost Worlds of Jewish Spa Culture.* Translated by William Templer. Philadelphia: University of Pennsylvania Press, 2014.

# Index

Numbers in **bold italics** indicate pages with illustrations

Adler, Ernst 126, 128, 129, 135, 140, 148, 149, 156–157, 162–163, 195, 197, 198
Adler, Katharina 16, 56, 58, 108, 177, *182*, 200, 204
Adler, Kurt Herbert 16, 132, 134–134, 135–136, 137–138, 139, 140–141, 144, 145, 148–149, 150, 151, 155–156, 162–163, 170–171, 173, 175, 177–178, 180–181, 182–183, 197, 198; married life 168–170, 179, 182; *see also* Miller, Nancy Goodhue; Moellner, Gertrude (Trudl); Warfel, Diantha 141, 160, 167, 168, 173, 179–180, 182
Alsergrund 43–44, 45, 129–130, 131
Anna O. 5, 6, 9, 10, 16, *25*, 26, 27, 33–34, 98, *98*, 183, 186, 195, 196, 201; *see also* Breuer, Josef; Freud, Sigmund; Pappenheim, Bertha
*Anschluss* 173, *174*, 176, 198
anti-Semitism 6, 7, 13, 40, 52–53, 56, 62, 82, 88, 114, 133, 144, 173, 181, 200

Bauer, Ida 9, 10, 13, 14, 16–17, 28, 30, 44, 45, *45*, 46, 135, 188, 196, 198; ailments 6, 7, 10, 46, 47, 48, 54, 55, 57, 58, 65–66, 73, 74, 75–76, 83, 85, 87, 88, 122, 139-140, 156–158, 159, 163, 177, 180–181, 184; aunt 7, 47, 65, 85, 120 (*see also* Bauer, Malvine); bridge (card game) 141, 161-162; brother *45*, 46, 55, 56–57, 58, 121, 129, 149, 155 (*see also* Bauer, Otto); dreams 80, 101–102, 104, 105, 107, 109–110, 200; early life 44–45, 55; education 13, 33, 60–61, 82, 83, 87–88, 121; father 55, 56, 57, 88, 95, 139 (*see also* Bauer, Philipp); fleeing Austria 170–171, 173–175, 177; governess 60, 82, 83; Hans Zellenka, seduction by 7, 14, 70–71, 73–75, 85, 91, 97, 106, 121, 122 (*see also* Zellenka, Hans); health treatments 10, 20, 55, 75, 76, 77; husband 126, 128–129, 131, 132, 136, 156–157, 158, 159, 163 (*see also* Adler, Ernst); life in America 179, 180-181; mother 56, 58, 59, 88, 93, 95, 158 (*see also* Bauer, Katharina [Käthe]

Gerber); Peppina Zellenka, bridge partner of 161, 162; relationship with 64–65, 70, 71, 83–84, 91, 177 (*see also* Zellenka, Peppina); religious conversion 7, 132, 133, 154, 166, 168, 200; sexuality 95–96; son 15, 133, 137, 141, 151, 155, 156, 158, 160, 175, 180-181 (*see also* Adler, Kurt Herbert); suicidality 7, 66, 88, 91, 92, 94; Zellenka children 14, 68, 70, 72, 73, 84–85, 91, 121, 125
Bauer, Katharina (Käthe) Gerber 10, 14, 42–43, 44, 47–48, 54, 56, 57, 58–59, 197; ailments 10, 58, 59, 139; cleanliness ("housewife psychosis") 7, 10, 14, 42, 54, 58–59, 100, 120, 144, 158, 163, 203; marital estrangement 59, 69–70
Bauer, Otto 14, *45*, 46, 55, 57–58, 60, 121, 140–141, 142, 143–146, 149, 163, 164, 167–168, 173, 175–176, 198; marriage 145, 176; socialism 14, 143–144, 145, 147, 151, 154–155
Bauer, Philipp 14, 45, 47, 135, 137–138, 139, 197; Hans Zellenka 62, 68–69, 70, 89 (*see also* Zellenka, Hans); health issues 14, 47, 54–55, 56, 58, 69–70, 139, 148–149; interactions with Freud 14–15, 70, 89, 93, 94, 122, 196, Peppina Zellenka, affair with 70, 83, 84, 85, 89, 116, 121, 144, 199 (*see also* Zellenka, Peppina); venereal disease 10, 14, 41, 44, 45, 55, 58, 69, 70, 196, 203
Bauer Friedmann, Malvine 36, 65, 85, 120, 197, 202, 205
Bernays, Martha 23, *98*, 99–100, *100*, 195, 196, 201
Bernays, Minna 97–98, *98*, 201
Biedermann family 53, 63–64, 205; bank 64, 66, 68–69, 141
Breuer, Josef 9, 10, 12, 24, 25–27, 33–34, 92, 94, 195, 196, 200, 201 (*see also* Anna O.); Freud, Sigmund
Bohemia 13, 14, 36–37, 38, 43, 44, 135, 149, 202

**219**

# Index

Charcot, Jean-Martin 23-24, *24*, 32-33, 78, *79*, 196, 201
countertransference 3, 4, 10, 109, 116, 123–124, 146, 184, 185, 188, 190, 191, 207

Deutsch, Felix 157-159, 198
Deutsch, Helene 157
Dollfuss, Engelbert 167, 168

Emperor Joseph II 37-38
Empress Elizabeth of Austria (Sissi) *50*, 51–52, *52*, 64

Fliess, Wilhelm 21, 27, 30, 185, 201-202
Franzensbad *51*, 56, *57*, 59, 76
Frau K. 7, 14, 53, 66, 89, 102, 106, 107–108, 204; *see also* Zellenka, Peppina
Freud, Amalia Malka Nathansohn *11*, 21, 31–32, *113*, 114
Freud, Anna *2*, 13, 32, 34–35, 166, 198, 201
Freud, Jakob *11*, 30, 31, *112*
Freud, Sigmund *2*, *11*, *77*, *79*, *100*, *112*, *113*, 115, 153, 187–188, 195; case study, Anna O. 26, 27, 33, 34, 196; case study, Dora 2-3, 4, 15, 16, 58, 62, 65, 88, 93, 96, 101, 103, 104, 110, 111, 116–117, 123, 124, 132–133, 184–185, 186, 188–189, 190, 191, 192–193, 197, 199, 201, 203, 208, 209; daughter *see* Freud, Anna; death 187, 198; dreams, interpretation of 101–108, 116, 129, 199–200; dream work 15, 21, 28, 80, 92, 93, 96, 100–101, 112, 113, 114–115, 190; early life 21–23, *22*, 30–32; father 30, 112, 113–114 *see also* Freud, Jakob; fleeing Vienna 166, 198; hypnosis 21, 25, 26, 27, 200; Ida Bauer, analysis/treatment of 15, 35, 58, 65, 76, 79, 85, 94, 95, 96, 102, 108, 111, 116–117, 122, 129, 143, 197, 199; Ida Bauer, countertransference; *see* countertransference; Ida Bauer, dreams, interpretation of 101, 102, 103, 104–108; Ida Bauer, termination of therapy 15, 103, 108, 109–110, 111, 115, 117, 120, 122, 123; Ida Bauer, transference *see* transference; Josef Breuer, collaboration with 9, 24, 26, 27, 32–33, 34, 92, 94, 196, 200 (*see also* Breuer, Josef); mother 31, 32, 112, 114 (*see also* Freud, Amalia Malka Nathansohn); museum *2*, *77*, 131, 201; Nazi invasion 166; Peppina Zellenka *see* Zellenka, Peppina; professional life 89, 114, 142, 149–150, 187, 197; publications 9, 16, 27, 92, 123, 146, 196, 197; self-analysis 28, 112–114, 115; sister-in-law 32, 97, *98*, 99, 100, 111, 207–208 (*see also* Bernays, Minna); talk therapy ("talking cure") 10, 21, 24, 25, 26, 27, 76 (*see also* psychoanalysis); wife 23, 32, 99–100, 201, 207 (*see also*

Bernays, Martha); women, relationships with 29, 32, 42, 89, 124, 186–187, 201

Herr, K. 7, 14, 71, 74, 89, 95, 96, 102, 204; *see also* Zellenka, Hans
Hitler, Adolf 12, 17, 137, 163, 164, 165, *165*, 167, 172–173, 174, 198
Hohenems 53, 63
hysteria (conversion disorder) 9, 21, 24, 27, 78, 93, 94, 96, 102, 107–108, 111, 143, 185–186, 190, 191, 196, 200

Jung, Carl 30, 123, 149, 184, 202

Königswarter Foundation 68, 204

Leopoldstadt 21-22, 39-40, *40*, 203

Magner, Martin 177-178, 212
Merano (Meran, South Tyrol) 47–48, 49–55, 56, 69, *69*, 150, 204, 205
Miller, Nancy Goodhue 182
Moellnitz, Gertrude (Trudl) 168–169

Nazi invasion, Austria 53, 164-165, *165*, 168, 170, 172-173, 174, *174*, 176-177, 198
Nuremberg Laws 168, 173, 175, 198

Pappenheim, Bertha 24, 25, *25*, 26-27, 33-34, 98, 186, 195, 196, 201; *see also* Anna O.; Breuer, Josef; Freud, Sigmund, case study, Anna O.
Pappenheim, Sigmund 98, 201
Pitié-Salpêtrière Hospital 23–24, 78, *79*
Preminger, Otto 167
psychoanalysis 1, 21, 28, 78, 92, 93, 109, 117, 183, 185, 186, 188, 190, 196

Reichenberg 85, *86*, *87*, 197
Reinhardt, Max 141, 160
Ritten von Sonnenthal, Adolf 126–128, *127*, 135

Schleicher, Cölestin 25
Schleicher, Mathilde 25–26, 196, 201

"talking cure" *see* Freud, Sigmund, talk therapy ("talking cure")
transference 3, 4, 10, 21, 93, 96, 103, 109, 116, 117, 159, 184, 188, 190

Vienna 39-40, *40*, 78, 137, *165*, 172; anti–Semitism 12, 15, 22, 40, 82, 88, 114, 133, 137, 138, 154, 165, 170, 173, *174*, 175, 176-177, 181; bridge (card game) 15, 141, 161-162; culture 39, 43, 87, 88, 128, 130, 131, 134-135, 172; decline 150, 154, 162, 164,

165, 170; growth, Jewish population 12, 38, 39, 43-44
Von Schuschnigg, Kurt 164, 168, 172–173

Walter, Margarethe 186-187
Warfel, Diantha 169, 179, 182
Woolf, Leonard 187
Woolf, Virginia 187

Zellenka, Hans 66-69, 205; *see also* Bauer, Ida, Hans Zellenka, seduction by

Zellenka, Peppina 63–65, 66, 68, 70, 85, 181–182; *see also* Bauer, Philipp, Peppina Zellenka; Biedermann family
Zellenkas 6, 7, 53, 62–63, 67–68, 139, 141, 199, 200; Bauer family relations 61, 62, 67, 68, 71–72, 84, 86, 204; children 67–68, 84–85, 121, 181; marriage 62–63, 66, 67–68, 70, 85, 196